MW00677027

Earnings From Learning

SUNY series, Frontiers in Education
Philip G. Altbach, editor

Earnings From Learning

The Rise of For-Profit Universities

Edited by
David W. Breneman,
Brian Pusser, and
Sarah E. Turner

STATE UNIVERSITY OF NEW YORK PRESS

Published by
State University of New York Press, Albany

© 2006 State University of New York

All rights reserved

Printed in the United States of America

No part of this book may be used or reproduced
in any manner whatsoever without written permission.
No part of this book may be stored in a retrieval system
or transmitted in any form or by any means including
electronic, electrostatic, magnetic tape, mechanical,
photocopying, recording, or otherwise without the prior
permission in writing of the publisher.

For information, contact State University of New York Press, Albany, NY
www.sunypress.edu

Production by Michael Haggett
Marketing by Fran Keneston

Library of Congress Cataloging in Publication Data

Earnings from learning : the rise of for-profit universities / edited by
David W. Breneman, Brian Pusser, Sarah E. Turner.
    p. cm. — (SUNY series, frontiers in education)
  Includes bibliographical references and index.
  ISBN 0-7914-6839-9 (hardcover : alk. paper) — ISBN 0-7914-6840-2
(pbk. : alk. paper) 1. For-profit universities and colleges—United
States. 2. Education, Higher—Economic aspects—United States. I.
Breneman, David W. II. Pusser, Brian. III. Turner, Sarah E., 1966- IV.
Series.

LB2328.52.U6E37 2006
338.4'3378—dc22

ISBN-13: 978-0-7914-6839-5 (hardcover : alk. paper)
ISBN-13: 978-0-7914-6840-1 (pbk : allk. paper)

2005026765

10 9 8 7 6 5 4 3 2 1

Contents

PART 3. POLITICAL ECONOMY

Illustrations

FIGURES

TABLES

Introduction

David W. Breneman

The present volume had its origin in fin-de-siècle twentieth-century America, when the enthusiasm for anything new related to the Internet and to the teaching of skills required by the "New Economy" dominated discussions about higher education. Among the developments capturing attention in that frenzied atmosphere was the growth of for-profit, degree-granting institutions of higher education, the University of Phoenix (UOP) being the most visible member of a group that includes DeVry, ITT Educational Services, and Strayer. Traditional higher education, while highly competitive in its own way, was not used to competing with institutions oriented toward making a profit, and there was much worry and dismay within the traditional sector about this turn of events. Those who sought to transform traditional institutions found this new development useful in order to advocate change as required for survival; others argued that the academy was being sullied, and that the academic profession was threatened by "barbarians at the gate." Still others expressed surprise that institutions such as Phoenix could earn a profit when competing with state-subsidized colleges and universities, as well as private, nonprofit institutions with sizable endowments and the ability to raise tax-favored contributions from alumni and friends. What was lacking in much of the discussion at the time was a knowledge base about these relatively new institutions. The authors in this volume took it as their task to understand and learn more about these new entrants; to provide a conceptual framework for thinking about them; and to explore aspects of the new environment, of which these institutions are very much a part.

It must be noted that this arena is rapidly developing and changing in ways that traditional higher education does not; hence, it is difficult to pin down specimens for study in a definitive way. While we have reached some tentative conclusions about the significance of these new entrants, we do not claim that our view is the only one possible, or that future developments may not alter our conclusions. Uncertainty is particularly strong regarding the eventual impact of distance learning and educational technology, where the shape of the educational future remains, to us, at best foggy. Before turning to brief introductions of the chapters that follow, it will help the reader to know what judgments we have reached.

First, there is no question that the model of an accredited, degree-granting, for-profit college or university has been proven feasible, as well as highly successful financially. Concern that such institutions would necessarily exploit consumer ignorance to "rip off" potential students by providing poor quality in fly-by-night operations, while always a possibility and an occasional reality, does not typify the majority of accredited, degree-granting, for-profit institutions. Indeed, a moment's reflection will suggest that any organization seeking to thrive in a market heavily influenced by word-of-mouth endorsements from existing customers has little incentive to defraud consumers. While state approval still remains an issue for some of the institutions in some of the states, we have no doubt that every state will eventually license those companies whose goal is to deliver educational services in this fashion.

Second, we do not believe that for-profit institutions are a significant competitive threat to most of traditional higher education, despite views to the contrary expressed by some observers. (This conclusion could change if the financial circumstances of traditional higher education were to change, e.g., if state support for public institutions were to erode substantially.) Our findings suggest that most of these for-profit programs extend the market to students who, in many cases, would otherwise not enroll at all. This finding seems to be particularly clear with regard to the older, adult students who are a mainstay of many of these programs. Many traditional institutions have not viewed such students as a priority for recruiting and serving, thereby leaving untapped markets available for new entrants. It is also clear that for many traditional college-age students seeking full-time residential programs, for-profit schools are unlikely to be included in their choice set. For example, the student applying to the Universities of Virginia, Duke, and Chapel Hill is unlikely to consider DeVry as a fourth choice.

Having said that, it should also be noted that there are numerous programs where non-profit institutions have found themselves in competition with for-profits. Any college or university that does take part-time adult students seriously will find a for-profit competitor either present or potential. University schools of continuing education, which often run as revenue producers for the host university, are perhaps the most immediately competitive, but two-year colleges and their continuing education units also serve similar markets and undoubtedly lose some students to the new suppliers. We are also aware of the wise observation that new technologies and new activities are often overrated in the short term but underrated in the long term. We believe that the period of the late 1990s was a time when these new entrants (including distance learning) were overrated, and we may be in danger of now underrating their potential. Nonetheless, we argue that extending the market is the most accurate way to view the impact of the for-profits thus far.

Third, we do not see room for the entry of multiple organizations the size of the University of Phoenix in the U.S. educational market. Higher education in the United States is a mature industry, with over thirty-six hundred non-profit institutions, both public and private, blanketing the states. While the University of Phoenix is located in over half the states today, and continues to expand at the rate of one to two states per year, we do not foresee another dozen entities like the University of Phoenix springing to life and adding to the competition. In short, the for-profits have successfully identified niche markets in specific professional/technical areas where they can compete successfully, but there are natural limits to the size of this market, and we suspect that those limits are close to being reached in the United States. Indeed, the greatest potential for these institutions may be abroad in developing countries, where the demand for higher educational opportunities and the need for investment capital are enormous.

Fourth, we believe that most traditional institutions have lessons to learn from these new for-profit competitors, as the very success of these newer entities indicates that they are meeting needs that the traditional colleges and universities are not. What typifies the successful for-profits is a clear focus on education and training for employment, coupled with an emphasis on the student as client, or consumer, rather than as supplicant. Courses are offered at convenient times, in convenient places, with ample parking, and with time-saving procedures. Every effort is made to permit the student to complete a program quickly and with a minimum of downtime. Whereas traditional institutions are often described as more faculty-centered than student-centered, that would never be the case with a for-profit, where the student is sovereign. This approach has been particularly effective with the adult market, and those colleges and universities working that terrain and competing with for-profits will increasingly be forced to match these operating procedures.

Fifth, while it is common for many casual observers to connect for-profit higher education with distance learning, such a linkage does not distinguish this sector from the nonprofits. One finds distance learning offered in both for-profit and nonprofit universities, just as one finds bricks and mortar and face-to-face instruction occurring in both sectors. It is largely coincidental that the rise of for-profit, degree-granting higher education took place at the same time as the growth of the Internet and the World Wide Web, although this coincidence probably explains the presumed connection between the two. Similarly, the dot.com boom and bust had relatively little to do with the prospects of for-profit higher education. While one can expect for-profit providers to make use of distance learning if it promises to be profitable, many nonprofit universities are also motivated to explore the potential of this new form of educational delivery.

Sixth, just as distance learning is not a distinguishing feature between for-profit and nonprofit institutions, neither is accreditation, the process of self-regulation practiced within higher education. DeVry and Phoenix were both regionally accredited in the 1970s, by one of the same agencies (North Central) that accredits traditional institutions. True, national accreditation is available for the for-profit world, and some for-profits eschew regional accreditation, but in both instances the accrediting bodies warrant a minimal level of quality and certify the eligibility of the institution to receive and administer federal student financial aid.

In short, we see the for-profit sector as an active, viable, and financially successful piece of the landscape of postsecondary education, and assume it will continue to grow, just as we foresee growth for the nonprofit sector. While we see some overlap among the sectors, we also see distinct market niches for each group. We believe the regulatory environment will not be an obstacle to the expansion of for-profit higher education, nor do we believe it should be. We believe, given the knowledge-based economy in which we live, that there is ample market opportunity for both for-profit degree providers as well as for the thirty-six hundred traditional institutions. We do not hold an apocalyptic vision—as do some observers—regarding the potential inroads that the for-profit sector may make in the nonprofit market, nor do we believe some of the more exaggerated statements one hears about the unlimited growth potential of the for-profits. We tend to take an ecological view and believe that both forms of life can cohabit in the rich market for postsecondary education and training that exists in this country. That having been said, we also note that scholarly investigation of this newly developing sector is relatively primitive, and it will behoove scholars of higher education to continue to follow closely the further development of this relatively new sector of the industry.

CONTRIBUTIONS OF THE PRESENT VOLUME

The eight chapters that follow are grouped into three parts: Theory, Practice, and Political Economy. The first chapter, written by Breneman, Pusser, and Turner, presents an overview of both demand and supply sides of the market for postsecondary education. Data are provided on both the number of suppliers and the number of degrees awarded by each sector over several decades. Basic demographic facts are presented, showing the growth of the traditional college-going population of 18–22-year-olds, and the growth of the adult population. The reader quickly learns that the for-profit sector, while growing rapidly, remains a small part of the total postsecondary universe as measured by degrees granted, but also learns about the potential demand that has given rise to this new source of educational supply. This chapter follows an economic paradigm as an introduction to the reader.

In chapter 2, Pusser broadens the framework with a political/social model of higher education and the public good. The reason why higher education has been provided historically through non-profit suppliers is discussed, reflecting the context of social and cultural values that are preserved and transmitted through our traditional institutions. The for-profit phenomenon clearly reflects private financial values and calculations in which the student and college are motivated primarily by the private return on investment in postsecondary education and training. While such motivation is certainly present in the nonprofit sector and for its students, the rationale for public subsidy has always harkened to the broader nonprivate and nonexclusive values of an educated citizenry. Indeed, higher education is thought to create externalities of both a financial and nonfinancial form not captured by the student, and we subsidize enrollment so as to ensure the creation of these nonprivate benefits. The tension between private and public values in the provision of postsecondary education is laid out effectively in this chapter as a key factor in shaping wise public policy.

In chapter 3, Turner returns to the economic model but supplements it with an approach that considers higher education as an industry. In particular, she explores geographic areas of opportunity within the United States where a combination of population growth plus relatively limited supply of traditional institutions produces opportunities for entry by for-profit providers. The focus of her chapter is on the examination of where for-profit colleges and universities have made the largest inroads in providing collegiate opportunities for nontraditional students. The empirical strategy is to compare the institutional growth of for-profit colleges and universities across metropolitan areas with measures of demand conditions and the existing capacity of traditional collegiate providers. Because there are significant barriers to the formation of new public institutions, for-profit colleges are most likely to enter markets where there is an undersupply of college options and a high demand for skilled workers. An obvious extension of her analysis is the realization that underserved markets overseas represent an even greater opportunity for expansion; hence, one is not surprised to learn that the Apollo Group, Inc. (APOL), parent company to the University of Phoenix, among others, has created an international arm that is developing educational programs in Brazil, China, India, and in other developing nations.

Part 2 begins with chapter 4, by Breneman, which is a detailed look at the University of Phoenix (UOP), treated here as the poster child of the for-profit sector. Breneman provides educational and financial data about the company as well as a brief history of its founding and development. The educational model employed by UOP is discussed at length, noting that it differs from that used by many of the other for-profits. The lesson is that no single educational model dominates the for-profit sector; some schools, such as Phoenix, use primarily part-time practitioner faculty who have full-time day jobs, while others, such as DeVry, employ their own full-time faculty. Breneman explains the economic/business model for Phoenix, which relies heavily on the university's ability to attract a practitioner faculty labor supply. Features of the educational model that make possible this labor supply are developed and explained. The chapter concludes with observations on the governance structure of the university, i.e., how it balances academic and financial objectives, as well as some observations of educational strengths and weaknesses in the Phoenix model.

In chapter 5, Dudley Doane and Pusser present a comprehensive study of an emerging entrepreneurial component of nonprofit institutions, the summer sessions, as they are operated in twenty-five public flagship institutions. They suggest that summer sessions serve as a useful site for the study of entrepreneurial revenue generation close to the academic core, a new terrain for a set of activities more generally associated with auxiliary enterprises. They also address the role of summer sessions in contributing to a well-defined component of the academic mission at their respective institutions, internationalization. Doane and Pusser find that the summer sessions in this study are able to generate revenue to meet, and in many cases exceed their costs, while serving an academic function and contributing to the institutional mission. They conclude with a discussion of the challenges and choices that nonprofit institutions face as they balance revenue needs with academic imperatives.

Although we noted earlier that distance learning is a separable topic from for-profit higher education, the linkages between new educational technologies and both nonprofit and for-profit institutions suggests that this is an area requiring exploration. Chapter 6, by Saul Fisher, fills in this gap with a thorough look at developments in the market for higher education at a distance. The author's primary goal is to assess the root cause of the move by traditional institutions to enter the for-profit sphere, namely, an interest in exploiting new instructional technologies. Fisher argues that traditional colleges and universities have in many cases misunderstood the extent to which such technologies can aid entry into a commercial higher education marketplace. The well-publicized failures of NYU Online and Fathom (a creature of Columbia University and other partners) indicate the traps that lie in wait for certain for-profit subsidiaries. In order to explain these situations, the author examines the projected efficiencies of instructional technology as the source of much promise (vis-à-vis market entry), and much disappointment. What had been so widely promoted as an inexpensive means for institutions to expand their reach in fact faces tremendous costs—some hidden, some less so—that are true barriers to entry. Much of Fisher's analysis applies to the issues confronting for-profit institutions that would enter this arena, where traps also await the unwary.

Chapters 7 and 8 shift the focus to the final part of the volume—Political Economy. By that term we mean aspects of the surrounding environment within which for-profit higher education must function. Chapter 7, by Andreas Ortman, examines why Wall Street fell in love with higher education, that is, why those with financial capital saw fit to invest in this sector. With about two initial public offerings per year, the number of publicly traded degree-granting providers of postsecondary education in the United States has grown steadily ever since the Apollo Group went public in December 1994. To sell investors on ownership in companies that compete against traditional providers that do not have to produce profits, often receive substantial state subsidies, and are favored by numerous regulatory and tax breaks (including tax-deductible donations), investment bankers and market analysts must have "compelling" stories to tell. This chapter presents an inventory of the arguments typically employed as well as an attempt to quantify their relative importance through a questionnaire sent to stock-market analysts who follow the education industry. Ortman finds the analysts' arguments reasonably congruent with modern economic and managerial theories of firms and markets. In short, Wall Street had good reasons for falling in love with this sector of the education industry.

Finally, in chapter 8, Pusser and David A. Wolcott explore the political world of lobbyists in the rise of for-profit higher education. The chapter contains a wealth of information regarding contributions to political action committees (PACs), as well as contributions to particular members of Congress who are in a position to influence legislation of interest to the for-profit sector. The chapter discusses efforts by for-profits to gain access to increased public funding for students (grants and loans), and to reduce regulations (incentive compensation and the 12-hour rule) that constrain the growth of the for-profit market share and profitability. The chapter concludes with observations on for-profit lobbying and the reauthorization of the Higher Education Act (HEA), and implications for the regulation and coordination of nonprofit and for-profit higher education.

It is our hope that this book will stimulate others to write and do research about this fascinating and rapidly evolving sector of higher education. We have just scratched the surface of this complex topic, and as better economic data are forthcoming, it will be possible to undertake studies that eluded us, such as measuring the economic rate of a return to for-profit degrees. The education world has been unalterably changed, however, and our understanding of its future evolution will require thoughtful empirical work of the sort we have attempted to model.

Part 1

Theory

Chapter 1

The Contemporary Provision of For-Profit Higher Education

Mapping the Competitive Market

David W. Breneman, Brian Pusser, and Sarah E. Turner

INTRODUCTION

It has become an article of faith in popular accounts that the next decade will be a period in higher education defined by significant competitive gains by for-profit providers of degrees, educational services, and products (Odening and Letsinger, 2003; Newman and Couturier, 2001; Ruch, 2001). As one sign of the rapid pace of change, the growth in the number and the nature of contemporary for-profit providers, in the United States in particular, was described by one experienced observer as "shocking" (Levine, 1997). Reports from market analysts have evoked images of an imminent collision between efficient, technologically innovative, well-capitalized edu-corporations, and a host of tradition-bound, inefficient, revenue-challenged, postsecondary institutions (Odening and Letsinger, 2003; Farrington, 1999). Inherent in these presentations is the presumption that the competitive environment in higher education is changing rapidly and that colleges and universities in the public and nonprofit sectors are inefficient and failing to meet market demands.

The entrance of for-profit providers suggests the potential for dramatic changes in the market for higher education, affecting the range of programs available to potential students and the costs associated with different courses of study. The nonprofit higher education sector in the United States alone encompasses over 3,900 institutions, some 14 million students, and annual expenditures of over $200 billion. Despite the importance of the topic and the initial headlines, to date little empirical research has been devoted to a documentation of the changes in the number, distribution, and characteristics of for-profit education providers over the past three decades.

3

This chapter begins with a discussion of the historical evolution and variation in the organizational form of institutions in higher education. The second section presents an overview of the current demographics in the market for higher education, with particular focus on the size of the for-profit sector. The third section turns to the analytic framework and discusses the shifts in supply and demand that determine equilibrium in the market for higher education as well as the growth opportunities that the for-profit institutions experience. The final section provides a discussion of the public policy implications associated with the rise in the for-profit provision in the rise in higher education services. Data are drawn from Integrated Postsecondary Education Data Systems (IPEDS) *Institutional Characteristics*, and from over twenty semi-structured interviews conducted in 1999 with institutional leaders in the for-profit and nonprofit higher education sectors, as well as venture capitalists and education industry analysts.

CONTEXT AND HISTORY

The sustained dominance of the public and private nonprofit institutions in higher education throughout much of the twentieth century suggests that these institutional structures hold advantages beyond historical precedent (Goldin and Katz, 1999; Clark, 1983). One argument for the extensive role of nonprofits in the delivery of higher education concerns the very nature of the product. Unlike many commodities, which are well-defined and singular in consumption, the benefits of a higher education experience may be difficult to measure with precision in the short term and may also provide benefits to society beyond the gains to the individual student. To the extent that higher education is characterized by these conditions—"information asymmetries" and the "public goods characteristics"—there is a potential role for nonprofit provision.[1]

"Higher education" is not a single output but a range of different educational products. Degree programs vary markedly along a number of dimensions including how they are subsidized, the extent to which the course of study provides general or job-specific skills, the selectivity of admission requirements, and the mode of instructional delivery. As such, it is not surprising that the distribution of organizational forms varies appreciably across the range of educational providers.

History has played a significant role in the institutional evolution of the provision of higher education. Both technology and public policy have shaped the degree to which education has been provided by nonprofit or for-profit institutions, as well as the extent to which higher education has been financed by public or individual sources.

Well into the nineteenth century proprietary education, though often not degree granting, was a source of basic skills in areas such as teaching, medicine, law, and accounting that enabled individuals to make the transition to professional employment (Goldin and Katz, 1998; Honick, 1995; Geiger, 1986; Veysey, 1965). Rapid industrial growth at the turn of the century led to a proliferation of commercial schools that offered training in a number of new technologies, including the typewriter and stenographic machines (Honick, 1995). Yet, the latter portion of this period was less kind to proprietary schools, as the Progressive political movement and advocates of public vocational training placed increased constraints on the provision of for-profit education (Honick, 1995; Trivett, 1974). The release of the Flexner report in 1910 severely curtailed for-profit medical education programs and led to further calls for regulation and oversight of the entire proprietary sector.

Concurrently, the basic dynamics of the production process of higher education shifted in the early decades of the twentieth century with the advent of the comprehensive research university (Goldin and Katz, 1998). These institutions became characterized by economies of scale and scope, brought about by substantial changes in the natural sciences and in the public policies furthering the application of academic science in local industry. These emerging research universities operated with an increasing division of labor and degree of specialization. At the same time, complementarities in production emerged among undergraduate education, graduate training, and basic research. Combining these activities under one umbrella proved to be more efficient than the independent production of each education service (Paulson, 2002; Ehrenberg, 2000; Lowen, 1997). These comprehensive research universities were also predominantly nonprofit and public institutions. The entrance of the research universities ushered in an era of collective public investment in higher education, accompanied by increasing public funding for, and public oversight of, higher education (Goldin and Katz, 1998; Veysey, 1965).

The period from 1945 to 1975 is often cited as the "golden era" of American higher education. That phrase generally refers to the expansion in enrollments and expenditures at existing public and private nonprofit institutions (Clark, 1983, 1971; Kerr, 2003, 1991). As part of a general expansion of the public support for educational programs beginning with the *Sputnik* and continuing through the Great Society initiatives, this period represented a golden age of public funding for higher education; furthermore, the federal government provided substantial infrastructure through research grants to universities and financial aid to students (Brinkman and Leslie, 1986; Bowen, 1968). This period also encompassed the emergence and growth of a significant public policy debate over the appropriate forms of university adaptation and the balance of public and private funding in the provision of higher education (Pusser, 2002; Tierney, 1999; Calhoun, 1998).

The Resurgence of For-Profit Providers

One of the more significant events in the period was the passage of the Higher Education Act (HEA) of 1972. HEA augmented the amount and types of student loans and significantly increased the amount of direct financial awards to students, primarily through Basic Educational Opportunity Grants, subsequently renamed as Pell grants. HEA offered key benefits to for-profit educational providers as several types of for-profit schools and their students were made eligible for federal financial aid. Given the portability of Pell grants, HEA also shifted control of the largest share of federal financial aid dollars from institutions to individuals.[2]

More recently, a number of market factors have driven a substantial transformation in the for-profit sector and strong projections for growth into the foreseeable future. On the supply side, investments in new technology and improved organizational practices may enable for-profit providers to deliver a variety of higher education services at lower costs than those provided by public and nonprofit providers. On the demand side, the rising return to college training, combined with the increasing size of the college-age population, changed the opportunities for entry among for-profit providers.

DEMOGRAPHICS OF THE FOR-PROFIT HIGHER EDUCATION SECTOR

A major problem in conceptualizing specific changes in the for-profit degree-granting sector is the conflation of statistics and reports on the growth of the overall "education industry" in the United States with data on the growth in the specific arena of degree-granting, for-profit education. The total education industry is estimated at about $826.6 billion in 2003. Higher education expenditures are generally estimated at about $315.4 billion in 2003, for an enrollment of about 17.4 million students (U.S. Department of Education, 2005). The corporate education and training market comprises another $75 billion, and is expected to grow more rapidly than any other segment (Altbach, 2001). The for-profit degree granting industry is, to this point, significantly smaller.

The three degree-granting institutions most cited in contemporary accounts, the University of Phoenix, DeVry Inc., and Strayer Education Inc., together account for well over 100,000 students and over $1 billion in sales. The largest provider, Phoenix, has seven times as many students as the third largest provider, Strayer. These are significant numbers—particularly in relation to the average scale of long-established institutions in the public and non-profit sectors—but the overall scale of the degree-granting proprietary sector currently remains relatively small.

TABLE 1.1
Title IV Postsecondary Institutions by Control, Academic Year 2002–03

Institution Type	N
TOTAL	6,354
For-profit	2,382
Nonprofit Private	1,921
Nonprofit Public	2,051

Degree Granting		Non-Degree Granting	
4-year		4-year	
For-profit	297	For-profit	3
Nonprofit Private	1,538	Nonprofit Private	20
Nonprofit Public	631	Nonprofit Public	1
2-year		2-year	
For-profit	494	For-profit	270
Nonprofit Private	127	Nonprofit Private	124
Nonprofit Public	1,081	Nonprofit Public	74
		Less than 2 year	
		For-profit	1,318
		Nonprofit Private	112
		Nonprofit Public	264

Source: U.S. Department of Education, National Center for Education Statistics. *Integrated Postsecondary Education Data System (IPEDS): Institutional Characteristics*, Fall 2002.

The basic demographics of the for-profit sector of the higher education market are not well documented. The empirical analysis of the sector is complicated by the observation that definitions and terminology developed for quantifying various types of provision of higher education in earlier decades may be insufficient to capture the myriad new forms in this emerging sector.[3]

It may come as something of a revelation that there are currently nearly as many for-profit postsecondary institutions as there are nonprofit postsecondary institutions.[4] The 2002–3 census of institutions by the National Center for Education Statistics documents 2,382 for-profit institutions, 1,921 private nonprofit institutions, and 2,051 public nonprofit institutions (Table 1.1). Distinguishing institutions by degree-granting status and length of study changes the distribution markedly, with the 297 for-profit institutions accounting for about 12% of all postsecondary institutions with four-year courses of study. Of the total number of institutions identified as for-profit, the majority (55.3%) offer programs that are less than two years in length and award certificates rather than traditional degrees like the BA or MA (Table 1.1).

A focus on the institutional level in the for-profit sector among degree-granting institutions points to the substantial concentration in this market.

TABLE 1.2
Trends in BA Degrees Awarded by Institution Type

	Number of BA Degrees				Distribution of BA Degrees		
	Total	Proprietary	Private Nonprofit	Public Nonprofit	Proprietary	Private Nonprofit	Public Nonprofit
Number of Institutions	3,353	200	1,660	1,493	6.0%	49.5%	44.5%
Year							
1970	786,478	641	266,238	519,599	0.1%	33.9%	66.1%
1975	926,575	968	288,569	637,038	0.1%	31.1%	68.8%
1980	939,113	1,939	309,980	627,194	0.2%	33.0%	66.8%
1982	962,715	2,419	320,892	639,404	0.3%	33.3%	66.4%
1985	988,874	4,778	328,838	655,258	0.5%	33.3%	66.3%
1990	1,058,197	5,510	351,349	701,338	0.5%	33.2%	66.3%
1995	1,166,901	7,744	377,996	781,161	0.7%	32.4%	66.9%
2000	1,237,875	20,062	406,958	810,855	1.6%	32.9%	65.5%
2001	1,244,171	23,032	408,701	812,438	1.9%	32.8%	65.3%
2002	1,291,900	26,398	424,322	841,180	2.1%	32.8%	65.1%

Source: Author's tabulations for 1970 to 1995 are based on institutional level data from the CASPAR compilation of the HEGIS/IPEDS *Earned Degrees Conferred Surveys* using institutions with identifiable classifications and for the years 2000 to 2002 from the National Center of Education Statistics IPEDS data.

Examination of data on degrees granted compiled through the CASPAR system indicates the extent to which providers differ markedly in their market representation. Baccalaureate level degrees awarded by for-profit institutions are a small share of the total, accounting for just 2% of degrees awarded, even in recent years (Table 1.2). While the growth rate in degrees awarded by public and private nonprofit institutions has been about 30% from 1982 to 2002, baccalaureate degrees awarded by for-profits increased by 10% (Table 1.2). The story is parallel but more exaggerated at the MA level. In the late 1960s and early 1970s, MA degree production was extremely small, representing awards by one or two institutions. In 1982, fewer than 400 MA degrees were awarded by for-profit institutions, relative to more than 300,000 degrees awarded by public and private nonprofits (Table 1.3). By 2002, MA degree production among the for-profits increased more than fortyfold to over 14,000 degrees; still, this number represents only 3% of the market for MA degrees (Table 1.3). It is reasonable to conclude that it is not the current level of participation of the for-profits in the degree-granting sector that is of policy interest. Rather, it is the growth potential of these institutions that merits consideration.

It is also useful to look at the degree of concentration within each degree-granting sector. While the overall categorization of institutions describes

TABLE 1.3
Trends in MA Degrees Awarded by Institution Type

	Number of MA Degrees				Distribution of MA Degrees		
	Total	Proprietary	Private Nonprofit	Public Nonprofit	Proprietary	Private Nonprofit	Public Nonprofit
Number of Institutions	3,353	200	1,660	1,493	6.0%	49.5%	44.5%
Year							
1970	208,354	11	73,822	134,521	0.0%	35.4%	64.6%
1975	292,561	48	99,017	193,496	0.0%	33.8%	66.1%
1980	298,832	280	110,893	187,659	0.1%	37.1%	62.8%
1982	296,306	376	113,549	182,381	0.1%	38.3%	61.6%
1985	286,729	1,462	115,177	170,090	0.5%	40.2%	59.3%
1990	323,862	1,261	136,922	185,679	0.4%	42.3%	57.3%
1995	397,292	2,950	170,243	224,099	0.7%	42.9%	56.4%
2000	457,056	10,308	203,591	243,157	2.2%	44.6%	53.2%
2001	468,476	11,633	210,789	246,054	2.5%	45.0%	52.5%
2002	482,118	14,264	218,034	249,820	3.0%	45.2%	51.8%

Source: Author's tabulations for 1970 to 1995 are based on institutional level data from the CASPAR compilation of the HEGIS/IPEDS *Earned Degrees Conferred Surveys* using institutions with identifiable classifications and for the years 2000 to 2002 from the National Center of Education Statistics IPEDS data.

nearly 300 for-profit institutions as both degree granting and offering programs at least four years in length, far smaller numbers of institutions can be identified as actually awarding BA and MA level degrees. Thirty-six for-profit institutions awarded BA degrees over the three decades for which institutional data are available and only ten institutions awarded the MA degree. In the early years, two institutions—Armstrong College and Madison Junior College of Business—awarded all the BA degrees granted by the for-profit sector, with Armstrong also awarding all of the MA degrees until 1971. While these two institutions have not been part of recent expansion, the market remains similarly concentrated. At the baccalaureate level, six campuses of DeVry, Strayer, and the University of Phoenix award nearly 80% of the BA degrees awarded by the for-profit sector. The University of Phoenix and Keller School of Management have awarded more than 80% of the MA degrees in the for-profit sector since the mid-1980s.

A FRAMEWORK FOR ANALYSIS

In framing the evolution to date of the for-profit sector and expectations for future growth, it is helpful to conceptualize the transformations in terms of

supply side and demand side factors. This framework is also useful for thinking about global for-profit providers, and the commodity value of higher education goods and services, as well as degrees (Altbach, 2001; Marginson and
Considine, 2000). The supply side factors represent changes in the costs of
inputs and innovations in the "technology" of higher education that affect
profit opportunities. Changes in the labor market returns to higher education,
and the demographics of the population, help determine the demand side of
the market. Policy variables—including the level of student subsidies provided
through financial aid programs, and barriers of regulation and accreditation
also play an important role in the changing institutional compositions in the
market for higher education.

The Supply of For-Profit Education

Existing research on the supply of for-profit education, while not extensive,
offers quite different perspectives on these questions. Interview data collected
for this research reveal significant variation in perspectives on the future
prospects for growth in for-profit provision in the United States and around
the world. Institutional researchers in the United States capital markets and
for-profit leaders suggest that the for-profits will be extremely successful in
competing with the nonprofits. They cite increased availability of investment
capital, excellent job placement records, freedom from traditional curricula,
lower costs through increased productivity, economies of scale, and state-of-
the-art technology as key assets of the for-profits. Taken together they see
these factors enabling the for-profit degree-granting institutions to capture
market share from the nonprofits, and their perceptions are in accord with
those expressed by investment industry analysts and for-profit providers
(Odening and Letsinger, 2003; Ruch, 2001; Ortmann, 2000).

Others, including a number of higher education institutional leaders who
were interviewed, suggested that there will be a competitive struggle at the less
prestigious institutions, but they saw little possibility that for-profits will be
able to supply a product that can match the peer effects and signaling value of
elite nonprofit higher education institutions. It is in those institutions with low
prices and high capital requirements where the distinction between nonprofits
and for-profits in their access to capital markets may prove to be most deci-
sive. While both nonprofits and for-profits have access to capital through the
bond markets, a key (and unresolved) question is whether costs of capital are
identical through debt financing. For-profit institutions have direct access to
equity markets while that source of capital can only be accessed by nonprofit
institutions that work in partnership with for-profit entities or that create for-
profit subsidiaries (Pusser, 2002). Michael A. Olivas (2004), Pusser (2002),

Slaughter and Leslie (1997) have argued that the competition will be more legal and political than economic, and that the exploitation of faculty knowledge and course materials as revenue sources can occur in both for-profit and nonprofit institutions.

With regard to costs, it has been argued that the different institutional norms of the for-profit institutions may enable these providers to reduce costs and achieve greater efficiencies than their peers in the nonprofit sector (Kirp, 2003; Marchese, 1998). The spiraling costs of higher education, at public and private institutions, and the increased burden on individual students, are creating enormous pressure on the nonprofit institutions in the United States and around the world (Duderstadt and Womack, 2003; Ehrenberg, 2000). This in turn suggests increasing competitive leverage in the for-profit sector if those institutions are able to utilize capital investments and lower wage scales to maintain lower overall operating costs, while highly structured labor markets and the institution of tenure limit the ability of nonprofit providers to adapt quickly to changes in student demand.[5]

On the pricing dimension, for-profit institutions may also be more likely to break with the traditional "one price" model of nonprofit higher education (Paulson, 2002; Rothschild and White, 1993). Challenges to the "one-price" model raise the following question, if the cost of educating a student in the physical sciences is higher than the cost of educating a student in the humanities, why do they pay the same tuition? Although differential fees for graduate and professional education are increasingly fundamental to the pricing structure of nonprofit higher education, the for-profit enterprises are likely to endeavor to expedite and extend the "unbundling" of higher education pricing, charging individual students at all levels, prices more closely matched with underlying costs.

Winston (1999) has suggested that barriers to the entry of for-profits in higher education may be inversely related to the degree of subsidy for each student at the institutional level. The degree of subsidy is, in effect, the amount of public subsidy (broadly defined) combined with donative contributions from private gifts and endowment income, devoted to subsidizing tuition prices. Accordingly, the high subsidies at the most selective liberal arts colleges and research universities create essentially insurmountable barriers to entry by for-profits. Similarly, Hansmann (1998) suggests that at the most selective level, where access is highly allocated and subsidies the highest, consumers are fundamentally interested in the attributes of their fellow students. That market, where higher education becomes an "associative good" is also virtually unobtainable by existing for-profit providers.

While research universities and liberal arts colleges provide undergraduate programs targeted to full-time residential students, much of the growth in enrollment in the last two decades has occurred among older, nontraditional students (Seftor and Turner, 1999). The type of skills demanded by this new group of students is in some respects quite different from the broad, general training provided in the traditional four-year residential experience. As one education industry analyst has written, "these for-profit institutions are not offering education as much as they are offering careers" (Soffen, 1998).[6] The University of Phoenix, where nearly half of all students have their tuition subsidized by their current employers, has also been conceptualized as being in the business of "degree-granting corporate outsourcing" (Pusser and Doane, 2001). Nor is there evidence that the contemporary degree granting for-profits will overcome the traditional challenges to vocational training programs; the difficulty of transferring credits from vocational programs to more broadly oriented baccalaureate programs, the sensitivity of vocational education programs to declines in the rate of job creation, and the rapid obsolescence of vocational skills (Levin, 2001; Grubb, 1997, 1995).

The Regulatory Environment

Starting a for-profit higher education institution is more challenging than entering many competitive markets because the product—the awarding of degrees—is heavily regulated by state and regional accrediting bodies. The various layers of regulation, and the variation in requirements for accreditation in different regions of the United States create significant barriers to entry in for-profit higher education (Eaton, 2003).

It has been noted that for-profit institutions seeking accreditation can be generally divided into three categories (Eaton, 2003). The first group consists of those institutions that are already accredited, as in the case of the University of Phoenix, and DeVry Inc. A second group includes those institutions that are not accredited and do not need accreditation. These are for the most part institutions that do not require Title IV financial aid.[7] These institutions, such as the IBM global campus and the Oracle corporate-training section, are primarily interested in providing employer-subsidized training and credentials. The third group consists of those organizations that seek rapid accreditation through partnerships with existing accredited institutions. Examples include the acquisition of Huron University by Whitman Incorporated.

There are two components of accreditation that are key to shaping the competitive environment in higher education. First, accreditation is central to the information asymmetries mentioned earlier. Accreditation sends a signal to potential students about the threshold quality of education provided. Second, accreditation is a prerequisite for student eligibility for federally sponsored financial aid under Title IV. Recently some analysts have suggested that large and publicly traded for-profits, such as the University of Phoenix, may ultimately provide all of the loans and grants needed by their students from institutional funds generated in alliance with investment firms (Goldstein, 1999; Soffen, 1998). In that case, if it proved to be in their interests to do so, they might also be able to forego the traditional accreditation process, as is the case with many of the largest international for-profit education programs (Tooley, 1999).

The Demand for Higher Education Services

The demand conditions faced by for-profit schools can be conceptualized as part of the more general demand for the training, skills, and credentials offered in higher education. The level and character of demand determine the particular implications for the for-profit sector. Overall, we can gauge the demand for higher education—and the services provided by higher education—in terms of the "prices," the levels of subsidy, returns in the labor market, the demographics of the population of potential students, and state and local norms affecting access. Whether one regards the return to a BA degree or the return to a single credit, the evidence is incontrovertible that the relative return to postsecondary training has increased since the early 1990s. This transformation in the labor market is a significant determinant of the probability of for-profit entry (Pusser and Turner, 2004). However, for-profit enrollments are nevertheless sensitive to broader economic shifts (Tables 1.2 and 1.3).

Among high-achieving recent high school graduates, the demand for college training may be largely insensitive to changes in labor market conditions or college costs, as those students seek elite (and highly publicly subsidized) training and credentials. However, for older and nontraditional students, demand for training is likely to be quite sensitive to cost, as well as to labor market conditions. A further issue is the extent to which for-profit degree programs will appeal to the largest portion of the degree market, traditional-aged students seeking their first degrees. The ultimate growth of the for-profit degree-granting institutions may depend on their ability to tap into the demand for this group of students. At issue is whether students—and the labor market—view the educational products offered by these institutions as close substitutes to the options provided by traditional colleges and universities.

If for-profits can provide narrowly tailored skills that lead to specific, high-value job placement, older students in particular may prefer this otherwise "no-frills" approach to higher education to institutions providing a wide array of student services and recreational activities (Sperling and Tucker, 1997; Ruch, 2001). While survey data including the Higher Education Research

Institute's "American Freshman Survey," report an increase in the share of freshmen citing the desire to "be well-off financially" (Astin and Parrott, 2003), this trend may not predict an increase in enrollments at the for-profit institutions. The increasing returns to college quality documented by Hoxby (1997), Turner (1997), and Brewer, Eide, and Ehrenberg (1999) would suggest that the largest increases in demand among traditional undergraduate students would be among the most highly selective institutions in the nonprofit and public sectors. It is also the case that traditional nonprofit institutions, residential as well as nonresidential higher education providers, are increasingly seeking to enter the competition for adult student training and degree granting, through innovative degree programs, continuing education, and extension programs (Pusser and Doane, 2001).

A number of these issues are manifest in contemporary responses to the shortage of teachers. The problem of how to rapidly recruit, train, and retain able young people in the teaching force is a challenge that may benefit from market competition (Turner, 2000; Raphael and Tobias, 1997). Whether for-profit provision of teacher training will help to resolve the shortage and enhance the quality of entering teachers is an open question (Turner, 2000).

The proportion of students who will be served by the emerging for-profit sector, and at what cost, is an outcome determined by the intersection of supply and demand forces. Public policy initiatives such as the availability of federal financial aid also serve to influence this equilibrium. Changes in the availability and specifications of aid such as Pell grants or Stafford loans affect the budget constraints faced by students and their families. At issue is the extent to which these demand shifts are countered by increases in the prices charged by the colleges and universities, and whether the for-profit schools respond differently than the nonprofit institutions.

IMPLICATIONS AND AREAS FOR FUTURE RESEARCH

As the data presented here demonstrate, for-profit providers currently represent a tiny fraction of the total degree-granting activity in American higher education. While the capital markets' excitement over the rapid growth in enrollments and the number of degrees granted by for-profits brings with it a very loud "buzz," that enthusiasm must be tempered to some degree by the very small base from which that growth is measured, and by the uncertain prospects for the continuation of the current rate of growth. There are, however, a number of key public policy issues that must be considered in light of the shifting economic, political, and social conditions that have given rise to the growth of for-profit participation in higher education.

Much of the concern over the growth of for-profit education reflects an historical debate over the risks associated with the private provision of an essential public good (Pusser, 2002; Weisbrod, 1998; Labaree, 1997; Veysey, 1965). Traditional arguments address the possibility of opportunistic behavior on the part of profit-seeking providers, the information asymmetry between consumers and providers, and the likelihood of uncertainty leading to under-investment (James, 1998). More recently, public higher education has been seen as a key arena for the redress of historical inequities in access to education and leadership positions (Bowen and Bok, 1998; Kerr, 1994; Carnoy and Levin, 1985). It has been argued that the expansion of nonprofit education in the postwar period, and the concurrent implementation in those institutions of public policies on affirmative action and gender equity, have contributed significantly to increased access and diversity in higher education (Breneman, 2003; Hurtado and Navia, 1997). Hansmann (1998) predicts that increasing stratification and privatization will present significant challenges to efforts to maintain equity and efficiency in higher education. How competition from for-profit providers will affect the distribution of access to higher education is a key public policy question going forward.

The impact of for-profit providers on curricula in higher education has also been raised by several researchers (Paulson, 2002; Marginson and Consadine, 2000; Raphael and Tobias, 1997; Rhoades and Slaughter, 1997). Raphael and Tobias examined the competition for the provision of teaching credentials in Arizona between the University of Phoenix and a number of nonprofit institutions. They found that while nonprofit providers had requirements that went beyond the state minimum for credentials, the University of Phoenix gained some competitive advantage by requiring only the state minimum of their students. A number of researchers have expressed concern that the determinant of curricular standards will increasingly be the political arena, where for-profit institutions are active financial contributors and nonprofits are prohibited from many aspects of lobbying (Aronowitz, 2000; Apple, 1999).

Initial research on "hybrid" institutional forms (Pusser, 2002) suggests that the increasing adoption of commercial behavior in nonprofit higher education institutions represents a potentially problematic convergence of non-profit and for-profit forms. The long-term effect of the growth of auxiliary enterprises, credit and noncredit continuing education programs, industry-university partnerships, and the creation of for-profit subsidiaries of nonprofit institutions are not yet clear. A key challenge for this research is to explain what factors distinguish educational products in which convergence appears, from those in which increased stratification dominates the landscape such as the changing dimensions of baccalaureate programs in the national market (Pusser and Turner, 2004; Hoxby, 1998).

Another important area of future research addresses the extent to which competition among for-profit and nonprofit institutions leads to a socially optimal level and distribution of educational attainment. A key aspect of this question is whether increased competition promotes productive efficiency—or getting an output at the least cost—in the education sector.[8] It is often argued that the competitive effects associated with the entry of new producers improves efficiency. Yet, such claims may not translate to a mixed-market context in which the underlying product is difficult to observe and encompasses collective benefits as well as individual rewards. Finally, higher education in the United States has not historically been equitably distributed between various racial-ethnic and socioeconomic groups. While changing demographics and increased efforts to access high-quality higher education by traditionally underrepresented groups will be key factors in shaping future demand, the nature of that demand and how it will affect the provision of higher education is at this point unclear.

NOTES

1. Hansmann (1987) provides a useful taxonomy of the potential economic motivations for the provision of goods and services. Social scientists disagree about the extent to which there is an appreciable "public goods" character to higher education. While it is widely argued that the provision of basic education (e.g., literacy skills) has a widespread public value in facilitating smoother social functioning (Labaree, 1997), and that higher education is a key component of State efforts to increase equity (Pusser and Ordorika, 2001; Carnoy and Levin, 1985) it is also argued that the returns to higher education may be largely confined to the individual. Still, one of the most compelling motivations for the subsidization of particular types of training in higher education (e.g., advanced scientific study) is that the social rate of return may well exceed the private return.

"Information problems" or "contract failures" are certainly a potential problem for students in higher education as it may well be difficult to ascertain if a student received the quantity or quality of education that he or she expected. While for-profit firms may have an incentive to take advantage of customers by providing an inferior education to increase their profits, the ability of agents of nonprofits to benefit personally through the provision of inferior services is limited by the nondistribution constraint.

2. An unanticipated consequence of that shift was a significant increase in the share of Pell grants allocated to students in for-profit institutions. For example, while only 7% of Pell revenue went to students at for-profit institutions at the start of the program in academic year 1973-1974, that share climbed to a peak near 30% in the late 1980s (McPherson and Schapiro, 1991, Table 2.5). Subsequent revelations of financial irregularities in awarding Pell grants and student loans (largely among trade schools) led to increased federal scrutiny and to a decline in the for-profits' share of those funds.

3. For example, an "institution" is a frequent unit of analysis that is used to refer to a single governing body with a single campus, while in the for-profit sector, an institution may have many campus affiliations.

4. These include degree-granting and nondegree-granting programs and institutions.

5. Nonprofits, out of necessity, have already begun to find new efficiencies in order to remain price competitive with one another as state block funding decreases (Blustain, Goldstein, and Lozier, 1998; Duderstadt, 1998). Rhoades and Slaughter (1997) point to the increasing and widespread use of nontenured and part-time faculty as an example of rapid cost reductions that have been implemented in the nonprofit sector. Other studies of nonprofit universities point to the increasing concentration of institutional resources in those disciplines and in professional schools perceived to yield the most favorable labor market outcomes (Kirp, 2003; Marginson, 1997; Slaughter and Leslie, 1997).

6. Beyond changes and adaptations in curricular content, for-profit providers may be better positioned to utilize innovative technologies for delivering program content, primarily through the use of the Internet (Ruch, 2001; Graves, 1998; Marchese, 1998; Levine, 1997). The three largest for-profit degree-granting concerns, the University of Phoenix, DeVry and Strayer, generally make relatively little use of the Internet in their delivery, though Phoenix currently has about 15% of its population, nearly 15,000 students, pursuing degrees online. It is also important to note that each of these institutions uses a predominantly synchronous learning process with instructor-led classes offered at convenient times in relatively unconventional locations, including shopping malls and industrial parks that are easily accessed by their largely adult and employed student bodies. The increasing incidence of "virtual degrees" is not, however, limited to the for-profit sector, as indicated by the offerings of the nonprofit case of Penn State's World Campus.

7. Title IV financial aid refers to federally subsidized loans and grants, including Pell grants.

8. There is of course little agreement on how best to define or measure the outputs of higher education (Levin, 2001).

References

Altbach, P. G. (2001, May 11). Why higher education is not a global commodity. *The Chronicle of Higher Education, Chronicle Review*, B20.

Apple, M. (1999, April 30). Rhetorical reforms: Markets, standards and inequality. *Current Issues in Comparative Education, 1*(2). Retrieved from http://www.tc.columbia.edu/cice/articles/ma112.htm

Aronowitz, S. (2000). *The knowledge factory*. Boston: Beacon.

Astin, A. W., & Parrott, S. A. (2003). *The American freshman survey 2003*. Los Angeles: Higher Education Research Institute, Graduate School of Education and Information Sciences: UCLA.

Block, H. M., & Dobell, B. (1999). *The e-bang theory. Illuminismo, 2.* San Francisco: Banc of America Securities Equity Research Division. Retrieved from http://www.masie.com/masie/researchreports/ebang.pdf

Blustain, H., Goldstein, P., & Lozier, G. (1998). Assessing the new competitive landscape. In R. N. Katz and Associates (Eds.), *Dancing with the devil: Information technology and the new competition in higher education* (pp. 51–72). San Francisco: Jossey-Bass.

Bok, D. (2003). *Universities in the marketplace: The commercialization of higher education.* Princeton: Princeton University Press.

Bowen, H. R. (1968). *The finance of higher education.* New York: McGraw Hill.

Bowen, W. & Bok, D. (1998). *The shape of the river: Long term consequences of considering race in college and university admissions.* Priceton: Princeton University Press.

Breneman, D. W. (2003, Spring). Declining access: A potential—if slow moving—train wreck. *National Crosstalk, 11(2).* Retrieved from http://www.highereducation.org/crosstalk/ct0203/voices0203–declining.shtml

Breneman, D. W., & Finney, J. E. (1997). The changing landscape: Higher education finance in the 1990s. In P. M. Callan and J. E. Finney (Eds.), *Public and private financing of higher education: Shaping public policy for the future* (pp. 30–59). Phoenix: ACE and the Oryx Press.

Brewer, D. J., Eide, E. R., & Ehrenberg, R. (1999). Does it pay to attend an elite private college? Cross-cohort evidence on the effects of college type on earnings? *Journal of Human Resources, 34*(1), 104–123.

Brinkman, P., & Leslie, L. L. (1986). Economies of scale in higher education: Sixty years of research. *Review of Higher Education, 10*(1), 1–28.

Calhoun, C. (1998). The public good as a social and cultural project. In W. W. Powell and E. S. Clemens (Eds.), *Private action and the public good* (pp. 20–35). New Haven: Yale University Press.

Carnoy, M., & Levin, H. M. (1985). *Schooling and work in the democratic state.* Stanford, CA: Stanford University Press.

Clark, B. R. (1983). *The higher education system: Academic organization in cross-national perspective.* Berkeley: University of California Press.

Clark, B. R. (1971). Belief and loyalty in college organization. *Journal of Higher Education, 42,* 499–515.

Duderstadt, J. J. (1998). Can colleges and universities survive in the information age? In R. N. Katz and Associates (Eds.), *Dancing with the devil: Information technology and the new competition in higher education* (pp. 1–26). San Francisco: Jossey-Bass.

Duderstadt, J. J., & Womack, F. W. (2003). *The future of the public university in America: Beyond the crossroads.* Baltimore: Johns Hopkins.

Eaton, J. (2003). Is accreditation accountable? The continuing conversation between accreditation and the federal government. *CHEA Monograph Series, 1.* Washington, DC: Council for Higher Education Accreditation.

Ehrenberg, R. G. (2000). *Tuition rising: Why colleges cost so much.* Cambridge: Harvard University Press.

Farrington, G. C. (1999). The new technologies and the future of residential undergraduate education. In R. N. Katz and Associates (Eds.), *Dancing with the devil: Information technology and the new competition in higher education* (pp. 74–94). San Francisco: Jossey-Bass.

Flexner, A. (1930). *Universities, American, English, German.* New York: Oxford University Press.

Flexner, A. (1910). *Medical education in the United States and Canada: A report to the Carnegie Foundation for the Advancement of Teaching.* New York: Ayer.

Friedman, M. (1955). The role of government in higher education. In R. A. Solo (Ed.), *Economics and the public interest* (pp. 123–44). Rutgers University.

Gay, K. (1998). *The age of knowledge: The growing investment opportunity in education, corporate training and childcare.* Equity Research Department, NationsBanc: Montgomery Securities.

Geiger, R. L. (1986). *To advance knowledge: The growth of American research universities, 1900–1940.* New York: Oxford University Press.

Goldin, C., & Katz, L. F. (1999). The shaping of higher education: The formative years in the United States, 1890–1940. *Journal of Economic Perspectives 13*(1), 37–62.

Goldstein, M. B. (1999). Capital ideas. *University Business,* 46–53.

Graves, W. H. (1998). Developing and using technology as a strategic asset. In R. N. Katz and Associates (Eds.), *Dancing with the devil: Information technology and the new competition in higher education* (pp. 95–118). San Francisco: Jossey-Bass.

Gumport, P. J., & Pusser, B. (1999). University restructuring, economic and political contexts. In J. C. Smart (Ed.), *Higher education: Handbook of theory and research, 14.* New York: Agathon Press.

Gumport, P. J., & Pusser, B. (1997). Restructuring the academic environment. In M. Peterson, D. Dill, and L. Mets (Eds.), *Planning and management for a changing environment.* San Francisco: Jossey-Bass.

Hansmann, H. (1998, September). *Higher education as an associative good.* Paper presented at the Symposium of the Forum for the Future of Higher Education, Aspen, Colorado.

Hansmann, H. (1987). Economic theories of nonprofit organization. In W. Powell (Ed.), *The nonprofit sector: A research handbook.* New Haven: Yale University Press.

Honick, C. A. (1995). The story behind proprietary schools in the United States. In D. A. Clowes and E. Hawthorne (Eds.), *Community colleges and proprietary schools: Conflict or convergence?* San Francisco: Jossey-Bass.

Hoxby, C. (1997). *How the changing market structure of U.S. higher education explains tuition.* (NBER Working Paper 6323).

Hurtado, S., & Navia, C. (1997). Reconciling college access and the affirmative action debate. In M. Garcia (Ed.), *Affirmative action's testament of hope: Strategies for a new era in higher education* (pp. 105–130). Albany: SUNY Press.

James, E. (1998). Commercialism among nonprofits: Objectives, opportunities, and constraints. In B. A. Weisbrod (Ed.), *To profit or not to profit: The commercial transformation of the nonprofit sector* (p. 340). Cambridge, United Kingdom: Cambridge University Press.

Kerr, C. (2003). *The gold and the blue. Vol. 2, A personal memoir of the University of California.* Berkeley: University of California Press.

Kerr, C. (1994). Expanding access and changing missions: The federal role in U.S. higher education. *Educational Record, 75,* 27–31.

Kerr, C. (1991). *The great transformation in higher education, 1960–1980.* Albany: SUNY Press.

Kerr, C. (1963). *The uses of the university.* Cambridge: Harvard University Press.

Kirp, D. L. (2003). *Shakespeare, Einstein and the bottom line: The marketing of higher education.* Cambridge: Harvard University Press.

Labaree, D. F. (1997). Public goods, private goods: The American struggle over educational goals. *American Educational Research Journal, 34*(1), 39–81.

Levine, A. (1997). How the academic profession is changing. *Daedalus, 126*(4), 1–20.

Levin, J. S. (2001). *Globalizing the community college: Strategies for change in the twenty-first century.* New York: Palgrave.

Lowen, R. S. (1997). *Creating the Cold War university.* Berkeley: University of California Press.

Marchese, T. (1998, May/June). Not-so-distant-competitors: How new providers are remaking the postsecondary marketplace. *AAHE Bulletin 50*(9), 37.

Marginson, S. (1997). *Markets in education.* Melbourne: Allen & Unwin.

Marginson, S., & Considine, M. (2000). *The enterprise university.* Cambridge, United Kingdom: Cambridge University Press.

McPherson, M., & Schapiro, M. (1991). *Keeping college affordable.* Washington, DC: Brookings Institution.

Newman, F., & Couturier, L. K. (2001, October). The new competitive arena: Market forces invade the academy. *Change 33*(5), 11–17.

Noble, D. F. (1998). Digital diploma mills: The automation of higher education. *First Monday, 3*(1). Retrieved from http://www.firstmonday.org/issues/issue3_1/noble/index.html

Odening, G., & Letsinger, K. (2003, April 8). Online degree demand just getting started. *Initiating Coverage* (pp. 1–12). Jeffries & Company.

Olivas, M. A. (2004). The rise of nonlegal-legal influences on higher education. In R. G. Ehrenberg (Ed.), *Governing academia*. Ithaca: Cornell University Press.

Ortmann, A. (2001) Capital romance: Why Wall Street fell in love with higher education. *Education Economics, 9*, 293–311.

Oster, S. (1997). *An analytical framework for thinking about the use of for-profit structures for university services and activities.* Paper presented at the Symposium of the Forum for the Future of Higher Education, Aspen, Colorado.

Paulson, K. (2002). Reconfiguring faculty roles for virtual settings. *Journal of Higher Education, 73*(1), 123–140.

Prager, C. (1995). Ties that bind: Default, accreditation, and articulation. In D. A. Clowes and E. Hawthorne (Eds.), *Community colleges and proprietary schools: Conflict or convergence?* San Francisco: Jossey-Bass.

Pusser, B. (2003). Beyond Baldridge: Extending the political model of higher education governance. *Educational Policy, 17*(1), 121–140.

Pusser, B. (2002). Higher education, the emerging market, and the public good. In P. Graham and N. Stacey (Eds.), *The knowledge economy and postsecondary education.* Washington, DC: National Academy Press.

Pusser, B., & Doane, D. J. (2001). Public purposes and private enterprise: The contemporary organization of postsecondary education. *Change, 33*(5), 18–22.

Pusser, B., and Turner, S. E. (2004). Nonprofit and for-profit governance in higher education. In R. G. Ehrenberg (Ed.), *Governing academia*. Ithaca: Cornell University Press.

Pusser, B. & Ordorika, I. (2001). Bringing political theory to university governance: The University of California and the Universidad Nacional Autónoma de México. In Stromquist (ed.), *Higher education: Handbook of theory and research*. Vol. XV. New York: Agathon Press.

Raphael, J., & Tobias, S. (1997). Profit-making or profiteering. *Change, 29*(6), 45–50.

Rhoades, G., & Slaughter, S. (1997). Academic capitalism, managed professionals and supply-side higher education. *Social Text, 15*(2), 9–38.

Rothschild, M., & White, L. (1993). The university in the marketplace: Some insights and some puzzles. In Clotfelter and Rothschild (Eds.), *Studies of supply and demand in higher education.* Chicago: University of Chicago Press.

Ruch, R. S. (2001). *Higher education, inc.: The rise of the for-profit university*. Baltimore: Johns Hopkins.

Seftor, N., & Turner, S. E. (1999). *Changes in adult collegiate enrollment: The role of federal student aid policy.* University of Virginia, mimeo.

Slaughter, S., & Leslie, L. L. (1997). *Academic capitalism: Politics, policies, and the entrepreneurial university.* Baltimore: Johns Hopkins Press, 276 pp.

Soffen, S. (1998, September). *For-profit, post-secondary education: Profiting from a knowledge-based economy.* Equity Research Industry Analysis. Baltimore: Legg Mason Wood Walker.

Sperling, J. (2000). *Rebel with a cause: The entrepreneur who created the University of Phoenix and the for-profit revolution in higher education.* New York: John Wiley.

Sperling, J., & Tucker, R. W. (1997). *For-profit higher education: Developing a world class workforce.* New Brunswick: Transaction.

Stallings, D. (1997). The virtual university is inevitable: But will the model be nonprofit or profit? *Journal of Academic Librarianship, 23*(4), 271–280.

Strosnider, K. (1998, January 23). For-profit higher education sees booming enrollments and revenues. *Chronicle of Higher Education,* A36.

Tierney, W. G. (1999). *The responsive university: Restructuring for high performance.* Baltimore: Johns Hopkins.

Tooley, J. (1999). *The global education industry.* London, United Kingdom: IFC Press.

Trivett, D. A. (1974). *Proprietary schools and postsecondary education.* Washington, DC: American Association for Higher Education.

Turner, S. E. (1997). *Increasing returns to college quality: Evidence from the PSID.* University of Michigan, mimeo.

Turner, S. E. (1999). *The new market for higher education: For-profit colleges and the transformation from mature to emerging industry.* University of Virginia, mimeo.

Turner, S. E. (2000). The evolving production functions of schools of education. In W. Tierney (Ed.), *Faculty roles and rewards in schools and colleges of education.* Albany: SUNY Press.

U.S. Department of Education, National Center for Education Statistics (2005). *Digest of Education Statistics* tables and figures retrieved from http://nces.ed.gov.

Veysey, L. R. (1965). *The emergence of the American university.* Chicago: University of Chicago Press.

Weisbrod, B. A. (1998). The nonprofit mission and its financing: Growing links between nonprofits and the rest of the economy. In B. A. Weisbrod (Ed.), *To profit or not to profit: The commercial transformation of the nonprofit sector.* Cambridge, United Kingdom: Cambridge University Press.

Winston, G. (1998, November). *For-profit education: Godzilla or Chicken Little?* Williams Project for the Economics of Higher Education, Williams College (Discussion paper No. 49).

Chapter 2

Higher Education, Markets, and the Preservation of the Public Good

Brian Pusser

If a nation expects to be ignorant and free, in a state of civilization, it expects what never was and never will be.
—Thomas Jefferson to Col. Charles Yancey, January 6, 1816

INTRODUCTION

One of the more remarkable aspects of contemporary research and analysis of higher education is the repeated invocation of the emergence of a market for postsecondary education and training (Newman, Couturier, and Scurry, 2004; Kirp, 2003; Collis, 2001; Ruch, 2001; Duderstadt, 2000, 1999; Munitz, 2000; Goldstein, 1999; Marchese, 1998). These accounts generally suggest that increased market competition is the inevitable result of economic and technological changes that are transforming higher education from "cottage monopoly to competitive industry" (Munitz, 2000, p. 12). They further suggest that under the market model, colleges and universities will be increasingly consumer driven (Peters, 2004); operated like firms (Washburn, 2005; Blustain, Goldstein, and Lozier, 1999; Garber, 1996); challenged by unprecedented competition (Breneman, 2005; Newman, Couturier, and Scurry, 2004); and will find their traditional forms of pedagogy and credentialing transformed by technological innovations (Geiger, 2004; Newman and Scurry, 2001; Adelman, 2000) and political economic shifts (Turner and Pusser, 2004; Aronowitz, 2000).

The inherent assumptions in the presentation of an emerging market for higher education are even more striking than the ubiquity of market metaphors themselves, yet it is not clear that those assumptions are valid. This chapter turns attention to three fundamental assumptions that shape predictions of an emerging competitive marketplace for higher education. The first is that higher education institutions operate in an environment and under conditions that can accurately be described as market competition. The second assumption is that a lack of institutional efficiency and productivity has

23

generated demands for market solutions and that market-like behaviors on the part of postsecondary institutions will increase efficiency and productivity in higher education. Finally, there is the assumption that market approaches to the provision of higher education will produce at least the same quantity and distribution of public and private goods as are generated by the present system. While each of these assumptions has been debated in contemporary research on higher education, the argument over the case for higher education as a public good has moved to the fore over the past decade (Pusser, in press; Marginson, 2004a; Slaughter and Rhoades, 2004; Levine, 2001). It is a conflict that is central to contests over access, finance, and accountability in the postsecondary realm and one that demands a reconsideration of the fundamental sources of legitimacy for postsecondary education. The notion that market provision of higher education will preserve the role of higher education as a public good challenges a number of traditional beliefs about the nature of education itself. John McMurtry (1991) put it this way:

> The defining principles of education and of the market-place are fundamentally contradictory in: (1) their goals; (2) their motivations; (3) their methods; and (4) their standards of excellence. It follows, therefore, that to understand the one in terms of the principles of the other, as has increasingly occurred in the application of the market model to the public educational process, is absurd. (p. 216)

The three assumptions have also engendered a degree of resignation to the expansion of market provision of higher education. While researchers may differ on whether a market approach is a positive development, the underlying question in contemporary accounts is not whether higher education institutions should adopt market-like behaviors, but whether they will be able to do so rapidly enough to remain competitive. As Newman and Couturier (2001) put it, "Whether policy makers and academic leaders are capable of addressing these issues in the months and years ahead or not, higher education will continue its inexorable evolution toward a market economy" (p. 9). That sense of inevitability in turn fosters demands for further adaptation of higher education systems in the United States and around the world (Levin 2001; Levin, 2005; Tooley, 1999; Clark, 1998). It is the argument here that market approaches to higher education should not be seen as inevitable, in part because they are largely ahistorical. Contemporary literature on the need to adapt to changing demands through market solutions does not sufficiently account for the evolution of the nonprofit institution as the dominant form for the provision of postsecondary education in the United States. Nor does contemporary research sufficiently explore the relative inability of market-based, consumer-driven systems to produce opportunities for universal access, leadership training, or the redress of social inequalities. In order to understand the continuing importance of nonmarket delivery of higher education in the service of the public good, we need to begin with an overview of the changing demands on the higher education system.

THE CHANGING ENVIRONMENT

Contemporary research on the contextual changes shaping higher education has focused on a number of issues, including labor market demands (Turner and Pusser, 2004; Adelman, 2000); the new demographics of postsecondary students and constituents (Geiger, 2004; Carnevale and Fry, 2001; Kohl and LaPidus, 2000); the rising cost of higher education (Ehrenberg, 2000); globalization (Marginson, 2004a; Levin, 2001); shifts in law and contracting (Olivas, 2004); new technologies (Mendenhall, 2001; Graves, 1999); governance (Pusser, 2004; Ordorika 2003); and intra-institutional competition as a driver of change in postsecondary structures and processes (Bowen, Kurzweil, Tobin, and Pichler 2005; Pusser and Turner, 2004; Slaughter and Rhoades, 2004; Kirp, 2003; Levine, 2001; Marginson and Considine, 2000).

Perhaps the most influential analyses have been those focused on changes in the finance of higher education over the past two decades (Breneman, 2005; Altbach, 2002; Heller, 2001; McKeown-Moak, 2000; Goldstein, 1999; Kane, 1999; McPherson and Schapiro, 1998). During that period increases in enrollments coincided with a retrenchment from state block grant support for higher education (Breneman, 2005; Winston, Carbone, and Lewis, 1998). In response, institutions have rapidly increased tuition, and students and parents have taken on a significantly larger portion of the finance of higher education (Burd, 2003; Altbach, 2002; Callan, 2001; Breneman, 2000). This shift in the burden of paying for higher education has revived a long-standing debate, one that encompasses considerably more than resource allocation, as it calls for rethinking the organization and delivery of higher education. In the United States and elsewhere around the world, that broader debate has recently centered on the role of market competition in the transformation of higher education and on the effect of market competition on the contributions of higher education to the public good (Pusser, in press; Marginson, 2004b; Altbach, 2001; Pusser and Doane, 2001; Currie and Newson, 1999; Tooley, 1999).

HIGHER EDUCATION AND THE PUBLIC GOOD

One of the few areas of agreement with regard to the public good is that it is a problematic concept. Even the phrase, "the public good," shares space in our discourse with "the common good" and "the public interest." There are also many references to a different concept, "public goods," in concert with the ascendance of market models and economic approaches to public life. The nature of public goods is also contested, though they are commonly identified by two characteristics, nonrivalry and nonexcludability (Samuelson, 1954). Public goods are presumed to be underproduced in markets, as those two fundamental characteristics constrain individual producers from generating sufficient profit (Marginson, 1997).

Mansbridge (1998) argues that the idea of the public good is a fundamentally unsettled, contested concept, one that is at the center of broader conflicts over public action. Similarly, Calhoun (1998) suggests that the public good is a dynamic and indeterminate social and cultural construct. Reese (2000) characterizes "the elusive search for the common good" as the struggle to find common social and political understandings in a pluralistic nation. Given that we grant the concept of the public good an indeterminate status at the limit, there are a number of outcomes of education that are widely agreed upon as contributing to the public good. These include the role of education in developing citizenship, building common values, and engaging democratic participation for the national good (Newman, Couturier, and Scurry, 2004; Cuban and Shipps, 2000), in stimulating economic growth and the diffusion of technology, as well as increases in social cohesion (Brighouse, 2000; Wolfe, 1995). Breneman (2001) notes that our ability to empirically measure the noneconomic contributions of higher education is weak and that consensus around the role of higher education in service of the public good will more likely be achieved though political and policy debate.

Acknowledgment of a public good emerging from the provision of higher education does not settle the question of how best to define or generate that public good. Since Plato pursued the meaning of "the good" and Aristotle the degree of materialism inherent in a "common good," philosophers and social theorists have contested these questions (Mansbridge, 1998). As he moved away from a medieval philosophy that set public good and private good as opposing forces, in the eighteenth century Adam Smith turned attention to the possibility that self-interest, in the aggregate, could most efficiently provide the common good. Smith's "invisible hand" has formed the foundation of contemporary neoliberal definitions of the public good as little more than the aggregate of private goods (Marginson, 1997).

A distinction also needs to be made between the degree to which different educational sectors contribute to the public good. There is a stronger consensus around the contributions to the public good made through the elementary-secondary system than there is for postsecondary education (Brighouse, 2000). Nonetheless, in the United States we have at various historical moments demonstrated a significant degree of consensus around creating elaborate and often costly postsecondary projects and policies in the service of the public good. The creation and expansion of higher education has been a key locus of collective commitment to the production of both public and private goods in the service of society. The land grant college movement, the expansion of the community college system after World War II, and the rapid increase in science and technology research programs in universities in the wake of *Sputnik* are oft-cited examples of promoting the public good through public investments in higher education. The creation and preservation of postsecondary institutions as public spheres has also been instrumental in shaping critical public space and social movements throughout the twentieth century (Pusser, in press). Over the same time frame, the nonprofit degree-granting institution in the United States has become dominant, in large measure to protect against moral hazard and underinvestment but also to ensure that the contributions of higher education to the public good will be widely disseminated (Pusser, 2000). Market production is generally understood as for-profit production, though Weisbrod (1998), Hansmann (1980), and others offer useful models of market-like competition between organizations.

Market competition also entails production closely following demand, if that demand leads to profit. Under market production, there is little if any provision for production in the absence of demand, and the market producer is theoretically indifferent to public goods (Marginson, 1997). These latter two cases, we shall see, form a key distinction between market production and public production in general and in higher education in particular. Public nonprofit production has long been the dominant model in higher education. Unlike market production, public nonprofit production has been oriented to public goods and to the common good, as well as to private goods. Public nonprofit production is also the only vehicle for ensuring the production of educational products and services that would not justify for-profit production. Public nonprofit production, in the contemporary policy environment, is challenged by the growth of for-profit production. There are limits to public subsidies and public support for education, and those subsidies will be distributed in a realm of political economic competition between market advocates and those who argue for public provision of higher education (Pusser, 2000).

Moving Away from Collective Support for Higher Education

Along with rising interest in market approaches for university adaptation, a related shift is taking place in public policy and planning from the public supply to the public subsidy of higher education. This shift is accompanied by a move from collective finance to individual finance and has significant implications for higher education as a public good. Both shifts are consistent with market approaches to the provision of higher education. An intriguing aspect of the policy debate is that the primary rationale for these changes is not the one advanced by neoclassical economists such as Gary Becker (1976), who argue that education is an investment in individual human capital and as such, is an appropriate investment for the individual to finance. Nor does the argument follow Howard Bowen's (1977) contention that since public subsidies have gone disproportionately to those who could matriculate without them, policy makers might appropriately shift the burden to those beneficiaries. Recent findings confirm Bowen's contention, as significant public subsidies continue to be available to students in middle- and upper-income brackets (Geiger, 2004; Winston, 1999) and financial aid continues to shift from need-based to merit-based provision (Ehrenberg, 2000). The primary rationale supporting the shift in resource allocation strategies is that market competition driven by consumer choice is the appropriate driver of reform in higher education (Pusser and Doane, 2001; Schmidt, 2001; Marginson and Considine, 2000). As a prime example, a report commissioned as part of the National Governors Association's initiative Influencing the Future of Higher Education (2001) predicted that

> Savvy states in the twenty-first century will focus on postsecondary customers; the learner, the employer, and the public who supports educational opportunities. In competitive states, resources will increasingly flow to the learner, and state regulatory policies will ease to encourage institutional flexibility. (p. 3)

This approach traces its lineage less to Becker or Bowen, although their findings are certainly influential, than to Milton Friedman. Friedman's *Capitalism and Freedom* (1962) emphasized the private benefits of higher education and called for a public retrenchment from funding. To the extent that government had a role, Friedman suggested that subsidies should go to individuals, not to institutions, and that competition should be increased throughout the system through the portability of financing instruments.

Despite the historical and contemporary references to the potential role of the market in postsecondary education, to date, empirical, discipline-based, and theoretical research that addresses the nature or impact of market models for higher education has received less attention than a quite different literature. The most visible accounts of the emerging market, new competitors, entrepreneurial forms of finance, and the like, come from the popular press, and more specifically, from those periodicals that cover business and the business of higher education. In part, this imbalance is due to an apparent preference in the press for reporting on economic, market-based, or profit-generating topics rather than academic ones. Add to the mix the rise of attention-garnering, publicly traded companies like the University of Phoenix, DeVry, and Strayer, and the partnerships between universities like Cornell and New York University with private venture capital funds, and an irresistible journalistic soup begins to emerge. Stir in a dollop of the dot-com revolution through virtual delivery of degrees and linkages between for-profit portal providers and higher education institutions, then add some business superstars like Glenn Jones (Jones International University) and Michael Milken (Cardean Learning Group) as the pot begins to boil. Add a growing chorus of protests over the rising costs of higher education, with a pinch of critiques of the higher education bureaucracy reminiscent of those leveled earlier at the elementary-secondary system by Chubb and Moe (1990), and familiar aromas will fill the metaphoric kitchen. Stoke the fire with research provided by groups relatively new to higher education: stock analysts (Block and Dobell, 1999; Soffen, 1998) and the presidents and administrative leaders of for-profit universities (Ruch, 2001; Sperling, 2000, 1989), and there may inevitably be considerably more heat than light shed on the subject.

THE APPEAL OF THE MARKET

It is not difficult to understand the appeal of market discourse and ideology. One can safely hypothesize that rapid changes are taking place and that higher education institutions may not be able to respond without significant adaptation. One could also confidently postulate that policy makers and many others believe that much of public higher education is priced too high, that it requires too much direct state funding, and that its fundamental organization is inefficient. It is also safe to say that the idea of putting the free market to work has considerable appeal to policy makers and legislators (Marginson and Considine, 2000). Faith in the market and its potential role in reforming the provision of higher education is based on a fundamental tenet of market ideology, that competition creates efficiencies, productivity gains, and cost savings. The problems appear to be precisely the ones that the market purports to remedy.

This is, however, a tricky terrain for researchers to navigate. Even the premise that higher education is too expensive is difficult to address without an agreed-upon metric for comparison (Ehrenberg, 2000). Too expensive compared to thirty years ago? One cannot begin to make that comparison without formulating a way to control for the vast changes in the structure, processes and outputs of higher education over that time. In which institutions is higher education too costly? The most expensive institutions, both public and private, are in many cases facing annual demand that considerably exceeds supply, a situation that in most market models would lead to further price increases

(Breneman, 2001; Winston, 1997). Yet the political and popular appeal of a commonly held perspective on a phenomenon is not easily dismissed. One of the contentions of this chapter is that the belief in market effectiveness, market efficiencies, and market gains drives the current policy fascination with markets and market competition in higher education, despite the paucity of empirical tests. It is also the case that the policy community does not necessarily wait for research results before taking action. A number of key policy actors have proposed significant shifts in the funding and production of higher education using market rhetoric and market models in their justifications (Burd, 2001; NGA, 2001). In the most dramatic example, in its 2004 legislative session, Colorado created a "College Opportunity Fund" that shifts a portion of the annual state postsecondary fund allocation into a fund that provides vouchers for eligible students (Hebel, 2005).

It has been suggested in prior research that using market models or market discourse to develop policy, where the conditions are inappropriate for market analysis, may lead to flawed assumptions and misguided policies (Leslie and Johnson, 1974). To fully understand the changes taking place in higher education today, and to formulate appropriate policies based on those changes, requires an evaluation of whether the contemporary context is appropriately defined as an emerging market environment and to what degree the market model is useful in this case.

MARKETS AND HIGHER EDUCATION

The history of theorizing on markets and market influences on higher education goes at least as far back as Adam Smith, who speculated in the eighteenth century on efficiencies that might be generated by linking faculty salaries to productivity (Ortmann, 1997). In a more contemporary realm, Milton Friedman's work on choice and education (1962) and Paul Samuelson's (1954) perspectives on public and private goods have done much to shape how we think about the potential for free market competition in higher education. Despite that long history, there are still a number of reasons to pause before applying a market model to an arena where the following conditions prevail: (1) the product is sold in the vast majority of cases for considerably less than it costs to produce; (2) some 90% of those seeking degrees are enrolled in nonprofit institutions; (3) of those enrollments, over 75% are in institutions that are nonprofit and public; (4) there are significant barriers to entry by new providers in many sectors; and (5) there are significant constraints on exit by the vast majority of providers. Before turning to these challenges in greater detail, it is also worth nothing that the American higher education system is, as a production story, arguably the finest in the world (Kerr, 2001).

CHALLENGES TO THE MARKET MODEL

For at least three decades, economists have pointed to difficulties in attempting to apply market models to higher education (Winston, 1997; Bowen, 1977; Leslie and Johnson, 1974). One fundamental question concerns whether collective goods, such as the benefits of increased levels of public education, are better generated by market or government production. Salamon (1995) suggests that collective goods are goods and services which, once produced, can be enjoyed by all, independent of whether the consumer helped pay for or produce the goods. This condition makes market production problematic, as few will pay for benefits they can enjoy without contribution (the "free rider" problem) and production will sink below optimal levels. Government, on the other hand, can use taxation as a way to ensure broader contribution to the cost of the collective good, but government production has its own shortcomings. Foremost of these is that government action is largely limited to the production of goods that a majority will agree merit production. Consequently, many goods desired by a minority of the polis will not be produced unless private nonprofit organizations are organized to produce those goods (Salamon, 1995). In innovative work produced shortly after the passage of the Higher Education Act (HEA) of 1965, Leslie and Johnson (1974) concluded:

> Upon considering collectively the major aspects of the higher education market, it becomes evident that while higher education can be generally and broadly discussed within the context of certain market terminology, the various market-related characteristics of higher education in no way approximate the sufficient conditions of the perfectly competitive market model. (p. 14)

It is no coincidence that the authors were theorizing about the nature of a market model for higher education on the heels of the passage of the HEA. With provisions for portable financing through guaranteed student loans and Basic Educational Opportunity Grants (now Pell grants), the HEA seemed to provide the foundation of a higher education market as envisioned by Milton Friedman. Yet what Leslie and Johnson surmised some twenty-five years ago, and what Gordon Winston (Winston, 1999; Winston et al., 1998) and others (Marginson, 1997; Slaughter and Leslie, 1997; Pusser, 2002) have suggested more recently, is that many characteristics of the production and consumption of higher education make developing a market model problematic. Those characteristics may also complicate predictions about the production of public and private goods through competitive markets in higher education.

Winston (1997) found six key factors that limit the utility of conceptualizing the contemporary provision of higher education as a free market. The first three factors, as Hansmann (1980) initially pointed out, result from the fact that the higher education arena has long been dominated by nonprofit production. Nor is that dominance an anomaly or historical accident. Nonprofit institutions have held a disproportionate share of enrollments and degrees produced throughout the twentieth century (Goldin and Katz, 1998; Clark, 1983).

Hansmann's three conditions also help to explain the success of the non-profit form. First, the production of higher education is characterized by information asymmetries. That is, higher education is a difficult commodity to assess in advance and often takes considerable time to consume and evaluate. Furthermore, producers of higher education generally have more information about the product than do the consumers. Given that the time required for a consumer to discover and redress the shortcomings of a poorly or fraudulently delivered education might be measured in years, that consumer is at considerable risk of exploitation. Second, the nondistribution constraint inherent in the nonprofit form protects the consumer from potential consequences of information asymmetry and other moral hazards, as it removes the possibility of profit-seeking as an incentive for producers to exploit their customers. Winston also suggests that since they operate under the nondistribution constraint, managers of nonprofits have alternative, generally more altruistic goals than managers of for-profits. Furthermore, higher education provides benefits to society beyond the gains to the individual student. Given that it is socially useful to cultivate the maximum social benefit from higher education, the nondistribution constraint allows any public investment to go directly to the production of social benefits and not to profit. When public investment is combined with direct public provision, in the case of public nonprofit production, the public has the greatest control and influence over the production of social benefits through higher education.

A third distinctive aspect of higher education production is that both public and independent nonprofit institutions generate revenue from a variety of sources beyond what they charge directly for admission. Because higher education institutions receive commercial revenue, tax revenue, and donations, they are appropriately characterized as "donative commercial nonprofits" (Hansmann, 1980). The mix of subsidies allows nonprofit higher education in the United States to be offered at a price far below its production cost (Winston, 1999, 1997). Winston estimated in 1996 that the average cost of a year of higher education in all schools in the United States was approximately $12,000, while the average price a student paid was just under $4,000. That average subsidy of around $8,000 was dwarfed by the subsidies offered at elite private institutions (Winston et al., 1998). These subsidies constitute a significant barrier to entry into the higher education arena.

A fourth limitation on conceptualizing the production of higher education in a market model is related to the asymmetry problem, as it has been noted that "the perfectly informed customer of economic theory is nowhere to be seen" (Winston, 1997, p. 4). Given the information problems noted earlier, this suggests that reputation and institutional history play a disproportionate role in consumer choice.

Two related factors also figure prominently here, the associative goods condition and institutional heterogeneity. Winston suggests that higher education is an associative good, and consequently one of an institution's most powerful resources is its own student body. This results in sharp competition between institutions for the most desirable students and between students wishing to attend those institutions enrolling their most highly recruited peers. What this suggests is that different institutions face quite different supply and demand conditions, and the same is true for students with differing levels of preparation and admissibility (Rothschild and White, 1993).

Marginson and Considine (2000), Ehrenberg (2000), Oster (1997), Slaughter and Leslie (1997), and others have built on the work of Winston and Hansmann to conceptualize a competitive environment of higher education composed of many different subcompetitions, based on subsidy levels, selectivity, geography, mission, and the like. Similarly, the internal allocation of resources in higher education institutions has been shaped to a large degree by organizational history, culture, and intent, as well as by competitive pressure (Slaughter and Rhoades, 2004; Marginson and Considine, 2000; Slaughter and Leslie, 1997).

This array of factors points to the complexity of developing either a production function or a theory of the firm for higher education (Winston, 1997; Masten, 1995). However, over the past two decades a quite useful body of research on the competitive responses of nonprofit institutions has emerged (Salamon, 1995; James and Rose-Ackerman, 1986; Weisbrod, 1988; Hansmann, 1980) and is quite helpful in understanding the contemporary higher education arena.

THE NONPROFIT FORM IN HIGHER EDUCATION

For over two hundred years, there have been publicly funded, publicly regulated, degree-granting postsecondary institutions in the United States. Perhaps more importantly, over the same period, there have also been publicly incorporated institutions that have been publicly funded and regulated, and they have become by far the dominant site of postsecondary enrollment and the provision of postsecondary degrees. The public—through the establishment of state nonprofit public universities, the provision of public funds to nonprofit public and independent institutions, and the establishment of accreditation and oversight functions—has long served as provider, subsidizer, and regulator of American higher education.

Over time the provider role has been most significant, as some 80 percent of postsecondary degrees are currently granted in public colleges and universities (Hansmann, 1999; Goldin and Katz, 1998). Given that approximately 85% of postsecondary enrollments are in public and independent nonprofit institutions, it is clear that public and independent nonprofit provision is the defining quality of the current system.

Public provision and finance of higher education, while not the original model, has long been the norm. Expanding the capacity of higher education has been a fundamental public project in the United States for two centuries. While hardly a linear expansion, the growth of nonprofit higher education has been more steady than often suggested, albeit punctuated by rapid expansion around the Morrill Act, the GI Bill, and the Great Society reforms (Cohen and Brawer, 1996; Breneman, 1992; Kerr, 1994; Hansen, 1991; Veysey, 1965). The reasons for the continued development of the nonprofit form in higher education, despite the growth of market provision in many sectors of American life over the past two centuries, deserve closer scrutiny. There are significant advantages and public benefits that can arguably only be generated by nonprofit provision. Powell and Clemens (1998) suggest that as a unique model of association within the public sphere, the nonprofit form itself is increasingly seen as a public good.

NONPROFIT PROVISION AND FINANCE

An analysis of the implications of demands for increased competition and market-like forms in higher education turns attention to earlier research on nonprofit competition (Hansmann, 1999, 1980; Weisbrod, 1998, 1988; Oster, 1997; James and Rose-Ackerman, 1986). In research on the role of the state in European higher education, Henry Hansmann (1999) has drawn a useful distinction between "public subsidy" and "public supply" of higher education and between "supply side" subsidies and "demand" subsidies for the support of higher education (p. 4). These distinctions are useful for understanding the changing provision of contemporary higher education.

PUBLIC SUPPLY AND PUBLIC SUBSIDY

Public supply here to the provision of higher education in public nonprofit institutions. Public subsidy refers to the allocation of public funds to public or private, for-profit or nonprofit institutions. Public subsidies may either be provided by state or federal entities to an institution as direct institutional grants (supply side subsidies) or to students in the form of grants, loans, tax credits, and the like (demand side subsidies) that the student may use at any accredited institution. Of course, public subsidies are most often used by students at public institutions. Hansmann (1999), James (1998), and Oster (1997) point to various trade-offs between public supply and public subsidy.

BENEFITS OF PUBLIC SUPPLY

The fundamental arguments for public supply are that it offers the most direct utilization of public subsidies and that it is the organizational type best suited to the rapid expansion of higher education (Hansmann, 1999). The argument for the benefit of public provision coupled with public subsidy is twofold. First, where education is provided in public institutions with public funds, the public has the greatest influence over the institution and its activities. Given the nonprofit status of public institutions, there is no diversion of the public subsidy to profit; hence, more of the subsidy goes to the production of preferred goods. Second, public higher education institutions can be rapidly built or expanded with public capital, while independent nonprofit institutions more often lack incentives and financing for such expansion (Oster, 1997). A salient example of public expansion is found in the history of public community colleges. The number of U.S. community colleges doubled from 1920 to 1950 and doubled again from 1950 to 1980. From a total of 8 community colleges at the turn of the twentieth century, by 1998 there were nearly 1,600 community colleges (Phillippe, 1999). The funding, authorization, coordination, and control of this level of capacity building required collaborative public effort (Cohen and Brawer, 1996). Public supply also provides the most direct mechanism for the production of public goods and benefits that would not be produced if consumer demand were insufficient to generate private nonprofit or for-profit provision or if private provision led to an undersupply of those goods and benefits. An example of this would be federal initiatives to integrate public higher education in the 1960s. Many of those initiatives were implemented through direct government intervention in public institutions where consumer demand had long been insufficient to effect social change (Gaston, 2001).

BENEFITS OF PUBLIC SUBSIDY

A primary argument for public subsidies to students for the purchase of higher education is that such subsidies may reduce underinvestment by reducing market constraints that prevent individuals from obtaining financing for higher education (James, 1998; Weisbrod, 1998). Public subsidies also serve to minimize the possibility that students will underconsume those forms of higher education which, while they might be socially desirable, entail uncertain individual returns (Hansmann, 1999).

The primary political appeal of public subsidy is the belief that the portability of financial aid increases consumer choice and that choice increases institutional efficiency (Chubb and Moe, 1990; Friedman, 1962). Using portable public subsidies, students as consumers may spend state and federal grant and loan funds at a variety of locations, including public and independent nonprofits, as well as for-profit institutions. While public subsidies do give legislators and other funders leverage over institutions, subsidy is not as effective as direct supply for generating specific outputs. Portability dates to the Serviceman's Readjustment Act (GI Bill), which financed entrance into higher education for two million returning World War II veterans (Bound and Turner, 1999). GI Bill grants for tuition and living expenses were awarded to individuals rather than to institutions and served as a forerunner to the subsequent creation of Guaranteed Student Loans and portable Pell grants in the Higher Education Act of 1965 and subsequent amendments. It is not often noted in contemporary higher education literature on market models and choice that portability of public subsidies originated some 60 years ago and was extended fairly universally nearly 40 years ago. It is also worth noting that the contemporary degree of enrollment choice and competition in American higher education is unprecedented in global higher education (Aronowitz, 2000). However, there is little empirical research to indicate that the choice provided by public subsidies has increased efficiency and productivity or led to lower costs of production. Given the increasing shift away from public supply, it is useful to also consider the implications of that shift for the creation of public and private goods.

THE PUBLIC INTEREST AND PUBLIC GOODS IN HIGHER EDUCATION

Higher education produces both collective (public) goods and private goods (Marginson, 2004a; Bowen, 1977). The Institute for Higher Education Policy (IHEP) has refined an effective framework for delineating the various forms of public and private goods generated by increased levels of higher education. That framework sorts the outputs of higher education into four categories: public economic benefits, private economic benefits, public social benefits, and private social benefits (IHEP, 1998).

A number of public economic benefits are generated as individuals acquire higher levels of education. These include greater levels of productivity, higher rates of consumer spending, increased tax revenues, enhanced workforce preparation, and decreased public expenditures for social services.

The list of private economic benefits that accrue to those with higher levels of educational attainment includes generally higher rates of employment and wages, increased levels of savings, increased labor market mobility, and enhanced working conditions.

The public social benefits generated by increased education are manifest in greater civic engagement, higher rates of voting, increased charitable giving and community involvement, and lower public health care costs. Bowen and Bok (1998) cite the production of a diverse cohort of leaders as a key public social benefit, while Bowen (1978) points to the contributions of university basic research and public service, the preservation of the cultural heritage of society, and the reduction of inequality as central public benefits. He notes, "Education has an advantage over other avenues toward equality—such as graduated taxes and public assistance—because it can reduce the inequality of what people are and what they can contribute, not merely of what they get" (p. 12).

Private social benefits that accrue to those with greater levels of education include better health and greater longevity, increased leisure time, and personal status, as well as access to better information for personal decision making (IHEP, 1998).

There are also significant interactions among these four categories. Higher individual income is a private benefit that also creates a public benefit—higher tax revenues. A higher level of civic engagement, a public benefit, in turn generates private benefits, as it enables individuals to live in more collegial communities.

David Labaree (1997) has suggested that the production of public and private benefits is shaped by three defining goals for education in the United States: democratic equality, social efficiency, and social mobility. These three goals are readily apparent in the contemporary higher education system. In the pursuit of cultivating democratic equality, the higher education system contributes to the production of such public social benefits as citizenship development and increased equality. Social efficiency suggests that collective investment is the way to reduce underinvestment in higher education and to produce a workforce appropriate for the contemporary labor market. Labaree's third goal, social mobility, is the fundamental driver of the production of private economic benefits through higher education. It suggests that education is a private good that enables individuals to succeed in social and economic competition. Labaree suggests that all three goals are political goals and that the production of public and private benefits is mediated by political processes. In public policy discussions and institutional analyses, it is increasingly the case that all three of these goals are subsumed under the overarching mission of economic development. While higher education institutions have contributed to economic production to some degree since the founding of the colonial colleges, today nearly all aspects of university mission are in some way linked to local, state, and federal economic development (Slaughter and Rhoades, 2004; Marginson and Considine, 2000; UCOP, 1996).

HIGHER EDUCATION AS A PUBLIC SPHERE

Another key concept that can be applied to thinking about higher education and the public good is the idea of the public sphere (Fraser, 1992; Habermas 1991, 1962). The public sphere is defined by Habermas as a space beyond the control of either the State or private interests where public conversation, deliberation, and innovation can take place. It is also a site of contest, where various perspectives on the State and on private interests can be freely and publicly debated, and where social identities may be forged (Frazer, 1992). Recent scholarship in higher education has argued that public universities have served as key public spheres (Giroux, 2002; Ambrozas, 1998) and that its role as a public sphere is an essential public good provided by the university (Pusser, in press; Giroux, 2002).

THE MARKET, CHOICE, AND THE PUBLIC GOOD

As evidenced by the quote from Thomas Jefferson at the beginning of this chapter, the public good and the public benefits of higher education have been discussed from nearly the founding of the country. As policy makers face pressure to increase competition and to adopt market models for the organization and finance of higher education, the emerging question is quite basic: What is the public role, and what are the potential impacts of market approaches on the contributions of higher education to the public good? Given the current organization of the higher education system, attention must also be directed to the future of the nonprofit form in higher education in the United States.

The gains to higher education that market advocates foresee are attributed to increased efficiency, driven by wider consumer choice. Yet thirty years of consumer choice supported by the portability of financial aid has done little to contain costs or to limit tuition prices in higher education. Nor is it clear that the intention of postwar public policy has been to contain prices;

rather, the effort seems to have been to increase capacity and choice and to preserve quality. Further reductions in state block grant allocations will likely result in significant tuition increases (Callan, 2001). Although this may to some degree "level the playing field" between public, independent, and for-profit institutions, it may well also level up the price structure (Ehrenberg, 2000). While tuition at nonprofit independent institutions varies widely, for-profit institutions on average are significantly more expensive than public nonprofit institutions.

A number of researchers have predicted that increases in net cost will reduce access to higher education by lower-income and traditionally under-served populations, as will a continuing shift from student grants to student loans (Callan, 2001; McPherson and Schapiro, 1998). Price sensitivity and loan sensitivity are significant challenges to access (Bowen et al., 2005; Heller, 2001; Winston, Carbone, and Lewis, 1998) and to the extent that market competition reduces public subsidies and levels prices, that competition may well increase stratification in the higher education system. The attention to the market also obscures the importance of the retreat from existing subsidies. While much has been written about the competition for public resources and the inevitability of state funding declines, there has been little speculation about what sort of education can be provided without the subsidies.

As state direct support declines, remedial education and other programs targeted to underprepared students may need to be funded from tuition increases, essentially a tax on better prepared students. Many other programs that are currently covered by state funds will also need to be funded through tuition increases. This sort of redistribution is increasingly unpopular at the state and federal levels, and there is little reason to assume it will be any more appealing in the long run at the institutional level. The decline in state support, the increasing use of tax credits as part of federal support for higher education, and the tilt from need-based to merit-based aid (Breneman, 2004) will likely further the divide in college going between those from higher and lower income strata.

There is also a great deal of uncertainty over how competition affects educational quality. While there is a growing literature on the educational outputs of contemporary degree-granting, for-profit institutions (Newman, Couturier, and Scurry, 2004; Ruch, 2001; Raphael and Tobias, 1997), these institutions constitute a very small fraction of the enrollments in postsecondary education and many have focused on adult enrollment. The success stories in this arena, the University of Phoenix and DeVry, offer fewer majors and courses of study than many public four-year colleges and universities. As one of the fastest-growing institutional sectors in postsecondary education, the for-profits' targeted approach may have significant implications for public institutions attempting to compete in an era of declining state support. Over time, the range of curricular choices may well decrease, as prices increase.

A decline in access and affordability is also likely to reduce the production of public and private social and economic benefits from higher education. Reduced levels of overall college attainment will lead to decreased civic engagement, charitable giving, and community service. It predicts for increased rates of unemployment, incarceration, and public health costs. While those who attain more years of postsecondary education and those who attend more prestigious institutions will enjoy greater social benefits and increased personal status, they may also be required to navigate an increasingly polarized and problematic society, as reduction in state support reduces social benefits and increases social costs.

The Future of Nonprofit Postsecondary Education

Calls for market approaches to higher education do not necessarily portend the end of the nonprofit form of provision. It is possible to imagine, at the very least, the elite nonprofit institutions continuing as a dominant form. In an environment of relatively equal funding for nonprofit and for-profit providers, it is conceivable that the nondistribution constraint may lead to higher quality education in the nonprofits and continued demand for nonprofit institutions. It is also the case that the divide between nonprofit and for-profit structure and process in higher education is narrowing. Such entrepreneurial commercial activities in nonprofit institutions as the provision of courses and degrees through continuing education, the growth of auxiliary enterprises, and the creation of partnerships with corporations and venture capitalists are increasing in every sector of the nonprofit education arena (Pusser et al., 2005). A number of researchers in higher education have suggested potential negative consequences to the growth in commercial enterprises (Slaughter and Rhoades, 2004; Marginson and Considine, 2000). As one example, it has been speculated that an increase in commercial enterprises may draw organizational attention away from core mission activities and require a "commercialization" of the managerial cohort. This in turn may decrease expertise in the nonprofits' core mission functions (Weisbrod, 1998; Oster, 1997).

Another significant issue is what the educational and social implications might be of an expansion of the for-profit form. Is there anything unique about the twenty-first century that has reduced the information asymmetries and moral hazards that have historically constrained for-profit expansion? It may be that better access to information through emerging technologies will increase consumer protection against exploitation in both nonprofit and for-profit institutions, but those who are most vulnerable to that exploitation also have the least access to information technology (Gladieux and Swail, 1999).

PRESERVING HIGHER EDUCATION'S CONTRIBUTIONS TO THE PUBLIC GOOD

Perhaps the most salient question is how higher education's contributions to the public good can be ensured if nonprofit public production gives way to a for-profit market. The fundamental mission of for-profit market production is to create private benefits for the producers and their customers. The historical mission of nonprofit production has been to create both public and private benefits. Public and private nonprofit higher education institutions have been key sites of access to leadership positions and to greater civic involvement for their graduates (Bowen, et al., 2005; Turner and Pusser, 2004; Bowen and Bok, 1998). Nonprofit institutions have been centers of social and political movements whose goals have been to achieve integration and the equalization of access to education. It is not at all clear that those goals can be realized through for-profit production. Public goals for the creation of public goods have been most effectively realized through direct public production of those goods.

The challenge before state, federal, and institutional leaders in higher education is to respond to a turbulent political economic environment while preserving the role of nonprofit and nonmarket provision of higher education in the service of the public good. The niche market success of the new wave of for-profit providers and the shifts to increasingly private funding of social welfare functions offer a tempting course of action: increased market competition in higher education. It may also be tempting to assume that competitive success at the periphery offers a guide to transforming the core, particularly in light of the plethora of calls urging that strategy. It isn't clear whether market approaches will induce effective transformations in higher education, but they are likely to be popular. The adoption of market initiatives may also produce expectations of greater choice, competition, and an increase in the public benefits from higher education. On the basis of existing research and the historical record, those expectations may well be for a state of grace which, as Mr. Jefferson suggested, never was and never will be.

ACKNOWLEDGMENT

An earlier version of this chapter appeared in 2002, as Higher education, the emerging market and the public good, in P. A. Graham and N. G. Stacey

(Eds.), *The knowledge economy and postsecondary education: Report of a workshop.* Committee on the Impact of the Changing Economy on the Education System, Center for Education, Division of Behavioral and Social Sciences and Education. Washington, DC: National Academy Press.

REFERENCES

Adelman, C. (2000). *A parallel postsecondary universe: The certification system in information technology.* Washington, DC: U.S. Government Printing Office.

Altbach, P. G. (2002, Spring). Who is paying for higher education—and why? *International Higher Education, 27*(3).

Altbach, P. G. (2001, May 11). Why higher education is not a global commodity. *Chronicle of Higher Education, 47,* B20.

Ambrozas, D. (1998). The university as a public sphere. *Canadian Journal of Communication, 23*(1).

Aronowitz, S. (2000). *The knowledge factory.* Boston: Beacon.

Becker, G. S. (1976). *The economic approach to human behavior.* Chicago: University of Chicago Press.

Block, H. M., & Dobell, B. (1999). *The e-bang theory.* Vol. 2. San Francisco: Bank of America Securities Equity Research Division.

Blustain, H., Goldstein, P., & Lozier, G. (1999). Assessing the new competitive landscape. In R. N. Katz and Associates (Eds.), *Dancing with the devil: Information technology and the new competition in higher education* (pp. 51–71). San Francisco: Jossey-Bass.

Bound, J., & Turner, S. E. (2002). Going to war and going to college: Did World War II and the G.I. Bill increase educational attainment for returning veterans? *Journal of Labor Economics 20*(4), 784–815.

Bowen, H. R. (1997). *Investments in learning: The individual and social value of American higher education.* San Francisco: Jossey-Bass.

Bowen, H. R. (1978). *The returns to investments in learning.* Occasional Paper Series 7. Charlottesville: University of Virginia, Center for the Study of Higher Education.

Bowen, W. G., and Bok, D. (1998). *The shape of the river.* Princeton: Princeton University Press.

Bowen, W. G., Kurzweil, M. A., Tobin, E. M., & Pichler, S. C. (2005). *Equity and excellence in American higher education (Thomas Jefferson Foundation Distinguished Lecture Series).* Charlottesville: University Press of Virginia.

Breneman, D. W. (2005, Spring). Entrepreneurship in higher education. In B. Pusser (Ed.), *Arenas of Entrepreneurship: Where nonprofit and for-profit institutions compete.* New Directions for Higher Education, *129,* 3–9.

Breneman, D.W. (2004) Are the states and public higher education striking a new bargain? Association of Governing Boards Public Policy Paper No. 04–02, June.

Breneman, D. W. (2001). *The outputs of higher education.* Paper presented at the Futures Forum 2001, Forum for the Future of Higher Education, Cambridge, MA.

Breneman, D. W. (2000, February 11). A tuition freeze accents the cockeyed economics of higher education. *Chronicle of Higher Education, 46,* A64.

Breneman, D. W. (1992). *Guaranteed student loans: Great success or dismal failure?* Washington, DC: United Student Aid Fund.

Breneman, D. W., Pusser, B., & Turner, S. E. (2000). *The contemporary provision of for-profit higher education: Mapping the competitive market.* Working Paper. Charlottesville: University of Virginia.

Brighouse, H. (2000). *School choice and social justice.* Oxford, United Kingdom: Oxford University Press.

Burd, S. (2003, May 2). High stakes on tuition. *Chronicle of Higher Education, 49,* 34–35.

Burd, S. (2001, February 2). Bringing market forces to student loan programs. *Chronicle of Higher Education, 47,* A26.

Callan, P. M. (2001). Reframing access and opportunity: Problematic state and federal higher education policy in the 1990s. In D. E. Heller (Ed.), *The states and public higher education policy: Affordability, access, and accountability* (pp. 83–99). Baltimore: Johns Hopkins.

Calhoun, C. (1998). The public good as a social and cultural project. In W. W. Powell and E. S. Clements (Eds.), *Private action and the public good* (pp. 20–35). New Haven: Yale University Press.

Carnevale, A. P., & Fry, R. A. (2001, March). Economics, demography and the future of higher education policy. In *Higher expectations: Essays on the future of postsecondary education.* National Governors Association.

Chubb, J. E., and Moe, T. M. (1990). *Politics, markets, and America's schools.* Washington, DC: Brookings Institution.

Clark, B. R. (1998). *Creating entrepreneurial universities: Organizational pathways of transformation.* Oxford, United Kingdom: Pergamon Press.

Clark, B. R. (1983). *The higher education system: Academic organization in cross-national perspective.* Berkeley: University of California Press.

Cohen, A. M., & Brawer, F. (1996). *The American community college,* 3rd ed. San Francisco: Jossey-Bass.

Collis, D. (2001). When industries change: The future of higher education. In *Higher Education Review, 65,* 7–24.

Cuban, L., & Shipps, D. (Eds.). (2000). *Reconstructing the common good in education.* Stanford, CA: Stanford University Press.

Currie, J., & Newson, J. (1999). *Universities and globalization: Critical perspectives.* Thousand Oaks, CA: Sage.

Duderstadt, J. J. (2000). *A university for the twenty-first century.* Ann Arbor: University of Michigan Press.

Duderstadt, J. J. (1999). Can colleges and universities survive in the information age? In R. N. Katz and Associates (Eds.), *Dancing with the devil: Information technology and the new competition in higher education* (pp. 1–26). San Francisco: Jossey-Bass.

Ehrenberg, R. G. (2000). *Tuition rising: Why college costs so much.* Cambridge: Harvard University Press.

Fraser, N. (1992). Rethinking the public sphere: A contribution to the critique of actually existing democracy. In C. Calhoun (Ed.), *Habermas and the public sphere* (pp. 109–42). Cambridge: MIT Press.

Friedman, M. (1962). *Capitalism and freedom.* Chicago: University of Chicago Press.

Friedman, M., & Friedman, R. (1980). *Free to choose: A personal statement.* New York: Hartcourt.

Garber, M. P. (1996, September). Wall Street Ph.D. *National Review,* 57–72.

Gaston, P. M. (2001). Reflections on affirmative action: Its origins, virtues, enemies, champions, and prospects. In G. Orfield and M. Kurlaender (Eds.), *Diversity challenged: Evidence on the impact of affirmative action* (pp. 277–293). Cambridge: Harvard Educational Publishing Group.

Geiger, R. L. (2004) *Knowledge and Money.* Palo Alto, CA: Stanford University Press.

Giroux, H. A. (2002, Winter). Neoliberalism, corporate culture, and the promise of higher education: The university as a democratic public sphere. *Harvard Educational Review, 72*(4).

Gladieux, L., & Swail, W. (1999, August). *The digital divide and educational opportunity. College Board Review,* 28–30.

Goldin, C., & Katz, L. F. (1998). *The shaping of higher education: The formative years in the United States, 1890–1940.* Working Paper 6537. Cambridge, MA: National Bureau of Economic Research.

Goldstein, M. B. (1999, October). Capital ideas. *University Business,* 46–53.

Graves, W. H. (1998). Developing and using technology as a strategic asset. In R. N. Katz and Associates (Eds.), *Dancing with the devil: Information technology and the new competition in higher education* (pp. 95–118) . San Francisco: Jossey-Bass.

Habermas, J. (1991). The public sphere. In C. Mukerji and M. Schudson (Eds.), *Rethinking popular culture* (pp. 398–404). Berkeley: University of California Press.

Habermas, J. (1962). *The structural transformation of the public sphere.* Cambridge: MIT Press.

Hansen, J. S. (1991, Summer). *The roots of federal student aid policy.* In J. P. Merisotis (Ed.), *New directions for higher education: The changing dimensions of student aid,* no. 74. San Francisco: Jossey-Bass.

Hansmann, H. (1999). The state and the market in higher education. *Mercato Concorrenza Regale, 3,* 475–496.

Hansmann, H. (1980). The rationale for exempting nonprofit organizations from corporate income taxation. *Yale Law Journal, 91,* 54–100.

Hebel, S. (2005, January 7). Christian university sues Colorado commission. *Chronicle for Higher Education, 51*(18), A35.

Heller, D. E. (2001). Trends in the affordability of public colleges and universities: The contradiction of increasing prices and increasing enrollments. In D. E. Heller (Ed.), *The states and public higher education policy: Affordability, access, and accountability* (pp. 11–38). Baltimore: Johns Hopkins.

Institute for Higher Education Policy (IHEP). (1998). *Reaping the benefits: Defining the public and private value of going to college.* The New Millennium Project on Higher Education Costs, Pricing and Productivity. Washington, DC.

James, E. (1998). Commercialism among nonprofits: Objectives, opportunities, and constraints. In B. A. Weisbrod (Ed.), *To profit or not to profit: The commercial transformation of the nonprofit sector* (pp. 271–286). Cambridge, United Kingdom: Cambridge University Press.

James, E., & Rose-Ackerman, S. (1986). *The nonprofit enterprise in market economics.* New York: Harwood Academic.

Jefferson, T. (1812). Letter to William Duane. ME 13:186. Washington, DC: Library of Congress.

Kane, T. J. (1999). *The price of admission: Rethinking how Americans pay for college.* Washington, DC: Brookings Institution.

Kerr, C. (2001). *The uses of the university,* 5th ed. Cambridge: Harvard University Press.

Kerr, C. (1994). Expanding access and changing missions: The federal role in U.S. higher education. *Educational Record, 75,* 27–31.

Kirp, D. L. (2003). *Shakespeare, Einstein and the bottom line.* Cambridge: Harvard University Press.

Kohl, K., & LaPidus, J. (Eds.). (2000). *Postbaccalaureate futures: New markets, resources, credentials.* Phoenix: Oryx Press.

Labaree, D. F. (1997). Public goods, private goods: The American struggle over educational goals. *American Educational Research Journal, 34*(1), 39–81.

Leslie, L. L., & Johnson, G. P. (1974). The market model and higher education. *Journal of Higher Education, 45,* 1–20.

Levin, H. M. (Ed.). (2001). *Privatizing education.* Boulder: Westview Press.

Levin, J. S. (2005, Spring). The business culture of the community college: Students as consumers; students as commodities. In B. Pusser (Ed.), *Arenas of Entrepreneurship: Where nonprofit and for-profit institutions compete.* New Directions for Higher Education, *129*, 11–26.

Levin, J. S. (2001). *Globalizing the community college: Strategies for change in the twenty-first century.* New York: Palgrave.

Levine, A. (2001). Privatization in higher education. In H.M. Levin (Ed.), *Privatizing Education* (pp. 133–150). Boulder: Westview Press.

Mansbridge, J. (1998). On the contested nature of the public good. In W.W. Powell and E. S. Clemens (Eds.), *Private action and the public good* (pp. 3–19). New Haven, CT: Yale University Press.

Marchese, T. (1998, May/June). Not-so distant-competitors: How new providers are remaking the postsecondary marketplace. *AAHE Bulletin*, 3–11.

Marginson, S. (2004b). Going global: Governance implications of cross-border traffic in higher education. In W. Tierney (Ed.), *Competing conception of academic governance: Negotiating the perfect storm* (pp. 1–32). Baltimore: Johns Hopkins.

Marginson, S. (2004a). Competition and markets in higher education: A 'glonacal' analysis. *Policy Futures in Education, 2*(2), 175–244.

Marginson, S. (1997). *Markets in education.* Melbourne, Australia: Allen & Unwin.

Marginson, S., & Considine, M. (2000). *The enterprise university.* Cambridge, United Kingdom: Cambridge University Press.

Masten, S. E. (1995). Old school ties: Financial aid coordination and governance of higher education. *Journal of Economic Behavior and Organizations, 28*, 23–47.

McKeown-Moak, M. P. (2000). *Financing higher education in the new century: The second annual report from the states.* Denver: SHEEO Finance Publications.

McMurtry, J. (1991). Education and the market model. *Journal of Philosophy of Education, 25*(2), 209–218.

McPherson, M. S., & Schapiro, O. (1998). *The student aid game.* Princeton: Princeton University Press.

Mendenhall, R. (2001). Technology: Creating new models in higher education. In National Governors Association, *Higher expectations: Essays on the future of postsecondary education* (pp. 37–44). Washington, DC: NGA.

Moe, T. (1996). *The positive theory of public bureaucracy.* New York: Cambridge University Press.

Munitz, B. (2000, January/February). Changing landscape: From cottage monopoly to competitive industry. *EDUCAUSE, 35*, 12–18.

National Governors Association (NGA). (2001). *The 21st century is upon us. Are we ready?* Washington, DC: NGA Center for Best Practices.

Newman, F., & Couturier, L. K. (2001, September/October). The new competitive arena: Market forces invade the academy. *Change, 33*(2), 10–17.

Newman, F., & Scurry, J. (2001, July 13). Online technology pushes pedagogy to the forefront. *Chronicle of Higher Education, 47*, B7.

Newman, F., Couturier, L. K., & Scurry, J. (2004). *The future of higher education: Rhetoric, reality, and the risks of the market.* San Francisco: Jossey-Bass.

Olivas, M. A. (2004). The rise of nonlegal legal influences on higher education. In R. G. Ehrenberg (Ed.), *Governing academia: Who is in charge at the modern university?* (pp. 258–275). Ithaca: Cornell University Press.

Ordorika, I. (2003). *Power and politics in university governance: Organization and change at the Universidad Nacional Autonoma de Mexico.* New York: RoutledgeFalmer.

Ortmann, A. (1997). How to survive in post-industrial environments: Adam Smith's advice for today's colleges and universities. *Journal of Higher Education, 68*, 483–501.

Oster, S. (1997). *An analytical framework for thinking about the use of for-profit structures for university services and activities.* Aspen: Forum for the Future of Higher Education.

Peters, M. A. (2004). Citizen-consumers, social markets and the reform of public services. *Policy Futures in Education 2*(3&4), 621–632.

Phillippe, K. A. (Ed.). (1999). *National profile of community colleges: Trends and statistics,* 3rd ed. Washington, DC: Community College Press.

Powell, W. W., & Clemens, E. S. (Eds.). (1998). *Private action and the public good.* New Haven: Yale University Press.

Pusser, B. (in press). Reconsidering higher education and the public good: The role of public spheres. In W. G. Tierney (Eds.), *Governance and the public good.* Albany: SUNY Press.

Pusser, B. (2004). *Burning down the house: Politics, governance and Affirmative Action at the University of California.* Albany: SUNY Press.

Pusser, B. (2000). The role of the state in the provision of higher education in the United States. *Australian University Review, 43*(1), 24–35.

Pusser, B., & Turner, S. E. (2004). Nonprofit and for-profit governance in higher education. In R. G. Ehrenberg (Ed.), *Governing academia: Who is in charge at the modern university?* Ithaca: Cornell University Press.

Pusser, B., & Doane, D. J. (2001, September/October). Public purpose and private enterprise: The contemporary organization of postsecondary education. *Change, 33,* 18–22.

Pusser, B., Gansneder, B. M., Gallaway, N., & Pope, N. S. (2005, Spring). Entrepreneurial activity in nonprofit institutions: A portrait of continuing education. In B. Pusser (Ed.), *Arenas of Entrepreneurship: Where nonprofit and for-profit institutions compete* (pp. 27–42, 129). New Directions for Higher Education.

Raphael, J., & Tobias, S. (1997, November/December). Profit-making or profiteering. *Change, 29*(6), 45–60.

Reese, W. J. (2000). Public schools and the elusive search for the common good. In L. Cuban and D. Shipps (Eds.), *Reconstructing the common good in education* (pp. 13–31). Stanford, CA: Stanford University Press.

Rothschild, M., & White, L. (1993). The university in the market place: Some insights and some puzzles. In C. T. Clotfelter and M. Rothschild (Eds.). *Studies of supply and demand in higher education* (pp. 11–42). Chicago: University of Chicago Press.

Ruch, R. S. (2001). *Higher ed, inc: The rise of the for-profit university.* Baltimore: Johns Hopkins.

Salamon, L. M. (1995). *Partners in public service: Government-nonprofit relations in the modern welfare state.* Baltimore: Johns Hopkins.

Samuelson, P. (1954). The theory of public expenditure. *Review of Economics and Statistics, 6*(4), 387–389.

Schmidt, P. (2001, January 4). Texas governor proposes radical shift n college financing. *Chronicle of Higher Education, 47,* A26.

Slaughter, S., & Leslie, L. L. (1997). *Academic capitalism.* Baltimore: Johns Hopkins.

Slaughter, S., & Rhoades, G. (2004). *Academic capitalism and the new economy: Markets, state, and higher education.* Baltimore: Johns Hopkins.

Soffen, S. (1998, September). *For-profit, postsecondary education: Profiting from a knowledge-based economy.* Equity Research Industry Analysis. Baltimore: Legg Mason Wood Walker.

Sperling, J. G. (2000). *Rebel with a cause: The entrepreneur who created the University of Phoenix and the for-profit revolution in higher education.* New York: Wiley.

Sperling, J. G. (1989). *Against all odds.* Phoenix: Apollo Press.

Tooley, J. (1999). *The global education industry: Lessons from private education in developing countries.* London: Institute of Economic Affairs.

Turner, J. K., & Pusser, B. (2004). Place Matters: The distribution of access to a state flagship university. *Policy Futures in Education, 2*(2), 388–421.

University of California Office of the President (UCOP). (1996). *UC means business: The economic impact of the University of California.* A Report by the University of California Office of the President. Oakland, CA: Author.

Veysey, L. R. (1965). *The emergence of the American university.* Chicago: University of Chicago Press.

Washburn, J. (2005). *University, Inc.: The corporate corruption of American higher education.* New York: Basic.

Weisbrod, B. A. (1998). The nonprofit mission and its financing: Growing links between nonprofits and the rest of the economy. In B. A. Weisbrod (Ed.), *To profit or not to profit: The commercial transformation of the nonprofit sector* (pp. 1–24). Cambridge, United Kingdom: Cambridge University Press.

Weisbrod, B. A. (1988). *The nonprofit economy.* Cambridge: Harvard University Press.

Winston, G. (1999, January/February). For-profit education: Godzilla or Chicken Little? *Change, 31,* 12–19.

Winston, G. (1997). Why can't a college be more like a firm? In Joel Meyerson (Ed.), *New thinking on higher education: Creating a context for change.* Bolton, MA: Anker.

Winston, G., Carbone, J. C., & Lewis, E. G. (1998). *What's been happening to higher education: A reference manual, 1986–87 to 1994–95.* Williams Project on the Economics of Higher Education. Amherst, MA: Williams College.

Wolfe, B. L. (1995). External benefits of education. In M. Carnoy (Ed.), *International encyclopedia of economics of education,* 2d ed. (pp. 159–164). New York: Elsevier Science.

Chapter 3

For-Profit Colleges in the Context of the Market for Higher Education

Sarah E. Turner

FOR-PROFIT COLLEGES IN THE CONTEXT OF THE MARKET FOR HIGHER EDUCATION

Provision of postsecondary, professional education by for-profit enterprises is not a uniquely modern development. Well into the nineteenth century, proprietary education was a source of training for professional occupations in areas such as teaching, medicine, law, and accounting (Goldin and Katz, 1998). Moreover, rapid industrial growth at the turn of the century led to a proliferation of commercial schools that offered training in a number of new technologies, including the typewriter and stenographic machines (Honick, 1995).

But, the advantage of the proprietary schools in these professional markets was eroded in the early twentieth century as public and nonprofit universities grew in scale and scope, offering both general education and specific technical training. The modern university had the capacity to combine the growing body of knowledge in the general sciences, such as chemistry, with professional applications. Moreover, the Flexner report (1910) severely criticized the range of small for-profit medical education programs and led to calls for regulation and oversight of the entire proprietary sector of medical education.

While the universe of public and nonprofit colleges matured through the twentieth century, it might be said that the for-profit sector was "reborn" in the 1980s and 1990s. Beyond the "mom-and-pop" schools offering sub-baccalaureate training in vocational fields like cosmetology and truck driving that proliferated in the 1970s with the availability of aid through the Pell grant program emerged a new breed of "corporate" for-profit university. These institutions like the University of Phoenix and ITT operated with the institutional controls of large corporations and entered BA and graduate degree markets in higher education. Active discussion of the for-profit providers in higher education suggests that the sector may have many of the characteristics of a growth industry.[1] For example, a *New York Times* article noted the promise of the for-profit sector to "turn the $700 billion education sector into 'the next health care'—that is, transform large portions of a fragmented, cottage industry of independent, nonprofit institutions into a consolidated, professionally managed, money-making set of businesses that include all levels of education" (Wyatt, 1999).

Understanding the organization of the market for higher education is imperative in assessing the prospects for these for-profit institutions providing opportunities that are, in some respects, substitutes for the traditional offerings of nonprofit and public colleges and universities. Because there is considerable diversity in the nature of the "product" in higher education, for-profit providers will have a relative advantage in some markets but not in others. The purpose of this chapter is to explore the geographic and product markets where for-profit providers of higher education have a competitive advantage with respect to their counterparts in the public and nonprofit sectors.

To be sure, there is considerable intersection between the activities of for-profit colleges and their nonprofit and public counterparts; in short, there is competition. But the overlap is far from complete. For-profit institutions specialize in degree programs that are relatively vocational or technical in orientation, while serving students who are often considerably older than recent high school graduates. Geographically, the entry of for-profit providers is the largest in states that do not meet their demand for college-trained workers from within-state capacity in higher education and in those states with relatively large growth in the size of the college-age population. The body of this chapter provides a motivation for why this differentiation is likely to exist and empirical evidence on its magnitude.

For-Profits in the Market in Higher Education

The popular discussion of *the* market for higher education suffers from an unfortunate lack of definition. In the industrial organization literature, responses to questions about the degree of competitiveness in a market presuppose a definition of both the product market and the geographic market.

In the context of education, the "product market" refers to the type, level, and quantity of skills provided by a college or university. Type or field distinguishes the range of specializations from engineering to health sciences to more broadly defined fields in the liberal arts. Beyond the high school degree, there are a number of levels of degree awards, with the most common: Associate, BA, MA, and PhD, as well as professional degrees in law and medicine. Specification of the product market within higher education is particularly important if one is to reasonably assess the degree of market competitiveness.

To take an example from the health care literature, a market with two hospitals—one specializing in cardiac care and the other in oncology—may be less competitive than suggested by a simple count of the number of hospitals, as these institutions are unlikely to compete for the same patients (Gaynor and Vogt, 1999). In the same vein, a college specializing in fashion design is unlikely to compete with an engineering school for students even if they are in quite close geographic proximity.

Geographic markets are defined by the boundaries of trade.[2] The geographic market for education consists of the range over which students will travel for a particular educational product. Note that, in education, some markets—for instance, high-quality undergraduate training—are effectively national, while others—for instance, technology-specific part-time training—are effectively local. Online degree offerings a new frontier as they change the boundaries of space and time.

The geographic definition of education markets has not been constant over time. Caroline Hoxby (1998, 1997) provides an excellent analysis of the causes and consequences of the increased geographic integration of the undergraduate market from the 1940s to the present. To illustrate, while over 93% of college students attended an institution within state in 1949, that figure dropped to under 75% in the 1990s (Hoxby, 1998). Changes in transportation costs, standardization of student performance (the introduction of the SAT), the advent of the National Merit program, and the GI Bill all contributed to a greater geographic range of choices for traditional undergraduate students.

Yet, while those in the market for a residential undergraduate experience are more likely to venture a considerable distance from home in recent years, students older than recent college graduates are likely to look explicitly for collegiate experiences close to their place of residence. Geographic proximity affords the opportunity to combine work and family with collegiate attainment, and the time cost of travel is likely to be an explicit barrier for many older students. For-profit colleges and universities specialize in providing collegiate opportunities in relatively local markets, and they are explicit in their efforts to bring education to their potential students, often offering several locations within a metropolitan area. The absence of the large "fixed" investments of substantial libraries and dormitories affords the capacity to serve many localities. To the extent that the costs of "entry" for a for-profit may be much lower than for a public university or nonprofit college as capital requirements are much lower,[3] for-profits may enter into geographic markets that are underserved. The result is the expansion of opportunities rather than a zero-sum game among institutional providers. Moreover, for-profit institutions are not likely to compete in all areas of study, but are likely to concentrate in areas where skill acquisition is relatively easy to certify.[4]

For-Profit Institutions and Public Policy

One of the unique characteristics of the market for higher education is the mix of nonprofit, public, and for-profit provision. For-profit universities award degrees of all types—from the PhD level to postsecondary certificates. To be sure, the distribution of degrees awarded differs by type of institution, as for-profit institutions award a disproportionate share of degrees at the subbaccalaureate and certificate levels while public and nonprofit institutions dominate in the production of degrees at the BA and graduate levels (Table 3.1). Overall, for-profit higher education is a relatively small share of headcount enrollment at about 3% of total enrollment in 2000. Yet, in particular categories of postsecondary outcomes such as the subbaccalaureate certificates, for-profit providers are responsible for nearly 15% of the educational attainment. Why for-profit providers are well-represented in some dimensions of education outputs but not others is tied to both the nature of the "products" and to the distribution of public subsidies.

Public institutions and private, nonprofit institutions receive subsidies that are not available to for-profit providers—direct appropriations, tax-favored treatment in exchange for more regulatory control, and the commitment to "charitable" purposes. Among the institutions with the greatest private subsidies are those that specialize in providing graduate education, research, and residential liberal arts studies. These are universities like Harvard and Princeton, as well as liberal arts colleges like Amherst and Williams, with substantial endowments per student.[5] As Winston (1998) notes, large endowments yield large subsidies per student, with students paying a relatively small share of the total cost of education. As such, these highly subsidized nonprofit institutions are unlikely to compete directly for students with for-profit institutions that must pass on the full cost of production in the form of tuition. To this end, programs receiving the greatest subsidies from these private sources including doctorate-level education at the universities and liberal arts programs at the colleges, are unlikely to be offered by for-profit providers.

Public sector institutions receive substantial direct subsidies in the form of state appropriations. For example, in the 1999–2000 academic year, public colleges and universities received more than $56 billion—36% of current fund revenues—from state sources (U.S. Department of Education, 2002, Table 334). As such, these institutions are able to offer some educational products well below the cost of production. Yet, state resources often bring state controls and regulations that limit the capacity of public institutions to adjust to changing market conditions.

While it is clear that public and nonprofit colleges and universities receive subsidies through channels largely unavailable to for-profit institutions, the latter are not untouched by public policy efforts to increase postsecondary

TABLE 3.1
Distribution of Degrees and Certificates Awarded by Control of Institution,
2000–2001 Academic Year

a. Enrollment	Insititutional Control		
	Public	Nonprofit	For-Profit
Undergraduate	10,617,567	2,300,053	412,183
Other Graduate Students	1,095,541	724,474	47,077
First-Time First-Professional	125,320	183,639	1,068
Total Enrollment Level	11,838,428	3,208,166	460,328

b. Degrees Awarded	Insititutional Control		
	Public	Nonprofit	For-Profit
Graduate Degrees			
Doctorate Degrees	28,280	15,991	797
First Professional Degrees	32,925	47,401	246
Master's Degrees	246,803	212,422	12,104
Bachelor's Degrees	820,514	416,560	23,234
Subbaccalaureate			
Associate's Degrees	459,803	46,950	78,857
2 But Less than 4-Year Certificates	10,221	1,215	1,198
1 But Less than 2-Year Certificates	99,799	7,503	23,035
Less than 1-Year Certificates	118,939	5,703	21,958

Source: Author's tabulation from WebCASPAR.

enrollment and attainment. Under the 1972 legislation reauthorizing the Higher Education Act, Congress employed the term *postsecondary education* rather than *higher education*, intending to broaden the range of options beyond traditional baccalaureate programs, which had been the focus of financial aid in the programs authorized under the Higher Education Act of 1965. The legislation authorizing the Pell grant program was explicit in opening the doors to a wider range of postsecondary providers and courses of study. As Lawrence Gladieux (1995) writes, "The intent was to break the stereotype that education beyond high school meant full-time attendance in a four-year academic program." The inclusion of proprietary schools among postsecondary institutions eligible for Title IV federal financial aid was an innovation in the 1972 reauthorization language and part of the general movement to widen the reach of federal support to include career and vocational education.[6] Pell grant recipients attending nonprofit colleges and universities are concentrated in baccalaureate institutions and those attending public institutions are slightly more likely to attend community colleges than four-year institutions. Among Pell grant recipients attending for-profit institutions, the majority of students are enrolled in relatively short duration programs; similarly, the majority of those attending less than two-year programs enroll at proprietary schools.[7]

TABLE 3.2
Distribution of Federal Student Aid by Institution Control, 2000–01

	Distribution of Federal Student Aid			
	Pell Grants	Campus-Based Programs	Subsidized Stafford Loans	Unsubsidized Stafford Loans
Public	68.0%	68.0%	50.1%	45.6%
Two-Year	(33.7%)	(35.0%)	(5.4%)	(4.4%)
Four-Year	(34.4%)	(33.0%)	(44.7%)	(41.2%)
Private Nonprofit	18.3%	17.9%	38.2%	40.6%
Proprietary	13.6%	14.2%	11.8%	12.9%

Source: College Board, 2003, Trends in Student Aid, Table 5.

Still, for-profit institutions share with public and private colleges and universities access to portable student aid programs, including Pell grants and student loans. Given that enrollment at for-profit institutions is about 3% of observed fall enrollment at all colleges and universities, students attending for-profit institutions garner a disproportionate share of student aid dollars, accounting for 13.6% of Pell grant recipients and 11.8% of subsidized Stafford loan recipients (Table 3.2). Two factors account for this very high student aid share. The first is that students at for-profit institutions may be disproportionately eligible for federal student aid. Independent students beyond the age where parental financial circumstances are considered in needs analysis are particularly drawn to for-profit institutions with their greater proximity to work and family. To this point, while about 55% of Pell grant recipients at private nonprofit institutions are classified as dependent, only about a quarter attending for-profit institutions are classified as dependent (Table 3.3). Length of course of study also affects the reported number of aid recipients: more than 55% of Pell grant recipients at for-profit institutions are enrolled in programs that are less than two years in duration; only about 2.8% of students at private non-profit institutions are enrolled in such very short-term programs (U.S. Department of Education, 2003, Table 18).[8]

Yet, there is also considerable variation among degree-granting for-profit institutions in the importance of Pell grants. A recent story in the *Chronicle of Higher Education* (Blumenstyk, 2004) tallied the ratio of Title IV financial aid (Pell grants and student loans) to annual revenue for publicly traded for-profit institutions. At one extreme, the ratio was 0.82 at Corinthian Colleges, 0.69 at Education Management colleges, and 0.67 at ITT schools. Other for-profit degree-granting programs, including those operated by Apollo (University of Phoenix), DeVry and Strayer, receive a somewhat smaller (0.62 to 0.55) share of revenues from Title IV programs as many students are employed full-time

TABLE 3.3
Distribution of Pell Grant Expenditures and Recipients by Type of Student and Control, 2002–2003

	Public		Private Nonprofit		Proprietary	
	Amount	*%*	*Amount*	*%*	*Amount*	*%*
Total Expenditures						
Total	$7,883,765,781		$1,968,766,154		$1,789,019,783	
Dependent Recipients	$3,623,907,290	46.0%	$1,111,650,235	56.5%	$469,918,067	26.3%
Independent w/o dependent	$1,411,037,071	17.9%	$311,256,667	15.8%	$305,275,938	17.1%
Independent w/ dependent	$2,848,821,420	36.1%	$545,859,252	27.7%	$1,013,825,778	56.7%
Total Recipients						
Total	3,263,602		757,050		757,855	
Dependent Recipients	1,424,886	43.7%	415,554	54.9%	190,965	25.2%
Independent w/o dependent	622,130	19.1%	122,384	16.2%	142,297	18.8%
Independent w/ dependent	1,216,586	37.3%	219,112	28.9%	424,593	56.0%

Source: U.S. Department of Education, 2003, Table 19.

(and often receiving tuition assistance from employers) or are graduate students and thus ineligible for most need-based federal aid. In fact, analysts have recently connected the dependence on Pell revenues to the extent to which institutions are likely to experience countercyclical swings in enrollment (Hughes, 2004).

What one should take away from this discussion is that the growth of for-profit higher education is in no way independent of federal and state higher education policy even though these institutions are unlikely to receive substantial direct subsidies from governmental sources. The effect of policy on the expansion (or contraction) of the for-profit sector operates through two channels. First, for-profit institutions are major beneficiaries of federal need-based financial aid; though the statutory beneficiaries are students, the economic incidence of these subsidies is more widely distributed, with for-profit universities gaining substantial revenues. Second, contraction in state appropriations per capita to public institutions increases the potential opportunities for for-profit providers in local markets as the relative "advantage" held by public colleges and universities is reduced.

What For-Profits Offer

Institutional control—whether an institution is a for-profit or a nonprofit—affects the expected course offerings in two related dimensions. First, nonprofits may have an advantage in offering degrees in which skills are difficult to certify.[9] Second, with nonprofit institutions and public institutions receiving substantial public and private subsidies, it is expected that for-profit institutions provide courses of study requiring little public subsidy beyond direct tuition revenues. As one observer of both the nonprofit and corporate sectors notes: "A for-profit board has an obligation to *get out* of a bad business while a nonprofit board may have an obligation to *stay in*, if it is to be true to its mission" (Bowen, 1994, p. 23).

Moreover, because individuals may be reluctant to contract with for-profit providers for the provision of difficult to observe skills, preprofessional and vocational skill development may be particularly well-suited to for-profit providers. Examples include business and accounting, computer programming, and some allied health fields. Several characteristics distinguish these courses of study and make them well-suited to provision by for-profit institutions:

- The "skills" are easy to certify through either direct assessment (e.g., certification examinations) or job placement.
- Experienced practitioners are good substitutes for research PhDs as instructors.[10]

- For-profits will also focus their energies on producing skills that are easily verifiable, and they will avoid training high-risk students.
- Modest physical plant and limited interdisciplinary requirements are necessary for degree completion.[11]

Liberal arts studies define one end of the spectrum that is unlikely to be served by for-profit providers because the "outcome" is hard to assess directly, and academic PhD-level instruction and significant capital infrastructure such as libraries and a wide range of field offerings are the norms. Still, there are a whole range of other specializations that are open to direct observation and testing. For example, it would seem to be reasonably straightforward to evaluate whether a student achieved proficiency in accounting or programming in a particular language.

Tables 3.4a and 3.4b show the distribution of Associate and BA degrees by type of institution. While two-year degrees are—in general—more vocationally oriented than BA degrees, two-year degrees offered by for-profit institutions tend to be concentrated in business, health professions, and engineering technologies. It is at the BA level that the biggest differences in concentration by institutional control are apparent. While public and nonprofit institutions award about 30% of BA degrees in arts and sciences disciplines such as English, economics, sociology, biology, and physics (Table 3.4b), less than 1% of BA degrees awarded by for-profit institutions appear in these categories. Instead, 56.1% of BA degrees awarded by for-profit institutions fall under the heading of "business." Engineering technologies and computer-related fields are also degree areas where for-profit providers are concentrated.

The Growth Markets and For-Profits

The demand for college education is a derived demand in the sense that it is conditions in the labor market, specifically the return to education, which determine the willingness of individuals to enroll. Changes in the geographic concentration of potential participants in higher education and the age at college attendance are two primary market forces affecting the growth of the for-profit colleges and universities.

Geographical Variation
The differences in the concentration of public and nonprofit colleges and universities across states are due in part to historical accident. Local politics, the structure of industry, and demographic characteristics dating back to the turn of the twentieth century contribute to the number of public and nonprofit institutions in a state and their location (Goldin and Katz, 1999). Against this

TABLE 3.4a
Distribution of Associate Degrees Awarded by Control of Institution and Field, 2000–2001 Academic Year

Field of Study	Number of Degrees			Percent Distribution		
	Public	Nonprofit	Profit	Public	Nonprofit	Profit
Total of All Instructional Programs	459,521	46,459	78,980			
Architecture & Related Programs	361	2	54	0.1%	0.0%	0.1%
Area, Ethnic, & Cultural Studies	63	244	0	0.0%	0.5%	0.0%
Biological Sciences/Life Sciences	1,461	62	3	0.3%	0.1%	0.0%
English Language & Literature/Letters	809	68	0	0.2%	0.1%	0.0%
Mathematics	664	28	3	0.1%	0.1%	0.0%
Philosophy & Religion	34	31	0	0.0%	0.1%	0.0%
Physical Sciences	1,198	21	48	0.3%	0.0%	0.1%
Psychology	1,338	182	34	0.3%	0.4%	0.0%
Social Sciences & History	4,843	304	0	1.1%	0.7%	0.0%
Arts & Sciences Subtotal	10,771	942	142	2.3%	2.0%	0.2%
Agricultural Business & Production Sciences	4,951	320	0	1.1%	0.7%	0.0%
Business Management & Administrative Services	66,888	12,131	15,615	14.6%	26.1%	19.8%
Communications	1,585	397	975	0.3%	0.9%	1.2%
Communications Technologies	1,522	167	331	0.3%	0.4%	0.4%
Computer & Information Sciences	13,467	1,990	11,324	2.9%	4.3%	14.3%
Conservation/Renewable Natural Resources	1,351	98	0	0.3%	0.2%	0.0%
Construction Trades	2,097	112	467	0.5%	0.2%	0.6%
Education	7,934	1,323	43	1.7%	2.8%	0.1%
Engineering	1,484	105	285	0.3%	0.2%	0.4%
Engineering-related Technologies	18,357	3,262	13,441	4.0%	7.0%	17.0%
Foreign Languages & Literatures	424	105	0	0.1%	0.2%	0.0%
Health Professions & Related Sciences	67,104	7,359	9,534	14.6%	15.8%	12.1%
Home Economics	707	218	23	0.2%	0.5%	0.0%
Law & Legal Studies	3,963	581	2,315	0.9%	1.3%	2.9%
Liberal/General Studies	188,312	8,417	174	41.0%	18.1%	0.2%
Library & Archival Sciences	103	0	0	0.0%	0.0%	0.0%
Marketing Operations/Marketing & Distribution	3,713	406	1,245	0.8%	0.9%	1.6%
Mechanics & Repairers	8,259	720	3,783	1.8%	1.5%	4.8%
Military Technologies	120	0	0	0.0%	0.0%	0.0%
Multi/Interdisciplinary Studies	10,289	113	40	2.2%	0.2%	0.1%
Parks, Recreation, Leisure, & Fitness	681	129	36	0.1%	0.3%	0.0%
Personal & Miscellaneous Services	2,183	3,975	4,272	0.5%	8.6%	5.4%
Precision Production Trades	7,245	347	4,023	1.6%	0.7%	5.1%
Protective Services	16,176	678	668	3.5%	1.5%	0.8%
Public Administration & Services	2,977	333	24	0.6%	0.7%	0.0%
Science Technologies	1,044	35	68	0.2%	0.1%	0.1%
Theological Studies & Religious Vocations	2	567	0	0.0%	1.2%	0.0%
Transportation & Materials Moving Workers	689	40	110	0.1%	0.1%	0.1%
Visual & Performing Arts	7,567	1,381	9,527	1.6%	3.0%	12.1%
Vocational Home Economics	7,402	76	217	1.6%	0.2%	0.3%

Source: Author's tabulations from WebCASPAR tabulations.

TABLE 3.4b

Distribution of BA Degrees Awarded by Control of Institution and Field,
2000–2001 Academic Year

Field of Study	Number of Degrees			Percent Distribution		
	Public	Nonprofit	Profit	Public	Nonprofit	Profit
Total of All Instructional Programs	820,417	414,701	23,261			
Architecture & Related Programs	6,552	1,902	68	0.8%	0.5%	0.3%
Area, Ethnic, & Cultural Studies	3,658	2,662	0	0.4%	0.6%	0.0%
Biological Sciences/Life Sciences	40,565	21,330	0	4.9%	5.1%	0.0%
English Language & Literature/Letters	34,918	16,557	0	4.3%	4.0%	0.0%
Mathematics	7,571	4,132	0	0.9%	1.0%	0.0%
Philosophy & Religion	3,417	5,163	0	0.4%	1.2%	0.0%
Physical Sciences	11,709	6,405	0	1.4%	1.5%	0.0%
Psychology	49,321	24,803	0	6.0%	6.0%	0.0%
Social Sciences & History	83,050	45,607	8	10.1%	11.0%	0.0%
Arts & Sciences Subtotal	*240,761*	*128,561*	*76*	*29.3%*	*31.0%*	*0.3%*
Agricultural Business & Production Sciences	13,813	643	0	1.7%	0.2%	0.0%
Business Management & Administrative Services	155,460	97,757	13,042	18.9%	23.6%	56.1%
Communications	40,294	18,138	46	4.9%	4.4%	0.2%
Communications Technologies	508	315	294	0.1%	0.1%	1.3%
Computer & Information Sciences	24,075	14,404	3,671	2.9%	3.5%	15.8%
Conservation/Renewable Natural Resources	7,409	1,663	0	0.9%	0.4%	0.0%
Construction Trades	50	124	0	0.0%	0.0%	0.0%
Education	76,798	30,927	28	9.4%	7.5%	0.1%
Engineering	44,751	14,078	180	5.5%	3.4%	0.8%
Engineering-related Technologies	10,264	1,829	2,057	1.3%	0.4%	8.8%
Foreign Languages & Literatures	10,306	4,926	0	1.3%	1.2%	0.0%
Health Professions & Related Sciences	48,501	25,240	838	5.9%	6.1%	3.6%
Home Economics	15,031	2,380	0	1.8%	0.6%	0.0%
Law & Legal Studies	1,095	832	45	0.1%	0.2%	0.2%
Liberal/General Studies	26,116	11,919	31	3.2%	2.9%	0.1%
Library & Archival Sciences	49	3	0	0.0%	0.0%	0.0%
Marketing Operations/Marketing & Distribution	2,496	1,834	173	0.3%	0.4%	0.7%
Mechanics & Repairers	74	34	0	0.0%	0.0%	0.0%
Military Technologies	21	0	0	0.0%	0.0%	0.0%
Multi/Interdisciplinary Studies	19,143	6,928	16	2.3%	1.7%	0.1%
Parks, Recreation, Leisure, & Fitness	14,402	5,199	10	1.8%	1.3%	0.0%
Personal & Miscellaneous Services	118	262	4	0.0%	0.1%	0.0%
Precision Production Trades	338	45	0	0.0%	0.0%	0.0%
Protective Services	18,912	6,901	199	2.3%	1.7%	0.9%
Public Administration & Services	13,672	6,223	2	1.7%	1.5%	0.0%
Science Technologies	131	138	0	0.0%	0.0%	0.0%
Theological Studies & Religious Vocations	0	6,986	0	0.0%	1.7%	0.0%
Transportation & Materials Moving Workers	1,472	768	7	0.2%	0.2%	0.0%
Visual & Performing Arts	34,263	24,615	2,458	4.2%	5.9%	10.6%
Vocational Home Economics	94	330	0	0.0%	0.1%	0.0%

Source: Author's tabulations from WebCASPAR tabulations.

institutional backdrop, for-profit higher education programs make decisions about "entry" (and "exit").

State governments are likely to be very slow and incomplete in adjustments to changes in the demand for education in local areas. Migration in response to the growth or the decline of industries necessarily changes the balance of population to higher education. Even when states like Arizona move to add new public institutions (e.g., the entry of ASU-West and ASU-East in the Phoenix metropolitan area) there remain substantial opportunities for entry among for-profit providers.

This point is illustrated by the simple correlation between growth in the population and the rise in the enrollment at for-profit institutions. Table 3.5 shows the change in for-profit enrollment and the change in college-age population between 1995 and 2000. While the secular increase in for-profit enrollment is remarkable, it is the states such as California, Colorado and Arizona that have experienced disproportionate increases in population that have the greatest increases in the for-profit enrollment. Taken together with variation in the growth rate of the college-age population across states, it is readily apparent that the prospects for the entry of for-profit providers vary markedly across states.

Older Students and the Competitive Advantage of For-Profit Universities

That participants in formal higher education are increasingly beyond the traditional college age of 18–22 raises interesting questions about the functioning of the higher education market and the labor market, while also providing comparatively rich opportunities for for-profit providers. Textbook models of the investment in education present models in which individuals invest in postsecondary education full-time and early in their careers. Yet, the observation that individuals over the age of 21 constituted 56% of enrollment in degree-granting institutions in 2000 and that 41% of students are enrolled part-time, suggests a need for some rethinking of the traditional modes of delivery (*Digest of Education Statistics*, 2002, Table 174).[12] For-profit educational institutions are likely to be explicit in their consideration of student time as a costly input, thereby organizing course offerings so as to minimize time costs from missed employment opportunities, with classes scheduled in extended blocks on weekends or in evening hours (Freeman, 1974). Because for-profit institutions treat student time as an input and maintain operations in a wide array of convenient geographic areas suggests that they are particularly well-suited to capture growth among older and nontraditional students.

The extent to which higher education institutions, combined with public policy initiatives, provide an efficient mechanism for individuals beyond the traditional college age to gain new skills, particularly in recessionary periods,

TABLE 3.5

Enrollment in Public and For-Profit Institutions and Population Growth, 1995–2000

	Fall 1995		Fall 2000		% Change Population 18–24
	Public	For-Profit	Public	For-Profit	1995–2000
Alabama	269,982	275	207,435	3,878	−2.5%
Alaska	28,368	204	26,559	486	17.7%
Arizona	254,530	14,413	284,522	46,876	17.1%
Arkansas	87,067	...	101,775	757	2.8%
California	1,566,008	22,632	1,927,771	75,913	4.3%
Colorado	213,955	9,744	222,227	18,427	18.8%
Connecticut	101,401	791	101,027	1,772	1.9%
Delaware	36,204	...	34,194	...	7.6%
Florida	530,607	13,480	556,912	36,077	8.2%
Georgia	247,919	6,923	271,755	10,326	9.2%
Hawaii	50,198	100	44,579	1,876	3.4%
Idaho	48,986	316	53,751	676	18.4%
Illinois	530,248	11,621	534,155	24,907	4.8%
Indiana	224,795	3,080	240,023	7,004	2.6%
Iowa	122,396	304	135,008	2,341	5.5%
Kansas	161,610	...	159,976	470	8.5%
Kentucky	148,808	3,878	151,973	8,353	−1.3%
Louisiana	172,769	901	189,213	4,624	3.1%
Maine	38,195	1,830	40,662	974	−2.7%
Maryland	227,760	517	227,969	3,419	8.6%
Massachusetts	176,777	38,459	183,248	1,844	2.2%
Michigan	461,321	...	467,861	3,101	0.8%
Minnesota	204,047	3,344	218,617	11,958	17.1%
Mississippi	110,600	...	125,355	409	−3.0%
Missouri	189,993	5,353	201,509	10,055	8.0%
Montana	37,435	...	37,387	...	13.3%
Nebraska	95,346	...	88,531	1,978	9.4%
Nevada	66,683	650	83,120	4,187	33.9%
New Hampshire	33,005	3,540	35,870	3,909	13.4%
New Jersey	271,069	4,550	266,921	6,975	4.0%
New Mexico	97,220	2,587	101,450	5,031	12.6%
New York	593,407	27,448	588,390	35,599	−0.4%
North Carolina	303,099	144	329,422	590	1.3%
North Dakota	36,810	...	36,014	111	10.6%
Ohio	410,500	13,215	411,161	13,674	2.4%
Oklahoma	158,026	1,310	153,699	3,134	2.7%
Oregon	144,147	611	155,336	3,020	13.2%
Pennsylvania	340,464	12,343	339,229	31,065	−0.2%
Rhode Island	38,653	...	38,458	224	−4.7%
South Carolina	148,706	491	155,519	757	13.9%
South Dakota	30,169	1,325	35,455	2,106	5.8%
Tennessee	193,136	1,727	202,530	5,571	10.2%
Texas	837,331	7,502	896,534	17,408	20.6%
Utah	110,560	2,647	123,046	4,744	7.4%
Vermont	20,470	...	20,021	337	0.5%
Virginia	293,127	9,990	313,780	17,134	12.5%
Washington	246,635	2,768	273,928	5,497	−9.4%
West Virginia	72,117	786	76,136	1,952	10.9%
Wisconsin	245,770	1,974	249,737	1,907	14.0%

Source: Author's tabulations from WebCASPAR and Census tabulations.

will have substantial implications for long-run economic growth and for the reduction of inequality in the distribution of earnings.

Federal funding provided through the Pell grant program also has the potential to enhance the role of postsecondary institutions as fiscal stabilizers.[13] Because cyclical downturns reduce the opportunity cost of time, it is expected that workers shift training investments to relatively slack labor market periods. In addition, shocks to labor demand may be tied to technological changes that make some skills obsolete (or open new opportunities in emerging industries). A final demand-side reason to expect enrollment funded through Pell grants to increase is that the capacity of individuals and families to finance college may also decline in cyclical downturns. As a result, some students become eligible for Pell grants who were previously ineligible.

Cyclical shocks measured by increases in state-level unemployment produce larger increases in Pell grant receipt among those attending for-profit institutions than in the public or nonprofit sector. A percentage point increase in the state-level unemployment rate is linked to an increase in for-profit enrollment in a state of 7–9% (Turner, 2004). Two important explanations follow. First, for-profit institutions may specialize in offering skill development in areas that are particularly suited to the needs of displaced workers and those underemployed in cyclical downturns. Second, on the supply-side of postsecondary education, nonprofit and public providers may be limited in their capacity to accommodate increases in demand because a significant share of resources comes from nontuition sources. Public institutions may face cutbacks in state appropriations driven by the same factors affecting transitory changes in the labor market.[14] Thus, while community colleges may be thought of as providing an "automatic stabilizer" to the local economy (Betts and McFarland, 1995), the capacity to perform this function may be limited by the cyclical nature of state funding. On the other hand, for-profit institutions do not rely on direct subsidies from the state; their supply response is likely to be somewhat more elastic.

CONCLUSION

The message from this analysis is that the product markets and factors affecting growth in for-profit institutions are not identical to those affecting public and nonprofit universities. (By the same token, the overlap in the markets is by no means zero.) The very nature of institutional control—with for-profit institutions explicitly maximizing profits—creates different areas of comparative advantage and specialization, as for-profit institutions are likely to gain ground in degree programs involving skills and expertise that are relatively easy to certify. For-profit universities also differ from other market peers in their capacity to respond to changes in local economic circumstances. These institutions are likely to be more responsive to the evolution of new demographic markets (e.g., the growth of the population in the Southwest) than public systems, which are likely to face political constraints and bureaucratic inertia in expansion. Moreover, many for-profit universities are likely to be better positioned to provide enrollment opportunities in the face of economic contractions than their counterparts in the public sector. Yet, to suggest that for-profit institutions are independent from policy decisions because they do not receive direct institutional appropriations like public universities, misses the important point that the funding and enrollment flows of for-profit colleges are often enabled by federal need-based aid programs.

NOTES

1. Beyond for-profit colleges, there are also a number of hybrid potential entrants to the educational marketplace including joint business-university ventures and distance learning. These innovations will also affect market structure. This chapter focused on the nonprofit/for-profit distinction for simplicity and clarity.

2. Elzinga and Hogarty (1973) provide an explicit metric through the analysis of shipments. In essence, a geographic market is large enough so that sales from sellers outside an area to inside buyers are small, and buyers outside an area from sellers within an area are also small. Thus, the definition of market boundaries should be expanded to the point where "importers" and "exporters" are a small part of total sales.

3. Entry among public universities is likely to also face substantial political barriers, with requirements for layers of bureaucratic approval before the establishment of a new institution or requirements for the addition of a branch to an existing institution.

4. Because it may be very difficult for students—or firms hiring students later in life—to observe the quantity or quality of learning that took place during college enrollment, there is the potential for contract failure in providing educational services. This problem may be particularly severe with for-profit providers, given the incentive to increase profits by providing an inferior education. The absence of residual shareholders reduces these incentives to cheat for nonprofit colleges and universities, as the behavior of management is limited by the nondistribution constraint.

5. For example, the most recent NACUBO survey placed the 2003 endowment of Harvard at $18.8 billion, the endowment for Yale at $11.03 billion, and the endowment for Williams at about $876 million.

6. Today, 53% of Pell grant recipients attend institutions that do not grant the BA degree and 11% attend institutions where the highest terminal degree or certificate is less than two years in length.

7. The introduction of the Pell program had a substantial effect on the postsecondary enrollment of students outside of the traditional college-going ages (Seftor and Turner, 2002). Eligibility for students claiming independent status has become more restrictive since the inception of the program. The 1986 amendments to the Higher Education Act required students to be at least twenty-four years old, married, or with children to qualify for aid as an independent student.

8. This point is also made in the recent Tebbs and Turner (2004) analysis. The number of Pell grant recipients is a count (or stock) throughout the course of the year, while the enrollment measures recorded by the Department of Education are based on a point in time (Fall). Thus, if a for-profit institution enrolled two independent half-year cohorts with 20% Pell recipients and a public institution enrolled one cohort with the same share of Pell grant recipients, our indicators would show twice as many Pell recipients at the for-profit institution (if the programs were of equal size).

9. This problem may be particularly severe with for-profit providers, given the incentive to increase profits by providing an inferior education. The absence of residual shareholders reduces these incentives to cheat for nonprofit colleges and universities, as the behavior of management is limited by the nondistribution constraint. In this sense, Hansmann (1987) has suggested that nonprofit or public provision may be a way to resolve the contract failure associated with the for-profit provision of educational services.

10. For example, it may be important for a researcher to be involved in the teaching of nuclear physics, while a practicing accountant may be qualified to teach bookkeeping in the classroom.

11. Goldin and Katz (1999) make a persuasive case that research universities evolved at the turn of the century into institutions defined by economies of scale and scope.

12. One possible cause of this trend is that students are increasingly credit constrained during the college years and are thus forced to combine school and work, thereby extending time-to-degree. Another explanation is that with an increased pace of technological change, workers are more likely to return to formal institutions to "retool" in the middle of their careers than they were several decades ago.

13. Unlike traditional social insurance programs that are statutory entitlement programs (or not subject to annual appropriations in the national legislative process), the Pell grant program requires regular federal appropriations and to this end is not an "automatic" stabilizer.

14. In addition, the educational production function, as well as the nature of the product, may affect responses to cyclical shocks. For those institutions where capital or long-term resources (e.g., tenured faculty) are an important part of the production process, short-term responses may be difficult. In contrast, institutions relying more heavily on variable inputs—rented space and untenured faculty—may be better positioned to adjust to changes in demand associated with local labor market conditions.

REFERENCES

Betts, J., & McFarland, L. (1995). Safe port in a storm: The impact of labor market conditions on community college enrollments. *Journal of Human Resources, 30*(4), 741–765.

Bowen, W. (1994). *Inside the boardroom: Governance by directors and trustees.* New York: Wiley.

Blumenstyk, G. (2004, May 14). For-profit colleges face new scrutiny. *Chronicle of Higher Education.*

College Board. (2003). *Trends in student aid.* http://www.collegeboard.com/prod_downloads/press/cost03/cb_trends_aid_2003.pdf

Elzinga, K., & Hogarty, T. (1973). The problem of geographic definition in antimerger suits. *Antitrust Bulletin, 18,* 45–81.

Freeman, R. (1974). Occupational training in proprietary schools and technical institutes. *The Review of Economics and Statistics, 56*(3), 310–318.

Gaynor, M., & Vogt, W. (1999). *Antitrust and competition in health care markets.* (NBER Working Paper No. 7112).

Gladieux, L. (1995). *Federal student aid policy: A history and an assessment.* http://www.ed.gov/offices/OPE/PPI/FinPostSecEd/gladieux.html

Goldin, C., & Katz, L. F. (1999). The shaping of higher education: The formative years in the United States, 1890–1940. *Journal of Economic Perspectives, 13*(1), 37–62.

Hansmann, H. (1998, September). *Higher education as an associative good.* Paper presented at the Symposium of the Forum for the Future of Higher Education, Aspen, Colorado.

Hansmann, H. (1987). Economic theories of nonprofit organization. In W. Powell (Ed.), *The nonprofit sector: A research handbook.* New Haven: Yale University Press.

Honick, C. (1995). The story behind proprietary schools in the United States, In D. A. Clowes and E. Hawthorne, (Eds.) *Community colleges and proprietary schools: Conflict or convergence?* San Francisco: Jossey-Bass Publishers.

Hoxby, C. (1998). *How the changing market structure of U.S. higher education explains tuition* (NBER Working Paper No. 6323).

Hoxby, C. (1997). *The changing market structure of U.S. higher education.* Harvard University, mimeo.

Hughes, M. (2004, July 9). *Education services: Review of for-profit education pricing.* Sun Trust Robinson Humphrey Report.

McPherson, M., & Schapiro, M. (1991). *Keeping college affordable.* Washington, DC: Brookings Institution.

Oster, S. (1997). *An analytical framework for thinking about the use of for-profit structures for university services and activities.* Paper presented at the Symposium of the Forum for the Future of Higher Education. Aspen, Colorado.

Seftor, N. and Turner, S. (2002). Back to school: Federal student aid policy and adult college enrollment. *The Journal of Human Resources, 37*(2), 336–352.

Sperling, J., & Tucker, R. W. (1997). *For-profit higher education: Developing a world class workforce.* New Brunswick: Transaction.

Tebbs, J., & Turner, S. (2005). College education for low income students: A caution on the use of data on Pell Grant recipients. *Change 37*(4), 34–43.

Turner, S. E. (2004). *Pell grants as fiscal stabilizers.* University of Virginia, Mimeo.

U.S. Department of Education, National Center for Education Statistics. (2003). *Digest of education statistics, 2002* (NCES Publication No. 2003–060) Washington: T. D. Snyder and C. M. Hoffman. Washington, DC.

U.S. Department of Education, Office of Postsecondary Education. (2003). *Title IV/Federal Pell Grant program 2002–2003 end of year report.* http://www.ed.gov/finaid/prof/resources/data/pell0203.pdf

Winston, G. (1998, November). *For-profit education: Godzilla or Chicken Little?* (Discussion Paper No. 49) Williams Project for the Economics of Higher Education, Williams College.

Wyatt, E. (1999, November 4). Investors see room for profit in nation's demand for education. *New York Times*, p. A1.

Part 2

_____

Practice

Chapter 4

The University of Phoenix

Icon of For-Profit Higher Education

David W. Breneman

By virtually any measure, the University of Phoenix (UOP) stands out as the leader in the for-profit, degree-granting, sector of American higher education.[1] Billing itself as the largest private university in the world, with total degree enrollments across all of its campuses of 255,600 students in 2004, UOP has been a clear financial and educational success. Among the leading for-profit providers, no single business or educational model predominates, so a detailed description of one organization cannot capture all the variation to be found; nonetheless, as the most visible and best-known member of this group, a close look at UOP provides insight into how this sector operates. A case study of UOP may also suggest implications for traditional, nonprofit colleges and universities.

EDUCATIONAL DATA

Students attending UOP were enrolled in a variety of Bachelor's, Master's, and Doctoral degree programs in 2004, a tenfold increase in enrollments since 1995. From its beginnings in 1976 through December 2004, the university has awarded 187,000 degrees. A profile of UOP students reveals that the average age is in the mid-thirties, with an average household income between $50,000 and $60,000. Thus, the first and most important point about UOP is that the focus is on working adults, not on traditional 18–22-year-old full-time students. The UOP mission statement expresses this focus clearly:

> The missions of the University of Phoenix are to educate working adults to develop the knowledge and skills that will enable them to

71

achieve their professional goals, improve the productivity of their organizations, and provide leadership and service to their communities.

Indeed, until recently, UOP required applicants to be at least 23^2 years of age, and, while not required for admission, the emphasis is clearly on those who have full-time jobs. In 2001, 69 percent of UOP students had been employed on a full-time basis for nine years or more. This fact leads to a key financing feature for UOP students in that 59 percent receive some amount of tuition reimbursement from their employers. With regard to diversity, 39 percent of the student population are racial and ethnic minorities, while 56 percent are female.

The UOP curricular offerings are concentrated in business administration and information systems and technology. Undergraduate business administration accounts for 41% of total enrollments, graduate business and management for 18%, and information systems and technology for 11%. Other programs offered include general and professional studies (8%), education (7%), health sciences and nursing (6%), social and behavioral sciences (8%), and advanced studies (1%). Thus, vast segments of the traditional university curriculum are not offered at UOP as degree-granting programs, including essentially the whole of the Arts and Science curriculum.[3] (A limited number of lower-division humanities and social science courses are offered as part of the general studies area for students who enter with fewer than 60 transfer credits, but beyond those courses, the UOP curriculum is centered on professional education.) Student motivation is largely based on the desire for professional and career advancement.

It should also be noted that UOP is accredited by the Higher Learning Commission of the North Central Association, one of several regional accrediting bodies in the United States. It also has specialized accreditation from the National League for Nursing Accrediting Commission, Inc. (NLNAC) and from the Council for Accreditation of Counseling and Related Educational Programs (CACREP), is licensed (as of 2004) in 35 states, and, because its parent company, Apollo Group, Inc. (APOL), is publicly traded, it is also regulated by the Securities and Exchange Commission. Among the first for-profit, degree-granting institution to be regionally accredited (1978), UOP faced a hostile educational community in its early years, as representatives from traditional colleges and universities sought to prevent their accreditation. That story, with all of its passion and intensity, has been told by the founder, the economist-historian John G. Sperling, in several publications.[4]

A distinctive feature of the UOP educational model is its heavy reliance on part-time, practitioner faculty, as opposed to full-time academic faculty. In 2004, UOP employed roughly 18,000 part-time practitioner faculty for teaching, and approximately 1,400 full-time faculty, who have both teaching and administrative duties. The basic explanation for UOP's profitability is to be found in these figures.

Most courses at UOP are taught in the evening and on an accelerated schedule, undergraduate courses last only 5 weeks and graduate courses last 6 weeks (the educational model will be discussed more fully later). Each practitioner faculty member teaches a class one night per week, for either 5 or 6 weeks, a time demand that is manageable for many professionals who have full-time jobs during the day. Practitioner faculty have Master's or Doctoral degrees and a minimum of 5 years of professional experience in the field that they teach (the average is 16 years of experience). They also must be professionally employed in their field of instruction. Within this labor force of 18,000 faculty, 37% are female, and 23% are from racial and ethnic minorities.

A common misperception of those who have only vaguely heard of UOP is the belief that it is a virtual university, with all instruction via online distance education. While UOP developed an online capacity beginning in 1989, the majority of students and courses are taught in the traditional, face-to-face manner, at night in leased facilities that are dedicated as UOP classrooms. Classes are typically small (15 to 20 students), and are managed as discussion seminars rather than as lectures. The online courses are low-tech, in that they are conducted via web and E-mail, without expensive production costs. Faculty members typically handle fewer students in this format, often limited to no more than 12, though the average online cohort is 9 students. The online component of UOP enrolled roughly 120,000 students in 2004, however, and is the fastest growing part of the system.

At this writing, UOP has a physical campus presence in 35 states and at over 157 locations. Campuses are concentrated in California, Arizona, New Mexico, Colorado, Utah, Nevada, and Florida. (Online courses are available in all 50 states and in 130 countries.) UOP has been adding campuses in about 2 new states per year, and will continue at that pace until the major markets are exhausted. Although they are regionally accredited, they often face stiff state requirements for licensure, which can delay their entry into specific markets. Although UOP, and its parent Apollo, will continue to develop new campuses in the United States, much of their future growth appears likely to be abroad.

FINANCIAL DATA

As an index of profitability, if one had purchased $10,000 worth of Apollo stock when first issued in 1994, by December 2004 it would have been worth roughly $1,034,743. In fiscal 2004, Apollo Group had revenues of $1,798.4

million and net income of $277.8 million; the online portion of net income was $139.9 million. UOP clearly has developed a business model that generates excellent cash flow and substantial profits, as well as a high rate of return on invested capital. Further discussion of the educational and business model will help to explain their ability to generate such impressive financial numbers.

For a variety of reasons, analysts continue to be bullish in their predictions about the value of Apollo Group stock.[5] Block and Johnston (2003) point to the strong recent performance of the company: "Apollo Group offered investors the appealing combination of high earnings visibility, high earnings growth, and high earnings quality, as qualified by cash flow growth that exceeded earnings growth during FY02 (56% versus 45%)" (p. 6). The rapid growth rate of for-profit institutions is another key driver of analyst optimism: "Since 1995, US enrollment in Title IV eligible institutions (95% of total enrollment) has languished at a meager Compound Annual Growth Rate (CAGR) of 1.67%. NCES estimates that enrollment will grow to 17.7 million by 2011, representing a decline in the meager CAGR to 1.16%" (Block, 2002). For-profit enrollment, on the other hand, has enjoyed CAGR of 7.6%, while increasing market share from 3.5% to 4.4%. According to Block (2002) one factor responsible for this growth has been the lack of consonance between the input needs of the economy and the outputs generated by traditional schools. For-profits have recognized this incongruence and succeeded in the market by providing more skills and credentials that are in demand.

BRIEF HISTORY OF UOP

Before turning to a discussion of the educational model of UOP, a few supplementary comments on the history of the university will be helpful. Sperling, its founder, has written several books in which he discusses the ideas and motivation that prompted him to create UOP, and only the relevant highlights need be mentioned here.[6]

Sperling was a faculty member at San Jose State University in California in the mid-1960s, and undertook a federally funded project to develop a twelfth-grade economics curriculum. This effort caused him to explore the field of pedagogy, and he subsequently moved on to projects involving the education of adults. Encountering frustration in his efforts to develop programs for working adults at San Jose State, he sought out a struggling private university, the University of San Francisco (USF), where his newly formed Institute for Professional Development could function and return a financial surplus to the university. All went well until the existence of his program and its budgetary surpluses attracted the attention of the Western Association of Schools and Colleges (WASC), the regional accrediting agency for USF. The leadership of WASC declared war on Sperling's institute, and threatened to withdraw accreditation from USF unless the institute was shut down. No college or university can survive for long without regional accreditation (essential, among other things, for eligibility to receive federal student aid), so USF had no recourse but to sever the relationship.

Incensed with the attitudes of WASC, Sperling and his associates moved to Phoenix where a different regional accrediting agency operates. Rather than connect with an existing nonprofit university, the decision was made to found a free-standing, for-profit university. Established in 1976, UOP received North Central Association accreditation in 1978, and the rest is history; accreditation by one agency carries over into states governed by other accrediting bodies. With that hurdle met, securing state licensure is the principal regulatory barrier to entry, with requirements varying by state. As noted earlier, as of 2004, UOP had been licensed to operate in 35 states.

UOP EDUCATIONAL MODEL

At the undergraduate level, a high school diploma or GED certificate is required for admission to UOP. Neither the high school GPA nor GPA at previously attended universities is considered, nor are SAT or ACT scores required for adult students, since these kinds of normed assessments have limited predictive validity for adults. The original emphasis at UOP was to enroll undergraduate students who had 60 or more transfer credits, so that the programs could concentrate on upper-division courses in the professional field of study. To that end, UOP has extremely liberal policies governing transfer credits, accepting all courses from accredited institutions, as well as providing the opportunity to earn credit through its Prior Learning Assessment Program. Under the latter program, students can present a portfolio of experiences that can earn college level credit, including such standardized testing found in CLEP. Up to 60 credits can be awarded through the Prior Learning Assessments Program, with a maximum of 30 credits each for professional training, experiential learning, or standardized testing. In short, every effort is made to accelerate the student toward the degree by awarding credit to virtually any form of prior educational experience.[7] It is safe to say that UOP places little emphasis on the general education portion of an undergraduate program, as general education is simply not the focus of the educational program.[8] Indeed, creation of a College of General Studies, complete with its own dean, was finally required as more and more students entered with fewer than 60 transfer credits. This is not an area in which one would expect significant educational investment to occur beyond the minimum required to qualify students for degrees.

Although admission is not selective at the undergraduate level, students must undergo a variety of assessments once enrolled. These provide adult students with useful information about their educational skills at entry, and it provides UOP with information about the efficacy of its programs and changes that might be necessary at exit. Students participate in an Adult Learning Outcomes Assessment that involves pre- and posttests in four areas: Cognitive Assessment, Professional and Educational Values Assessment, Critical Thinking, and Communication Skills. This process not only allows UOP to carry out extensive outcomes assessment, but also helps students identify areas needing improvement. In addition, all incoming undergraduate students demonstrate proficiency in writing, math, and critical thinking through a UOP-developed, web-based Proficiency Assessment System. Extensive support services exist to help students improve these skills, including an Online Writing Center and Saturday Math/Statistics labs at some of the campuses. A clear strength of the UOP educational model is this heavy emphasis on assessment, often not found in traditional colleges and universities.

The University of Phoenix also uses the ETS major field exams, such as the Major Field Test in Business, to compare their graduates' performance with those of a national comparison group. Data on this ETS test for a group of 205 undergraduate business majors at UOP compared favorably with a national comparison sample of more than 41,000 students. Sperling's motto of "Measure everything" is clearly evident in the UOP educational model.

As noted earlier, over 18,000 part-time practitioner faculty make up the teaching corps, supplemented by about 1,400 full-time faculty, who have more complex assignments. The selection of practitioner faculty is carefully done, with a review of credentials and an extensive orientation and training program. Preservice faculty are assigned an experienced faculty mentor and must take 10 workshops covering the following topics: Adult Learning Theory; Facilitation Techniques; Learning Team Management; Grading, Evaluation, and Feedback; Classroom Assessment; Human Equity; Copyrights and Copy "wrongs"; Administration, Organization, and Orientation; Internet Training; and Electronic Library. Only about 30 to 40 percent of all eligible applicants are approved to teach at UOP.

While no fixed faculty load is required, the typical part-time faculty member teaches 6 courses per year, while the full-time faculty average 9 courses per year. Remember that an undergraduate course lasts only 5 weeks and requires only 5 nights per faculty member per course, for a total of 20 classroom hours. For this effort, the pay is in the range of $1,000 to $1,600 per course. Graduate courses meet for 6 weeks, or 24 faculty contact hours, and have proportionately larger salaries. Interviews with over 20 long-time UOP practitioner faculty confirmed that few "do it for the money" but rather for the professional contact, the stimulation of teaching adult students in the faculty member's professional field, and for the prestige of being a faculty member. Whereas adjunct faculty in traditional universities are often made to feel like second-class citizens relative to the tenured faculty, UOP has no tenured faculty, and relatively few full-time faculty, so the practitioners are the faculty, and they reflect that pride.

The full-time faculty teach an average of 9 courses per year, which is viewed as a half-time load, and spend the other 50 percent of their time serving as Campus College Chairs (CCC). Essentially, each academic program at each major campus has a CCC, who helps to recruit part-time faculty, to guide curricular reviews, and to generally administer the department, much as a department chair does in a traditional university (the full governance structure is discussed later).

The academic calendar is a significant departure from that followed in traditional institutions, in that courses begin virtually every week of the year, and run for only 5 or 6 weeks, depending on degree level. Thus, a student can enter UOP in November, for example, and find courses to take at that time, rather than being forced to wait until January or September, as would be common in the nonprofit sector. Students are advised not to take more than 8 courses per year, but many are able to do that. Furthermore, when a student begins at UOP, they will meet with an adviser and plan the entire sequence of courses from beginning to end so that the student can plan well in advance to move through the program quickly and efficiently. These features are all part of the UOP philosophy of customer-centered convenience, with education provided to meet the student's needs and schedule, not that of the faculty.

One of the more controversial aspects of the educational model among traditional academics is the central production of common course syllabi, rather than the distinct creation of each course by each faculty member, as is common in the traditional sector. Designing one's own course and syllabus is a central feature of faculty autonomy in the traditional college or university, and to have the course handed to a faculty member already designed and developed, is simply contrary to traditional faculty culture. Derisive references to "McEducation" are often heard from faculty who learn about this feature of the UOP model. What it means for UOP is that the general outline and objectives of each course offered on one campus are roughly identical to those of the same course offered on any other campus, and various scale economies can be derived from this standardization. For example, publishers are more than willing to produce printed texts for a UOP course, for they know that demand for the text will be substantial throughout the UOP network. Over time, the more experienced faculty at UOP have an opportunity to customize the courses they teach to some degree, provided the educational objectives are all met. Indeed, one instructor's proposed changes may be considered for adoption into the common syllabus, thus becoming part of each instructor's program. Part of the reason why UOP can pay relatively low salaries to practitioner faculty is that the time-consuming task of course design is not part of each professor's burden. The common course design also means that a student who moves during the program to another state can continue the program with minimal disruption, as the courses are essentially identical in each location.

Mention was made earlier about Learning Teams, an essential feature of the UOP model. In every course, students are broken down into groups of 3 to 5 students who meet together without a faculty member for 4 hours each week during the course. In that setting, they work on projects or topics that are assigned as part of the syllabus, and often report on the results of their team work in the next full class session. In a 5-week course, therefore, there are 20 faculty contact hours, but 40 hours in which students are engaged in an organized learning activity. This feature of the UOP program is key to understanding the economics of the UOP model, and is discussed more fully subsequently.

Another key feature of the UOP model is the absence of bricks and mortar libraries, replaced with a totally online system. Each of its instructional sites has a Learning Resource Center with workstations and work areas that support use of the Digital Library. The digital collections are designed to support the curriculum, with access to multiple databases, including newspaper and journal collections. Reference librarians are available in person and online, and help the students locate needed materials. In several locations, UOP has negotiated agreements with full-service libraries, often in traditional universities, for UOP student use, supplementing the materials available online. The Digital Library is clearly designed for instructional support rather than research support, and can thus be limited to those items needed for the standardized courses. Economies of scale clearly generate efficiencies in this expensive area of educational support and service.[9]

As stated earlier, UOP normally leases their space, which is often designed and built to their specifications. The buildings appear to be traditional office buildings on the outside, and are usually located just off major freeways, with plenty of parking. Classrooms are traditional, and most facilities have computer labs, where various forms of instruction take place. Administrative and admissions offices are on-site, as is a limited bookstore, but the broad array of student services found on a typical campus (dining halls, large bookstores, gyms and other recreational venues, athletic fields, and dormitories) are not present, nor needed. Furthermore, with classes at night, the classrooms are generally empty during the day, with only administrative functions in operation. In short, the physical plant is designed to service the limited needs of part-time, adult students, comfortably but with no frills.

UOP ECONOMIC/BUSINESS MODEL

How is the University of Phoenix able to generate such large profits from an activity that in the nonprofit sectors of public and private higher education requires substantial subsidy? Tuition differences are not the answer, as tuition charges in most private, nonprofit institutions are as high as or higher than they are at UOP. Indeed, an undergraduate student at UOP would expect to pay about $8,000 for one year's course of study, a figure well below the tuition of many private colleges. As UOP is not eligible for charitable gifts, it does not have that revenue source, nor does it have an endowment or receive research grants. In short, it survives on tuition alone, and as its charges do not exceed those of many nonprofit institutions that require additional subsidies, the answer must be found on the cost side.

Before looking at specific issues, the overarching point is that a comparison of UOP and traditional institutions is really a case of apples and oranges. Traditional four-year colleges and universities cater to full-time residential students, in single physical sites, and with a vast array of related activities that UOP does not undertake. Universities are multiproduct firms that conduct research, graduate and professional education, undergraduate education, and public service. Their multipurpose nature entails extensive physical plant investments in dormitories, student unions, libraries, laboratories, and athletic facilities. Universities are not unlike small cities, and carry the cost consequences of that form of activity and organization. UOP is singularly focused on part-time adult students, and thus does not have to invest in most of this high-cost infrastructure. UOP also benefits from economies of scope and scale, as it spreads the cost of curriculum development and organization over hundreds of sites. Sperling and Robert Tucker make these observations in their 1997 book, *For-Profit Higher Education*, where they elucidate their model of an adult-centered professional university.[10]

In the remainder of this section, we will look briefly at the components of their business model, highlighting the factors that appear to be key to their success.[11]

Faculty Labor Supply. As noted earlier, the vast majority of the faculty are practitioners who are fully employed elsewhere than at UOP. They teach part-time in the evenings for UOP for a variety of reasons, many of them nonmonetary. The pay for a 5 or 6 week course is in the range of $1,000 to $1,600, not a bad hourly rate but hardly enough to motivate many of those involved purely for the pay. The nonmonetary benefits include faculty status linked to the professional field in which the practitioner works, contact with midcareer adults eager to learn more about the profession being studied, and an ability to keep abreast of developments in the professional field of study. As noted earlier, unlike adjunct faculty at traditional campuses, UOP faculty do not feel like second-class citizens—they essentially are the faculty of the university. In interviews, what came through was the sense of pride and ownership expressed by many faculty. The upshot is that UOP employs a faculty for a fraction of the cost borne by colleges and universities who hire mostly full-time personnel.[12]

A key factor often overlooked is the short time commitment required for each course taught. Essentially, a faculty member gives up 5 or 6 evenings per course, or between 20 and 24 hours of classroom contact. While there are some additional time requirements, the syllabi supplied by the university cuts down on one of the major activities that traditional faculty must undertake. It should also be noted that, unlike traditional institutions, faculty at UOP generate 3 or 4 credit hours per course with half the contact-hour input, that is, 20 to 24 hours rather than the 40 to 42 that is the normal requirement widely followed in higher education. To generate the conventional number of contact hours, UOP faculty would either have to meet 2 evenings per week, or else the classes would have to expand to 10 to 12 weeks. Given the type of faculty who work for UOP, it seems likely that fewer would be interested in teaching if it meant twice the hours of work, even though pay would presumably have to double as well.

The students, however, do meet for the conventional number of hours per credit because they do meet twice a week, once with the faculty member in class and a second time in learning teams of 3 to 5 students. The faculty member is not present when the learning teams meet. The learning teams engage in projects related to their course assignments, working as teams rather than on their own. UOP touts this method as developing the teamwork skills required by most modern jobs, and criticizes the traditional universities for emphasizing solo work and competitive intellectual development. Without taking a position on the pedagogical aspects of this model, it should simply be noted that the 5-week, 20-hour requirement for faculty is absolutely key to the successful economic functioning of the University. Without this approach, faculty labor supply would be sharply diminished, and/or labor costs would rise appreciably. The basic economics are simple and obvious. If the typical class enrolls 20 students at $800 tuition each, revenue equals $16,000. If the faculty member is paid $1,600 to $2,000, that leaves at least $14,000 to cover all other costs plus profit. So long as demand remains strong, UOP is a veritable money machine.

The University has encountered problems with regulations in some states that require the traditional number of faculty contact hours, and the University's response has been to argue that it is a mistake to rely upon input measures rather than output measures to evaluate educational quality. The heavy emphasis placed on evaluation is, no doubt, partly caused by the need to back up this argument, which is critically important to the University not only educationally, but also economically.

Student Time. A second key to the University's success has been a focus on making the best possible use of student time. Convenience and service are the hallmarks, and the student is viewed as a customer, not as a client or a supplicant.[13] Even the location of the classrooms in buildings adjacent to freeway off-ramps, with ample parking, is planned to maximize student ease of physical access. The fact that students can start courses during virtually any week of the year also minimizes lost time compared to the fall/spring pattern of traditional institutions.

Prior to beginning coursework at the University, a student meets with an enrollment counselor who evaluates past course work and lays out a plan of courses leading to degree completion. Thus, the student's course of study is fully mapped out before he or she begins.[14] The student can plan with certainty that courses will be offered on the schedule provided, a feature not always found in traditional universities. The entering student goes through an initial orientation session, learning how to use the electronic library and how to access various services such as writing and math/statistics laboratories. He or she also undergoes a variety of educational assessments for diagnostic and evaluation purposes, and learns how to order textbooks electronically, which are delivered directly to the home. Within a matter of days, the new student can be enrolled and working toward a degree.

Transfer credit falls into two categories: credits from a regionally accredited institution and those that are awarded through the university's Prior Learning Assessment program. The latter program assesses and awards credits based on participation in professional training, on standardized testing such as CLEP, and on life experience (experiential learning). To gain credit for experiential learning, students must enroll in a course that helps them prepare a portfolio for assessment and evaluation. A maximum of 30 credits can be earned for each of the following: professional training (e.g., courses given by the American Institute of Banking), experiential learning, or standardized testing. No student can be awarded a total of more than 60 credits through all types of Prior Learning Assessment, an extraordinarily generous allotment.

For those familiar with credit transfer in traditional institutions, UOP appears to be very liberal and nondemanding. One could say this policy is further evidence of the "student as customer" focus, as it clearly helps students to receive maximum feasible credit for prior work. It is further evidence of the limited interest UOP takes in the first 60 credits of general education, as the real focus of their program is in the upper division third and fourth years, which concentrate on the major field of study. The North Central Association criticized UOP in its 1992 evaluation for not having a rigorous general education component, and the University responded by creating a Dean for General Education and investing more in this area. It remains, however, a relatively weak part of the program.[15]

Course Syllabi. In my experience, many academics know (or think they know) two things about UOP. First, a surprising number of people believe that UOP is a virtual university, offering courses solely online. This perception, of course, is in error. The other thing they believe is that course syllabi are centrally produced and effectively franchised—the "McEducation" criticism. On the second of these two points, the perception is not wrong, albeit somewhat exaggerated. Course syllabi are produced collectively, with input from individual instructors, as well as from the full-time faculty in each area. (There exists a faculty hierarchical structure, which, in descending order, includes the Campus College Chair [CCC], Assistant Department Chairs [ADC], the Faculty Curriculum Coordinator [FCC], and practitioner faculty. Only the CCC is a full-time faculty member.) Once adopted, experienced faculty members are free to deviate and customize a course to some degree, providing they can demonstrate that the students are covering the material prescribed for the course.

These common syllabi mean that a new instructor is provided with the course plan in advance, together with faculty guides and related materials. This policy also means that a given course taught in one location will be virtually identical in content to the same numbered course in another location. Students who move before completing a degree, therefore, can shift from one campus to another with little academic disruption. It also means that UOP reaps significant economies of scale, which gives the University enormous buying power with book publishers. Given the size of the market, publishers are more than willing to produce customized texts for each course, made available only to UOP and its students. While most full-time faculty in traditional institutions take great pride in creating their own unique courses and syllabi, there is clearly something to be said for this type of collective course design and implementation.

Online Courses. Begun in 1989, Phoenix Online is the fastest-growing segment of UOP, and is treated as a distinct unit for financial analysis. (The online part of the University has its own "tracking" stock listed on the NASDAQ exchange.) In May 2004, nearly 109,800 students were enrolled in a Phoenix Online course. Many UOP students take some courses online and some in actual classes. The online course work is essentially the same as in the classes, and it is distributed in a relatively low-tech fashion, relying on E-mail and web-sites. Courses are typically smaller, around nine students, for the demands on faculty for E-mail contact are sufficiently time-consuming that fewer students can be taught via distance learning than in the group fashion of the classroom. Faculty members produce a weekly lecture, distributed as a text-formatted Word document rather than as a videotape. Parts of the course are asynchronous, but other parts are real-time discussions, enabled by group-collaboration software.

Many organizations have attempted to enter the distance-learning world, and few have thus far succeeded.[16] In some cases, companies have spent far too much on production values, rendering their offerings too expensive to return a profit. In other cases, universities and related spin-off ventures have overestimated the demand for such instruction. Another reason is the failure to invest as heavily as UOP has in the student service infrastructure for online students instead of trying to serve them with the same processes and staff as the ground-based students. The University of Phoenix would seem to be one of the few success stories in this area, generating and meeting substantial demand, keeping the technology simple and cost-effective, and turning a profit on the effort.

Facilities. Physical facilities are a major expense for traditional colleges and universities, but UOP has developed a cost-effective way to avoid large outlays. The needs of the University are far less than for traditional, residential colleges; UOP requires no dormitories, no athletic fields, and even no science laboratories, as they do not teach lab science courses. What they need are classrooms capable of holding 20–25 students, administrative space for staff and other full-time personnel, computer facilities, space for a Learning Resource Center (electronic library), and limited office space for faculty. These requirements are easily met by a normal office building near a well-traveled freeway, with easy access and plenty of parking spaces for staff and students. UOP leases their facilities from owners willing to construct new buildings, or to modify existing ones, to their specifications. Leasing obviously ties up much less money than owning buildings, and provides UOP with the ability to develop space for new campus sites quickly.[17]

Student Finance. With a student body composed of working adults with family incomes averaging between $50,000 and $60,000, student finance is not the severe problem for UOP that it can be for colleges and universities serving a younger population made of up full-time, low-income students. Nearly 60 percent of enrolled students at UOP receive some tuition assistance from employers, a much higher rate of such support than would be found in traditional institutions. Because UOP is an accredited institution, students are eligible for federal and state student aid programs if they meet the academic workload and income test standards set by the various programs. And, of course, many of the working students can afford to pay the $800 to $900 per course tuition from their own resources.

SUMMARY

UOP has been financially successful because it focuses on a narrow range of career-oriented programs that can be provided at low cost through the use of part-time practitioner faculty following a standardized curriculum that yields substantial economies of scale. UOP avoids many of the costs that traditional colleges and universities incur for residential programs and research activities, and they concentrate on a relatively high-income population that does not require substantial student aid. Students are treated as customers, and all UOP programs are focused on maximum student convenience and rapid degree completion. Their programs are sufficiently well regarded by employers that many of them pay the tuition for their students-employees. UOP online courses appear to be among the most successful in operation, in part because of relative simplicity, low costs, and integration with the array of regular classes. As the university expands each year into one or two new states, they are effectively saturating the adult, part-time market in the for-profit sector, and are discouraging other for-profits from attempting to compete with them on a broad scale. UOP has a very sound business plan, for which the market is compensating stockholders handsomely.

GOVERNANCE

In traditional colleges and universities, one speaks of governance and of administration, but less often of management. Sperling and Tucker argue that

> The University of Phoenix is unique in that it is both managed and governed. The University is a for-profit service corporation in which the Board of Directors sets policies and business strategies, and management carries out the policies and strategies. The faculty and its nominated academic governing body, together with the students and staff, oversee the quality of the educational services being delivered, and the teaching faculty and students create the dynamics of the teaching/learning process.[18]

Indeed, UOP has created parallel lines of authority, with academic issues brought up through faculty, Campus College Chairs, Deans, and ultimately to the Provost, while the financial dimensions are brought up through a parallel organization on the business side. The result is that there is a place for the advocacy of academic issues that is not automatically trumped by financial considerations. For example, the type of conflict that can arise may occur when an accrediting body for a professional field, such as Counseling, requires more course work than state licensure requirements. The academic side of the University will press for the accrediting standard, while the business side will argue for the more streamlined approach. Regardless of which side prevails, the structure supports this debate, which from an academic point of view, is to the

University's credit. The University appears to have taken an enlightened view of its long-run interest in not deciding all academic decisions on a purely short-run financial basis.

Whereas a traditional college or university has an enormous investment in the quality of its faculty, and provides numerous procedural safeguards, including tenure, to ensure academic freedom for teaching and scholarly work, the situation at UOP is different. Critics often argue that traditional institutions are more faculty-centered than student-centered, and while this may be an exaggeration, there is more than a grain of truth in that observation. There are reasons to be faculty-centered in that the reputation and scholarly productivity of faculty largely determine the prestige and status of the institution, which enhances the ability to attract high-quality students, research grants and contracts, and gifts from grateful alumni. With UOP, however, these considerations are distinctly secondary to the all-consuming focus on student satisfaction. If a practitioner faculty member receives consistently poor evaluations, that person is dropped. Even the full-time faculty spend half of their time administering programs, and thus are as much administrative as academic in their focus. UOP faculty, in short, are employees, do not have tenure, and can be let go, subject to laws that prevent wrongful dismissal. Under these circumstances, many of the governance issues that absorb time and energy in traditional institutions simply are not present. The models are simply different.

In a recent meeting with the provost and deans of the several schools at the University of Phoenix, we discussed how these academic leaders spend their time. Ironically, it became clear that the deans at UOP were free of the effort to raise money that increasingly dominates the lives of deans in non-profit colleges and universities. Each dean within the UOP system receives an annual expenditure budget, and there is no expectation that they will engage in any explicit effort to enhance that internal stream of dollars, through grant-procurement or private fund-raising. As a result, these individuals are expected to focus their efforts exclusively on the academic programs under their jurisdiction. I was impressed by the time and energy spent on matters academic and pedagogical. By contrast, as a dean in a public university, a substantial portion of my time is necessarily devoted to fund-raising and grant procurement. The ironies abound!

WEAKNESS OR QUESTIONS REGARDING THE UOP EDUCATIONAL MODEL

A central purpose of this study has been to determine what might be learned from successful for-profit, degree-granting institutions such as UOP, and to derive implications, if any, for the traditional sectors of higher education.

Before turning to that task, let me first identify those areas of UOP operation which, in my judgment, represent actual or potential educational weaknesses. Much of this chapter has emphasized the strong and successful features of the university, but those observations need to be balanced by a brief summary of areas that seem less positive, or at least open to question.

First, it seems apparent to this observer that UOP has relatively little interest in the general education aspect of their undergraduate programs,[19] focusing instead on the professional training that occupies the last two years. This criticism extends to the transfer criteria they apply, and the willingness to bend over backward to give credit for virtually any activity that can be construed as related to college work. This policy clearly reflects the fact that UOP does not convey a strong sense of broad educational purpose; its programs are intensely focused on training and immediate relevance to the workplace. While some may see this trait as a strength, it can also be seen as a weakness.

Second, the fact that UOP awards credits for half of the faculty input raises a question about educational production. I have some sympathy with the UOP view that education should not be measured exclusively by inputs, and they do a good job of testing and evaluating students along the way, that is, outcome assessment. Nonetheless, much hinges on the quality of the time that students spend in the learning teams, and a cynic might suggest that students have been known to shirk efforts that are not monitored. Furthermore, students in traditional universities often gather into informal study groups and undertake many of the same activities that presumably happen at UOP, and this on top of 40+ contact hours with a faculty member.[20] I am not in a position to render a conclusive judgment on this unique feature of the UOP learning model, but it remains a question unresolved to my satisfaction.

Third, the near total reliance on a part-time, practitioner faculty would be viewed in a traditional college or university setting as an absolute scandal, and the institution would be scorned by its peer institutions (assuming any would acknowledge it as a peer). Given the focus that UOP has adopted on providing professional skills to a part-time, employed adult population, this potential criticism seems to be less pertinent. Most programs of continuing education offered by traditional colleges and universities also rely on part-time faculty, although in many cases these are regular faculty teaching on overload. I suspect that were UOP to enter the market of full-time undergraduate education using the same educational model, the faculty issue would take on much greater salience, and be far more controversial.

UOP has had difficulties with some state regulatory bodies because of the lack of a bricks and mortar library. In some instances, they have had to enter into contracts with local universities to provide student access to a regular library collection. The narrow focus of the Phoenix programs may be the best response to this question, for students are rarely expected to engage in broad research beyond the bounds of the literature available electronically in the Learning Resource Centers. UOP is not about general education, and does not award degrees in liberal arts and science disciplines, where broad library resources are a prerequisite. Given their focus, I am not inclined to be critical of the approach they have taken to this educational resource.

Finally, it is worth noting that UOP could not exist were it not for the scholarly and publishing works of faculty in traditional institutions. Essentially, UOP rides on the availability of scholarly knowledge generated elsewhere, and packages that knowledge effectively for adult students. One might argue that a global economic analysis of UOP would have to credit traditional academia with generating an enormous externality for the benefit of UOP and its students, in that the educational materials used are derived from the scholarly works of faculty in nonprofit institutions. What this means is that an entire educational system populated only with UOP-type institutions would be intellectually barren and would not produce new knowledge. UOP thus depends critically upon the existence of the traditional sector for most of its intellectual input and for its ultimate success.[21]

IMPLICATIONS FOR TRADITIONAL HIGHER EDUCATION

A first lesson is the obvious success of UOP's emphasis on service and convenience for adult students. While many traditional institutions serve this constituency, often through divisions or schools of continuing education, few have gone so far as UOP to make the experience effective and efficient for the student. By starting a new type of University, the founders were able to dispense with many of the traditions and bureaucratic ways of doing things that slow or inhibit adaptation to new clientele on the part of older institutions. The availability of evening courses at convenient locations with good parking, the flexible calendar with courses starting every week, the five- and six-week course schedule, and superb support services have all contributed to the runaway success of UOP. All colleges and universities can learn from this student-centered approach.

The radically altered faculty role is potentially the biggest challenge presented by the UOP model, but it is far from clear that the way in which UOP manages faculty has meaningful implications for the rest of the enterprise. Faculty at UOP are part-time employees, and they are paid exclusively for teaching and for providing related student services. Scholarly work is not part of the job, and the institution of tenure is inconceivable. This approach would be more threatening to faculty in traditional colleges and universities if the UOP employed a large, full-time faculty, but since they rely primarily on part-time practitioners, the connections—and implications—are far from obvious.

While UOP competes on the margin with certain types of schools, our research suggests that they are largely extending higher education opportunities to a group of students who would otherwise not enroll in traditional programs. There are clear exceptions to this generalization for those traditional programs that focus on the part-time adult population, but this is not a core business to many colleges and universities. Indeed, Sperling was motivated to start UOP because he found that few universities took the part-time adult population very seriously. Where UOP does compete with traditional institutions, competition will generally be beneficial to students, and there is no reason to decry that outcome. On balance, the education of working adults has been strengthened and improved by the existence of UOP, and the nation is the better for it.

A Cautionary Note

A report released in September 2004 raises disturbing questions about the admissions practices of the University of Phoenix.[22] The U.S. Department of Education's forty-five page report described a corporate culture that puts enormous pressure on enrollment counselors at the University to meet or exceed admissions and recruitment targets. The report also describes compensation formulas for the counselors that explicitly tie salaries to numbers of students enrolled, in violation of the rules governing eligibility for Title IV federal student financial aid. Without admitting guilt, the University and the Department of Education settled the complaint for $9.8 million, the largest fine ever levied by the Department. Specifically, the Department of Education said that the University was in violation for the following reasons:

> (1) Hires its recruiters with the promise of lucrative compensation for success in securing enrollments, (2) Maintains a recruiter evaluation and salary system that provides incentive payments based both directly and indirectly on success in securing enrollments, (3) Provides substantial incentives to its staff to recruit unqualified students and students who cannot benefit from the training offered, and (4) Systematically and intentionally operates in a duplicitous manner so as to violate the department's prohibition against incentive compensation while evading detection.

Suffice it to say that such practices, assuming they occurred as described, are one of the key reasons why economists and others have doubted the wisdom of providing education through the mechanism of for-profit production. The temptation to exploit the differences in information available to potential students and to the supplier, and the nature of the service provided, suggests that for-profit production and sale of educational services is replete with opportunities for less-than-ethical behavior, particularly when a third party (the federal government) is paying for much of the service. The countervailing argument is that an institution such as the University of Phoenix has a huge stake in building and sustaining its reputation for quality, and that short-run profit maximization of the sort described in the report runs contrary to long-run profit maximization linked to reputation.

During my visit in December 2004, I had hoped to learn more about this incident, which the University disputes, but did not gain any clear evidence one way or the other. The episode was clearly embarrassing to those on the academic side of the enterprise, and they did not want to discuss it in detail. If there is any truth to the report, and any explanation for such behavior, it may be found in the growth expectations imposed on the company by Wall Street analysts, who continue to promote the stock based on extraordinary expectations of annual growth. Indeed, Apollo Group Chief Executive Todd Nelson, is devoting considerable time to meeting with industry analysts, attempting to explain that UOP is a mature enterprise, and that exceptional growth expectations need to be tempered.[23]

Whatever the truth behind this particular episode, it does suggest that constant vigilance on the part of those who accredit the University is necessary, not only for the protection of students and their employers, but also for the protection of UOP employees and shareholders, all of whom stand to lose if the University's reputation is sullied.

NOTES

Information in this and in subsequent sections are provided by UOP, including the author's participation in a site visit in August 2000 conducted by the Regents of the University of the State of New York, in connection with UOP's application to offer courses in that state. The author revisited the University's head office in December 2004, meeting with the provost and academic deans.

1. The University of Phoenix (including University of Phoenix Online), is part of the Apollo Group, Inc., which also includes the Institute for Professional Development, the College for Financial Planning, and Western International University.

2. While the University had recently lowered its age requirement from 23 to 21, in June 2004 it further announced a decision to admit students as young as 18. This announcement followed Apollo Group's creation of a new college aimed specifically at 18-to 23-year-old students, to be named Axia College. Opened in 2004, Axia operates from two campuses located in Phoenix, and appears to be an experimental effort to

determine the viability of serving this market. It is too early to pass judgment on this venture; the academic leaders at UOP with whom I met in December 2004, did not have much to say about it.

3. Leaders of the University of Phoenix commented on this chapter, and their remarks are included in this section to provide the reader with differing perspectives on matters of judgment. The first such UOP comment follows:

> We would merely respond that this is appropriate to an institution that serves the working adult population—especially so based on recent research by Carol Aslanian describing the educational needs and desires of this population. Between 40 and 45% of college and university students are now 25 and older; of those, 80% work full-time and 80%, presumably the same group, indicate that their primary reasons for returning for advanced education relates to career development.

4. See, for example, John Sperling, *Against all Odds* (Phoenix: Apollo Press, 1989); and *Rebel with a cause: The entrepreneur who created the University of Phoenix and the for-profit revolution in higher education* (New York: Wiley, 2000).

5. In November 2004, Apollo Group experienced an abrupt reversal of the previous 4¹/₂ years of growth (in which the price rose from $9 to $98), after the scandal (see chapter conclusion for details) which resulted in a 36% drop in price to 62.55. (See W. C. Symonds [2005, January 31]. Back to earth for Apollo Group? Higher marketing costs could slow growth for the University of Phoenix parent. *Business Week*, 50. Retrieved online from the Infotrac database). By year end 2004, stock prices were up to $80.71.

6. See Sperling, *Against all Odds.*

7. University of Phoenix Comment: "In doing so, the University adheres strictly to recommendations of ACE and CAEL (the Council for Adult and Experiential Learning) in awarding academic credit for prior experience."

8. University of Phoenix Comment:

> While we don't disagree with this statement, we don't think you place it in a proper context. We believe that we have created a general education program appropriate to an institution whose mission is to serve working adults who are enrolled in professional/managerial programs. These are not the 18–22 year-olds for whom most liberal education programs were designed. College is not a rite-of-passage. That doesn't mean that general education isn't important to us or our students but it clearly is an instrumental goal and, arguably, must be conceived of differently for a different kind of student.

9. The absence of a traditional library has been an issue in several states as UOP seeks licensure, but negotiated agreements with existing libraries have generally been accepted as meeting that requirement.

10. Sperling and Robert W. Tucker, *For-profit higher education: Developing a world-class workforce* (New Brunswick, NJ: Transaction Publishers, 1997), pp. 35–50.

11. In this section, the author draws in part on information gained while serving as a member of a New York Regents review team considering the application of UOP to begin offering courses in New York. The team spent three days in Phoenix and Tucson reviewing all aspects of the UOP operation, August 6–9, 2000. The author also made two additional visits, most recently in December 2004.

12. University of Phoenix Comment:

We know based on our earlier discussions that you believe this last sentence relating to the economics is the primary and overarching reason for the faculty model. While it certainly is one of the enabling "benefits" of the model— the truth is that the academic reason is, to us, the primary reason. We believe that the population we serve is better served by a practitioner faculty. It may be difficult for someone whose frame of reference is traditional higher ed to imagine that, given a choice, an institution might choose for any other than economic reasons not to employ a traditional faculty, but it's true.

13. University of Phoenix Comment: "This is an interesting point. Is it possible that there is a sense in which students can be both students (in one traditional sense of the word) and customers, when it comes to support services, program design, and model?"

14. The role of the enrollment counselor and the recent controversy surrounding that function will be discussed at the end of the chapter.

15. University of Phoenix Comment: "Using traditional standards and conventions one could make this argument—but, again, this area is the subject of constant evolution and development, and is appropriate to the population served."

16. Columbia University, for example, has discontinued its highly touted venture, Fathom, an online multi-institution, multimedia effort to enter this arena.

17. Sperling and Tucker, *For-profit higher education*, p. 42, indicate that UOP can be up and running at a new location within six months.

18. Ibid., p. 98.

19. University of Phoenix Comment:

We disagree with this characterization. A very small percentage of students actually use prior learning credits and of those who do, the average number of credits applied is 15. Further, there are specific requirements for the different areas of general education. Thus, some credits accepted may not fall into any needed general education area and even though they are transcripted and, therefore, students end up taking the requisite coursework after all. Your conclusions appear to be based on an implicit assumption that adult educators have contested for years and that led to the development of the prior learning assessment [PLA] system. That assumption is that the correct and acceptable place for education and learning is the classroom. In truth, of course, most of what we learn in life we learn outside of structured learning environments. [The] PLA . . . process is designed to recognize that college-level learning takes place elsewhere and it creates a system to evaluate that learning. Finally, our higher education system continues to operate under the fiction that students should go through a "coherent" program of study. In reality most students these days, even a good many of the traditional, full-time residential students (who now comprise only 16% of the student population) will transfer from institution to institution or bring in credits from a variety of places. Besides, the smorgasbord that now makes up general education in most institutions can scarcely be described as coherent.

20. University of Phoenix Comment:

Again, we're dealing with adults here, who bring an average 14 years of work (and adult life) experience to the classroom. There is much horizontal learning taking place and, in some real senses, these students are experts. More importantly, however, you seem to overlook the following points: (1) that the 40+ hours "scheduled" with a faculty member often does not represent contact with a faculty member at all (because students are most often not required to attend); (2) that the time spent in those 40+ hours do not all represent time on task; or (3) that the quality of contact is contextual—i.e., you can't argue that faculty contact in the large lecture sections that make for a great deal of the general education in most institutions (talk about an economic model—most agree that the lecture model to large numbers is the worst way to teach and yet it's the only way our system can balance the books) represents the same quality of contact, albeit fewer hours, in a 10-15 student classroom. Finally, we think you gloss over the outcomes argument. Why should students spend more time if the learning is equivalent?

21. University of Phoenix Comment: "This suggests that there is no scholarship taking place among our faculty, a conclusion that research proves squarely not to be the case. But suppose it were true: we make no suggestion that UOP is 'the' model for the future of higher education—just that it is 'a' model, and an appropriate one at that, for an institution with a specialized mission."

22. United States Department of Education. (2004). *University of Phoenix, OPEID 020988 00: Site Visit of 8/18/2003–8/22/2003* (Program Review Report PRCN 200340922254). San Francisco: Case Management & Oversight, Case Management Team, Southwest-San Francisco Team.

23. Symonds. Back to earth for Apollo group?

Chapter 5

Profit Centers in Service
to the Academic Core

Dudley Doane and Brian Pusser

INTRODUCTION

Since the late 1990s, the role of entrepreneurial revenue generation in the financing of public and private higher education in the United States has received significant attention (Pusser, 2002; Heller, 2001; McKeowan-Moak, 2000; Goldstein, 1999; Kane, 1999; McPherson and Schapiro, 1998). Interest in the topic can be traced to a variety of sources, including the following: declining state subsidies (Winston, Carbone, and Lewis, 1998); rising costs (Ehrenberg, 2000); changing demographics (Carnevale and Fry, 2001; Hudson, 2001); shifting operating environments (Levin, 2001; Adelman, 2000); competition with for-profits (Pusser and Turner, 2004; Marchese, 1998); and assumptions among some policy makers, researchers, and stakeholders that the organization and finance of higher education should be based on a market-production model (Munitz, 2000; Friedman, 1962).

For the purposes of this research, entrepreneurial revenue generation is defined as those institutional activities that produce revenue without significant direct state support. In many cases the revenue generated may significantly exceed costs (as in university development), although more generally these activities either break even or require institutional subsidy. It is worth noting that under this definition a great deal of revenue generation in private institutions, nonprofit and for-profit, can be characterized as entrepreneurial.

Entrepreneurial revenue generation in public institutions is in many ways a distinctly different phenomenon (Pusser, 2002; Slaughter and Leslie, 1997). State financial support of public nonprofit institutions has traditionally been provided for activities close to the academic core, fundamentally directed to undergraduate education and to other activities that have been seen as preferred and legitimate institutional activities (Slaughter and Leslie, 1997). Student tuition has also historically been tied to academic activities close to the core. Although tuition is not a form of direct state support, tuition levels and the uses of tuition revenue have historically required state approval, or at least tacit state political support. While the research presented in this chapter was conducted in public research universities, the issue of entrepreneurial revenue generation from core academic activities has significant implications for both public and private institutions.

NEW ENTREPRENEURIALISM

An enthusiasm for entrepreneurial approaches to academic organization in general, and to revenue generation in particular, has accompanied efforts to address the changing financial dynamic of postsecondary institutions (Ruch, 2001; Ehrenberg, 2000; Peterson, Dill, and Mets, 1997). The case for entrepreneurial reorganization has been most often made in literature on for-profit higher education (c.f. Sperling, 2000; Ruch, 2001) but is by no means limited to work on proprietary institutions. Researchers have also examined entrepreneurial activities and diversification of revenue sources among nonprofit public and private colleges and universities (Winston, 1999, 1997; Hansmann, 1980). S. Oster (1997) studied revenue-generating auxiliary enterprises within institutions that enjoy 501 c (3) status. More recently, many nonprofit universities have extended their reach and generated significant revenue by offering courses, degrees, and training through continuing education and extension programs (Levin, 2001; Pusser and Doane, 2001).

The importance of increasing nontraditional sources of revenue is leading both nonprofit public and private institutions to increase their production of what Burton Weisbrod (1998) labels "nonpreferred goods"—goods produced to generate revenue in support of preferred activities as opposed to the direct production of the preferred goods or activities themselves, those outputs that are directly related to the mission of the institution. Although the diversification of revenue sources has helped a number of public colleges and universities weather reductions in the proportion of their operating budgets covered by state funding, dependence on commercial activities, or the production of nonpreferred goods, to finance traditional or "preferred" activities may yield unintended consequences.

It has been argued that the variety and complexity of entrepreneurial revenue-generating activities can require substantial resources for support and oversight as part of a vast expansion of "academic capitalism" (Slaughter and Leslie, 1997). Units such as endowment offices, real estate foundations, and patent offices, are home to a growing cadre of professionals and numerous support staff (Ehrenberg, 2000). It has been observed that over the previous three decades faculty have ceded considerable influence to professional administrators (Marginson and Considine, 2000; Rhoades, 1998; Slaughter and Leslie, 1997). The growth in the production of nonpreferred goods by universities has also contributed to the increasing tension between legislatures and state public institutions. As universities have become ever more complex, conglomerate organizations, institutional demands for autonomy have increased while legislatures have countered with requests for even greater institutional accountability.

CLOSE TO THE CORE

To date, there has been little empirical investigation of the effect of entrepreneurial revenue generation close to the academic core. That is, there has been little attention paid to contemporary efforts to offer credit-bearing courses that originate in the disciplines and departments, using regular faculty and stand-alone revenue generation. One arena that generally operates under those conditions is the provision of summer sessions at public colleges and universities. Summer sessions at public institutions are not auxiliary operations, for instance, summer camps or special conferences and institutes, nonpreferred goods that might generate revenue for a university during a time when the physical plant and support staff of the institution are underutilized but that do not directly support the mission of the institution.

The courses and programs offered through summer sessions provide public institutions a means both to extend academic-year offerings and to enrich those offerings while utilizing their physical plant and facilities. Institutional mission is supported; preferred goods are produced. Decisions about course offerings and staffing are generally made by, or at least approved by, academic departments. Resident (nonvisiting) faculty and teaching staff commonly provide instruction to resident students. Faculty earn additional income, generally in the form of overload pay, and graduate teaching assistants can supplement their academic year stipends and gain classroom experience.

Despite this connection to, and support of, the academic mission of public colleges and universities and the production of preferred goods, summer sessions are generally not only self-supporting but also generate surplus revenue.

The Pressure to Profit

Many, if not most, summer session divisions at the public universities examined in this study are expected to collect tuition and fees that exceed basic operating expenses—in some cases by as much as 100 percent (AUSS, 2003, pp. 50–51), yet the outputs of these divisions tend to be curriculum-centered, and focused on students enrolled in a degree program. Again, the vast majority of summer students at the public universities included in this study enroll in classes at their home institution; they earn credits that they apply toward degree requirements. They are primarily taught by resident teaching staff, that is, faculty and graduate teaching assistants. Among a university's revenue generating units, the summer sessions division thus appear to be located close to the academic core of these universities.

The organization and financing of summer sessions at public institutions provides an interesting example of a self-supporting unit within universities that is entrepreneurial and required to operate on a surplus revenue generation model, yet is nested in core academic operations. In summer sessions, a set of activities that could be described as both "preferred"—tied to an institution's mission and subject to faculty influence—yield a "profit." How substantial fiscal responsibilities impact the mission and governance of summer sessions merits examination, particularly in light of growing pressure on the academic core of colleges and universities to become more economically entrepreneurial.

In order to better understand the tension between conforming to core academic values and surplus revenue generation, we present data on the role of summer sessions in support of one core academic value, internationalization. Internationalization is a process to which most leading U.S. universities have committed themselves—at least, rhetorically, through course work, overseas study options, and integration of international students and scholars. Data on international programming and revenue generation in summer sessions at the twenty-five public research universities that belong to the Association of University Summer Sessions (AUSS), along with case studies on internationalization at four of the institutions are analyzed to better understand how the need to generate surplus revenue influences the support of faculty, students, and a mission-specific activity—internationalization. The dilemma of summer sessions—the need for efficiency and profits on the one hand, and constituent interests and a larger institutional mission to internationalize on the other hand, provide a useful lens for evaluating contemporary demands for entrepreneurial behavior at the academic core.

THE SCOPE OF SUMMER SESSIONS

First introduced around the time of the Civil War, summer sessions have become an important source of academic offerings at many postsecondary institutions. This is particularly true among public colleges and universities. Summer sessions at these institutions frequently enroll substantial numbers of students, focus on resident students, and function as providers of key academic credits. Regular academic-year courses are offered in an intensive format, and,

TABLE 5.1
Enrollments at Individual Public AUSS Member Institutions: Summer 2003

Item	Min.	Max.	M	P25	P50	P75	N
Summer Sessions Enrollment 2003	3,422	18,448	10,487	7,344	10,663	14,044	24
Summer Sessions 2003 Enrollment as a Percentage of Fall 2002 Enrollment	21.1	84.1	38.9	32.8	37.9	43.2	24
Percentage of Summer Session Students Who Were Resident Students	63	95	83	73	86	91	15

Source: Author's tabulations from the *2003 Summary of Reports of the Association of University Summer Sessions.*

in many cases, courses not available during the traditional academic year are often available in the summer.

The scale of many summer session programs is significant. In 2003, the units generated through summer sessions at the University of California at Los Angeles (UCLA) equaled 27.4% of the units produced in the fall semester of 2002 at UCLA (AUSS, 2003, p. 34). Enrollment (nonduplicative) in summer sessions in 2003 at the University of Connecticut equaled 45.3% of the fall 2002 enrollment (p. 26). At the University of North Carolina at Chapel Hill (UNC), the proportion of UNC students in undergraduate and graduate summer courses was 85.5% and 76.1% respectively in 2003 (p. 24). At the University of Virginia (U.Va.), 44% of students who took an undergraduate degree in 2002–3 completed at least one summer session at U.Va. (Doane, 2004, p. 1). The data in Table 3.1 further illustrate that summer sessions at the twenty-four sample institutions, for which enrollment information was available, enroll substantial numbers of students, and primarily serve their own students.

The academic focus that was discussed in the two previous paragraphs, and the production of preferred goods, can be contrasted with the focus of summer offerings at a number of independent institutions, for instance, at some elite independent universities, where the typical summer student is not enrolled in a degree program at the host institution. While summer courses and programs at such a university may have a public service function and even provide an extension of academic resources for students enrolled in a degree program at the institution, the offerings are likely to serve a highly commercial function. Again, it should be noted, however, that a mix of academic and financial purposes generally characterize summer sessions programming. Even those summer sessions that appear to serve a chiefly academic purpose, are commonly expected to generate revenue in excess of direct costs. Summer sessions at the 25 public universities examined here, fulfill a substantial academic function, but at two institutions, in particular, summer courses and programs were found to also have a strong commercial orientation, that is, they generate substantial revenue through the enrollment of visiting students. Yet even here, one can argue that a preferred good was produced as access to the resources of each of the two elite institutions was expanded to students through summer sessions, and the visiting students earned credit that could be applied toward degree requirements.

Organization and Finance

Twenty-two of the 25 public universities that belong to AUSS are land-grant universities. Twenty-two of them are also flagship campuses. Just under one-third of them are considered highly selective with regard to undergraduate admission. Sixteen of the summer sessions administrative units (64%) are organized under academic affairs at their parent institution. The remaining 9 offices belong to a division other than academic affairs, usually as an individual unit within a division of continuing education or extension.

Sixteen of the 22 summer sessions units for which data were available, are financed through an annual budget allocation (AUSS, 2001a, pp. 1–55). Units are typically subject to an expenditure target as well as to a revenue target. Summer sessions are expected to generate revenue in excess of administrative and instructional costs[1] at all but 7 of the sample institutions, and 5 of those 7 institutions require summer sessions revenue to equal administrative and instructional costs (AUSS, 2003, pp. 50–51); thus, 92% of the institutions studied require summer sessions to generate revenue that meets or exceeds administrative and instructional costs. At 10 of the sample institutions, summer sessions revenue is expected to exceed costs by up to 50% while the fiscal obligations of the summer sessions at 3 of the sample institutions require revenue to exceed costs by 100% (pp. 50–51).

Eleven of the 22 units for which information was available, practice revenue sharing with schools or departments (AUSS, 2001a, pp. 1–55). Revenue in excess of costs at sample institutions at which revenue sharing is not the norm, generally goes into an account controlled by central administration, for instance, the office of the provost. In 2003, instate undergraduate tuition rates charged by the sample institutions in summer sessions ranged between $86/credit and $310/credit and averaged $161/credit.[2] Out-of-state undergraduate tuition ranged between $86/credit and $769/credit and averaged $400/credit. At 6 of the sample institutions, undergraduate summer tuition rates were not tied to domicile (pp. 39–43).

Internationalization

Conceptions of *internationalization* vary, but generally involve changes in curriculum; institutional practices; faculty and student culture; and education policy that lead to increased student and faculty mobility across borders, better integration of international students and scholars, broadened research agendas, and a desired level of *global competence* (ACE, 1998) among U.S. college graduates.

There is a vast literature on the internationalization of U.S. higher education.[3] Although much of it was composed during the last two decades, the central theme of the literature evolved through responses of the federal government and other institutions to the launch of *Sputnik* in 1957. In the common narrative, authors proclaim that the world is rapidly changing, that there is consequently a need for more international programs in higher education, and that other nations are doing a better job with international education than is the United States; thus, the United States needs to catch up. The possibility of the United States losing its position as the world's dominant economic, political, and cultural power is often, though not always, an issue. The proclamation is typically followed by a call for greater internationalization. This usually includes an appeal for the establishment of broad national goals for international education and for increased resources for international activities. Much of the literature is more normative than reflexive. Best or promising practices are frequently highlighted. Campus-based documents on international education have been shaped by this narrative.

Rationales

Rationales for internationalization are diverse and complex and can be found in a number of national reports such as *A Nation at Risk* (National Commission on Excellence in Education, 1983); *Integrity in the Curriculum* (Rudolph, 1985); *Internationalization of U.S. Higher Education* (Hayward, 2000); *Beyond September 11* (ACE, 2002a); *Toward an International Education Policy for the United States* (NAFSA, 2000); and *Internationalizing the Campus* (Green and Olson, 2003). Jane Knight (1999) identifies four categories of rationales for the internationalization of higher education: political, economic, academic, and cultural and social (pp. 17–20).

Political rationales may be driven by interests in foreign policy, national defense, technical assistance, peace and mutual understanding, national identity, or regional identity (De Wit, 2002, pp. 85–89). De Wit notes that a " . . . view of international education as a peacemaking force has been dominant in American politics and higher education for the past fifty years, and is still rather widespread. . . ." (p. 88). Economic rationales stem from interests related to economic growth and competitiveness, the labor market, national educational demand, and financial incentives for institutions and governments (pp. 89–92). De Wit divides cultural and social rationales into two categories, cultural, that is, the reproduction of culture, and social or personal development (pp. 92–95). Categories for academic rationales include providing an international dimension to research and teaching, extension of the academic horizon, institution building, profile and status, enhancement of quality, and international academic standards (pp. 95–99).

Recently, there has been a marked shift in the rationales for internationalization of higher education. Economic rationales for international activities at colleges and universities pervade the national reports issued by the American Council on Education (ACE) as well as the work of two major authors on the topic, de Wit (2002) and Knight (1999). Service to the economy seems to be commonly viewed with greater importance than does educating global citizens, the more traditional, liberal humanist rationale for international education.

Components of Internationalization

De Wit (2002), Hayward (2000), Knight (1999), and Ellingboe (1998) each provides a breakdown of the components of internationalization. Hayward and Ellingboe (1998) specifically address U.S. contexts. Ellingboe focuses on internal components of internationalization: leadership, faculty involvement in international activities, curriculum, overseas study opportunities, integration of international students and scholars, and cocurricular units and activities (pp. 206–8). Hayward (2000) adds several external components to Ellingboe's list of internal components: government policy and support (state as well as federal), outside funding, and attitudes of multiple stakeholders. Hayward adopts the language of Yershova, DeJaeghere, and Mestenhauser (2000); Mooney et al. (1998); Mestenhauser (1998), Johnston and Spalding (1997), and Vestal (1994), with regard to development of an international perspective and global competence.

Status Quo

Disappointment about the internationalization of U.S. colleges and universities has been high. In 2000, ACE published a preliminary status report on the
internationalization of U.S. higher education. Hayward (2000), the author of
the report, notes that ACE researchers had found little evidence to suggest
that the nation's institutions of higher education were equipping students with
the knowledge and skills needed to function effectively across nations and cultures (p. 5). In fact, ACE researchers could see few advancements of significance since ACE reviewed international education in the mid-1980s (p. 5). To
support these claims, Hayward cites low enrollments in foreign language
classes, low levels of proficiency among those students who do study a language in college, low numbers of course offerings in languages and international studies, low numbers of students who study abroad, limited exposure to
non-Western cultures and history, the declining number of undergraduate
programs that require a foreign language for admission, fewer institutions with
language requirements for graduation, shrinking numbers of area studies and
language faculty, and declining federal support for international areas in postsecondary education (pp. 1–4).

Green (2002), Sadlak (2001), Hayward (2000), NAFSA (2000), ACE
(1998), and Pickert and Turlington (1992) claim that in order for colleges and
universities to graduate substantial numbers of interculturally proficient citizens, individuals who can demonstrate global competence, efforts to internationalize will need both to expand and to take new forms. Advocates for
increased internationalization suggest that institutions have to find new ways
to infuse the curriculum with international perspectives and information; to
encourage all students to study languages beyond the low-intermediate level
and to become knowledgeable about other cultures through overseas experiences (study and internships); and to encourage and to reward faculty for
incorporating international topics and perspectives, in their teaching, research,
and service (ACE, 1998; Pickert and Turlington, 1992). Green (2002) calls for
an approach to internationalization that is "intentional, integrative, and comprehensive" (p. 16).

Contribution of Summer Sessions to Institutional Mission

Literature on summer and intensive courses suggests that these courses bear
certain characteristics that universities may exploit to overcome some of the
challenges associated with internationalization (DiGregorio, 1998, 1997;
Martin 1998, 1997; Alexander, 1997; Peca, 1997; Scott and Conrad, 1992).

Faculty and student availability to participate in study abroad programs; the benefits of immersion formats, particularly for the study of languages; opportunities to offer special courses, for instance, courses in less commonly taught languages and interdisciplinary programs such as area studies; and lower costs, both for providers and participants, are broad features of summer sessions that might be employed to facilitate internationalization. Summer may also serve as a desirable time of entry for incoming international students.

Given the fact that summer sessions at 92% of the 25 institutions studied must be self-supporting, and that 68% require summer sessions to generate tuition and fees that exceed costs, a central question emerges, to what degree do these fiscal responsibilities effect summer sessions' capacity to contribute to core academic mission among the 25 universities?

Data Collection and Findings
Data were collected through a questionnaire completed by the head of summer sessions at each of the 25 public research universities that belong to AUSS, and through summary documents published by AUSS, *Profiles of Summer Sessions* (2001a), and *Summary of Reports of the Association of Summer Sessions* (2003, 2002, and 2001b). Data from case studies on internationalization at four of the institutions were also reviewed. Case study data were collected through document review, on-site interviews, and institutional data banks.

Contributions of Summer Sessions

Although levels of international activity in summer vary among the sample institutions, unique international courses and programs are offered at nearly all of them. These courses and programs most commonly involve study abroad, intensive language study, or area studies. They are delivered in formats not offered during the traditional academic year, are taught by faculty who would otherwise not be available during the academic year, and are offered to students who also would not be available during the academic year. Additionally, summer sessions at several of the sample institutions attract a number of visiting international students.

Combined, these international activities show that summer sessions are a vehicle for international study opportunities, unique curricular offerings, support for faculty work, and the enrollment of visiting international students. Among the sample institutions, summer sessions courses, programs, and other activities, thus appeared to contribute to internationalization. These offerings can be classified as preferred goods as they reflect institutional mission. What is not clear is if, and, if so, how these contributions are reported, acknowledged, and connected to institutional goals.

The scheduling and organization of summer courses and programs are well-suited to support international programming. Data collected in the study showed that students and faculty benefit from these strengths among the majority of the sample institutions. Again, what is not clear, is if, and if so, how information about these strengths is shared with students, faculty, and university leaders. Despite the lack of an articulated connection, summer sessions among a majority of the sample institutions did appear to provide a preferred good with respect to internationalization, a good tied to the core academic mission. At the same time, evidence of successful mission-related entrepreneurial behaviors within these nonprofit institutions were identified. Summer international activities did not receive direct state support, and revenue, in the form of tuition or course fees, exceeded costs.

Organization, Role, and Function of Summer Sessions

The findings of the study illustrate that the organization, role, and function of summer sessions vary with regard to international programming at the sample institutions. While unique international courses and programs are offered in summer at nearly all the sample institutions, the number and types of international activities at the institutions differed, as did the level of involvement on the part of summer sessions staff.

Data showed, however, that the importance of summer international activities is increasing. Just under half of the administrators who participated in the study indicated that they are extremely involved with international activities. Large summer study abroad enrollments or the recruitment of large numbers of visiting international students generally required designated staff among the sample institutions.

The summer sessions administrative units that were studied typically have a dual purpose. They are to serve the academic community of the university, and they are to earn a profit. The latter can trump the former and, thus, impact summer international activities as well as other summer programming.

Pressure to earn profits can create strong incentives to pursue money-making activities, for instance, open enrollment for visiting international students in summer, which is practiced at one of the case study institutions, yet departments and faculty were found to exercise substantial authority over summer course offerings and faculty assignments among the sample institutions. Summer sessions at these institutions are largely faculty-driven operations, and this may counter pressure to pursue financial gain at the expense of academic quality. Revenue-sharing arrangements, however, may create incentives for departments and schools to focus on financial gain rather than on academics.

As professional administrators, the heads of summer sessions at the four case study institutions were found to interact with faculty and other middle-line administrators. In this role, they listened, advised, sometimes persuaded, and, most important, "made things happen," yet that did not mean that they were unable to promote international endeavors.

First, each summer session administrator controlled a budget that allowed her some flexibility. A new program could be subsidized for one or two years. Second, each administrator directed a support unit with a staff that could complete multiple tasks. The summer session administrators were thus able to make financial and human resources available to a faculty member.

Current Practices and Emerging Strategies

Intensive language programs, study abroad courses, area studies programs, and numerous courses with a global focus, are commonly offered in summer at the public research universities examined in this study. A number of these universities also attract visiting international students. A significant factor in the success of summer international activities appeared to be faculty and student availability. The activities frequently involved immersion formats and provided opportunities for extensive faculty—student interaction. Faculty ownership of courses and programs was found to be both important and standard.[4] In general, summer international activities reflected an academic mission and could be characterized as preferred goods.

In that these sessions are largely faculty driven, it was perhaps not surprising that the approach to summer international programming was found to be ad hoc at all but two of the sample institutions. Among the case study institutions, summer international courses and programs appeared to be tied to an individual or to a department, rather than to institutional policy or goals. Overall, however, international courses and programs appeared to be increasingly central in summer offerings among the sample institutions, which most likely reflects the increasing centrality of international activities in general among the sample institutions. There, thus, appears to be a reason for administrators of summer sessions to consider approaching the organization and delivery of internationally focused courses and programs more systematically.

Implications

That all but three of the summer session administrators who participated in the study indicated that internationalization is important at their university was not surprising. U.S. research universities operate in a global environment; few would deny the reality of interglobal connections and dependencies. The administrators were less certain about financial support for internationalization and whether or not internationalization is a priority at their university. Questions about the depth of commitment and the willingness and capacity to act on that commitment emerge. For leadership on internationalization, the summer session heads look first to the operating core of their respective universities, the faculty, and second to the strategic apex of their organization—the president, provost, and school deans.

For the most part, summer session administrators also believed that academic integrity was maintained in their programs despite the revenue-generating demands they faced. A number of those interviewed noted significant nonpecuniary incentives that motivated the institution to support international activities and substantial faculty control of the programs offered in summer sessions. For many students, summer sessions provide a means to address academic needs and interests that they cannot address during the academic year. Summer sessions can also provide a means for students to get more out of their university experience, but what they pay for these courses more than covers the costs of delivery.

A number of caveats also emerged from conversations with the summer session administrators. Entrepreneurial revenue generation entailed evaluating both the academic utility of a program and its commercial potential. Selectivity, prerequisites, the duration of a program, and many other factors shape both the academic rigor and the commercial potential of programs offered. In the cases studied here, administrators were confident that academic concerns outweighed the commercial potential of a program. How that dynamic will be affected by such emerging contextual factors as increasing demands for entrepreneurial revenue generation, rising costs, and increased intra-institutional competition is a key area for future inquiry.

The summer session units in this study provided fiscally sound academic programs that adequately served the academic mission. One key to their ability to accomplish this was the linkage of academic programming in summer sessions to specific faculty interests and departmental needs. As nonprofit pubic and private institutions contemplate increased entrepreneurial revenue generation close to the academic core, they would do well to incorporate a measure of faculty control in curricular development and delivery of courses and programs, as well as incentives for faculty to actively participate. Taken together, these findings suggest that before nonprofit institutions embark on significant efforts to generate greater revenue from core academic functions, they will need to give careful thought to values, both those that attract students and revenue, and those that emerge from the fundamental beliefs of the institution.

NOTES

1. Instructional costs generally include a salary for teaching a course plus federal payroll taxes of 7 percent. Contributions to a pension plan or toward the annual cost of health insurance for a resident, full-time faculty member with a nine-month appointment who teaches in summer are, thus, not deducted from a summer sessions office budget. In summer, most faculty essentially have part-time status and are only paid by a summer sessions office to teach. Summer sessions units, thus, do not incur costs associated with research and service. The full cost of administrative staff in a summer sessions office would be charged to the summer sessions budget.

2. Calculations performed by the author using data available in Summary of Reports of the Association of Summer Sessions (AUSS 2003, pp. 39–43).

3. See ACE (2002a, 2002b, 1998); Altbach (2002); de Wit (2002); Green (2002); Levin (2001); Hayward (2000); Knight (1999); Mestenhauser and Ellingboe (1998); Mooney et al. (1998); Johnston and Spalding (1997); Kelleher (1996); Vestal (1994); Harari (1992); Pickert (1992); Pickert and Turlington (1992); and Burn (1980).

4. Summer sessions are perhaps unique in that they are a support unit highly influenced, if not controlled, by faculty.

REFERENCES

Adelman, C. (2000). *A parallel postsecondary universe: The certification system in information technology.* Washington, DC: U.S. Government Printing Office.

Alexander, S. F. (1997). Summer session as an incubator: A case study of one university's success. *Summer Academe, 1,* 51–56.

Altbach, P. G. (2002). Farewell to the common good: Knowledge and education as international commidities. *International Educator, XI,* 4, 13–17.

American Council on Education. (1998). *Educating for global competence.* Washington, DC: Author.

American Council on Education (ACE). (2002a). *Beyond September 11: A comprehensive national policy on international education.* Washington, DC: Author.

American Council on Education. (2002b). *Promising practices: Spotlighting excellence in comprehensive internationalization.* Retrieved from http://www.acenet.edu/programs/international/promising-practices/

Association of University Summer Sessions (AUSS). (2003). *Summary of reports of the Association of University Summer Sessions.* Bloomington: Office of the Summer Sessions and Special Programs, Indiana University.

Association of University Summer Sessions (AUSS). (2002). *Summary of reports of the Association of University Summer Sessions.* Bloomington: Office of the Summer Sessions and Special Programs, Indiana University.

Association of University Summer Sessions (AUSS). (2001b). *Summary of reports of the Association of University Summer Sessions.* Bloomington: Office of the Summer Sessions and Special Programs, Indiana University.

Association of University Summer Sessions (AUSS). (2001a). *Profiles of summer sessions.* Bloomington: Office of the Summer Sessions and Special Programs, Indiana University.

Bok, D. (2003). *Universities in the marketplace.* Princeton: Princeton University Press.

Burn, B. (1980). *Expanding the International Dimension of Higher Education.* San Francisco: Jossey-Bass.

Carnevale, A. P., and Fry, R. A. (2001, March). Economics, demography and the future of higher education policy. In *Higher expectations: Essays on the future of postsecondary education.* National Governors Association. Retrieved from http://www.nga.org/files/pdf/HIGHEREDDEMOECON.pdf

De Wit, H. (2002). *Internationalization of higher education in the United States of America and Europe: A historical, comparative, and conceptual analysis.* Westport, CT: Greenwood Press.

DiGregorio, K. D. (1998). Getting a lot of education: College students' out-of-classroom interactions with faculty and the implication of summer session. *Summer Academe, 2,* 7–28.

DiGregorio, K. D. (1997). Essential encounters: Non-classroom interactions between students and faculty. *Summer Academe, 1,* 13–26.

Doane, D. J. (2004). *Summer session 2004 annual report.* Charlottesville: University of Virginia, Office of the Summer Session.

Ehrenberg, R. G. (2000). *Tuition rising: Why college costs so much.* Cambridge: Harvard University Press.

Ellingboe, B. J. (1998). Divisional strategies to internationalize a campus portrait: Results, resistance, and recommendations from a case study at a U.S. university. In J. Mestenhauser and B. Ellingboe (Eds.), *Reforming the higher education curriculum: Internationalizing the campus* (pp. 198–228). Phoenix: Oryx Press.

Friedman, M. (1962). *Capitalism and freedom.* Chicago: University of Chicago Press.

Garber, M. P. (1996, September). Wall Street Ph.D. *National Review,* 57–62.

Goldin, C., & Katz, L. F. (1998). The origins of state-level differences in the public provision of higher education: 1890–1940. *American Economic Review, 88,* 303–308.

Goldstein, M. B. (1999, October). Capital ideas. *University Business,* 46–53.

Green, M. F. (2002). Joining the world: The challenge of internationalizing undergraduate education. *Change, 34*(3), 13–21.

Green, M. F, & Olson, C. (2003). *Internationalizing the campus: A user's guide.* Washington, DC: American Council on Education.

Hansmann, H. (1999). The state and the market in higher education. *Mercato Concorrenza Regale, 3,* 475–496.

Hansmann, H. (1980). The role of non-profit enterprise. *Yale Law Journal, 89*, 835–901.

Harari, M. (1992). Internationalization of the Curriculum. In C. Klasek (Ed.), *Bridges to the Future: Strategies For Internationalizing Higher Education.* (pp. 52–79). Carbondale, IL: Association of International Education Administrators.

Hayward, F. (2000). *Internationalization of U.S. Higher Education: Preliminary Status Report.* Washington, DC: American Council on Education.

Heller, D. (2001). Introduction: The changing dynamics of affordability, access, and accountability in public higher education. In D. Heller (Ed.), *The states and higher education policy: Affordability, access, and accountability* (pp. 1–8). Baltimore: Johns Hopkins.

Hudson, L. (2002). Demographic and attainment trends in postsecondary education. In P. A. Graham and N. G. Stacey (Eds.), *The knowledge economy and postsecondary education: Report of a workshop* (pp. 13–57). Washington, DC: National Academy Press.

Johnston, J. S. Jr., & Spalding, J. R. (1997). Internationalizing the curriculum. In J. Gaff, J. Ratcliff, and Associates (Eds.), *Handbook of the undergraduate curriculum* (pp. 416–435). San Francisco: Jossey-Bass.

Kane, T. (1999). *The price of admission.* Washington, DC: Brookings Institution.

Kelleher, A. (1996). *Learning from Success: Campus Case Studies in International Program Development.* New York: Peter Lang.

Kirp, D. L. (2003). *Shakespeare, Einstein, and the bottom line: The marketing of higher education.* Cambridge: Harvard University Press.

Knight, J. (1999). Internationalization of higher education. In J. Knight and H. de Wit (Eds.), *Quality and internationalization in higher education* (pp. 13–28). Paris: Organisation for Economic Co-Operation and Development.

Krathwohl, D. R. (1997). *Methods of educational and social science research.* New York: Addison-Wesley.

Leslie, L. L., & Johnson, G. P. (1974). The market model and higher education. *Journal of Higher Education, 45*, 1–20.

Levin, J. S. (2001). *Globalizing the community college: Strategies for change in the twenty-first century.* New York: Palgrave.

Mangan, K. S. (1999, 21 September). U.S. students flocking to for-profit colleges for business degrees. *Chronicle of Higher Education.*

Marchese, T. (1998, May/June). Not-so distant-competitors: How new providers are remaking the postsecondary marketplace. *AAHE Bulletin,* 3–11.

Marginson, S. (2000). Living with the other: Higher education in the global era. *Australian Universities Review, 43*(1), 5–8.

Marginson, S. (1997). *Markets in education.* St. Leonards, Australia: Allen & Unwinn.

Marginson, S., & Considine, M. (2000). *The enterprise university: Power, governance and reinvention in Australia.* London: Cambridge University Press.

Martin, H. (1998). Student achievement in summer session versions of traditionally semester-length courses. *Summer Academe, 2,* 63–76.

Martin, H. (1997). Summer sessions: The centrality of their purpose to the academy's mission. *Summer Academe, 1,* 7–12.

McKeowan-Moak, M. P. (2000). *Financing higher education in the new century: The second annual report from the states.* Denver: State Higher Education Executive Officers.

McPherson, M. S., & Schapiro, M. O. (1998). *The student aid game.* Princeton: Princeton University Press.

Mestenhauser, J. (1998). Portraits of an international curriculum: An uncommon multidimensional perspective. In J. Mestenhauser and B. Ellingboe (Eds.), *Reforming the higher education curriculum: internationalizing the campus* (pp. 3–39). Phoenix: Oryx Press.

Mestenhauser, J. A., & Ellingboe, B. J. (1998). *Reforming the Higher Education Curriculum: Internationalizing the Campus.* Westport, CT: Greenwood Publishing Group.

Mingle, J. R. (2000). *Higher education's future in a "coporatized" economy.* Occasional Paper 44. Washington, DC: Association of Governing Boards of Universities and Colleges.

Mooney, M., Kawase, T., Reardon, M., Nunn, F., & Mashiko, E. (1998). A transnational model for internationalizing the curriculum. In J. A. Kushigian (Ed.), *International studies in the next millennium* (pp. 137–140). London: Faber and Faber.

Munitz, B. (2000, January/February). Changing landscape: From cottage monopoly to competitive industry. *Education Review, 35,* 12–18.

NAFSA: Association of International Educators. (2002b). *NAFSA News, 7*(35).

NAFSA: Association of International Educators. (2002a). Strategic task force on education abroad formed, begins work. *NAFSA: Association of International Educators Newsletter, 53*(5).

NAFSA: Association of International Educators (2001, November/December). Competing immigration security bills proposed. *NAFSA: Association of International Educators Newsletter, 53*(1), 28.

NAFSA: Association of International Educators. (2001). *NAFSA's 2001 public policy priorities and recommendations.* Retrieved from http://www.nafsa.org

NAFSA: Association of International Educators. (2000). *Toward an international education policy for the United States: A white paper for the president-elect's transition team.* Retrieved from http://www.nafsa.org

National Commission on Excellence in Education. (1983). *A nation at risk: The imperative for reform.* Washington, DC: National Institute of Education.

Newman, F., & Couterier, L. K. (2001, September/October). The new competitive arena: Market forces invade the academy. *Change, 33*(2), 10–17.

Ortmann, A. (2001). Capital romance: Why Wall Street fell in love with higher education. *Education Economics, 9*(3), 293–311.

Oster, S. (1997). *An analytical framework for thinking about the use of for-profit structures for university services and activities.* Paper presented at The Forum for the Future of Higher Education, Aspen, CO.

Peca, K. (1997). Intensive instruction: Lessons from the field. *Summer Academe, 1,* 57–62.

Peterson, M. W., Dill, D. D., & Mets, L. A. (Eds.) 1997. *Planning and Management for a Changing Environment.* San Francisco: Jossey-Bass.

Pickert, S. M. (1992). *Preparing for a global community: Achieving an international perspective in higher education.* ASHE-ERIC Higher Education Report 2. Washington, DC: George Washington University, School of Education and Human Development.

Pickert, S., & Turlington, B. (1992). *Internationalizing the undergraduate curriculum: A handbook for campus leaders.* Washington, DC: American Council on Education.

Pusser, B. (2000). The role of the state in the provision of higher education in the United States, *Australian Universities Review, 43*(1), 24–35.

Pusser, B., & Doane, D. J. (2001). Public purpose and private enterprise: The contemporary organization of postsecondary education. *Change, 33*(5), 19–22.

Pusser, B., & Turner, S. E. (2004). Nonprofit and for-profit governance in higher education. In R. G. Ehrenberg (Ed.), *Governing Academia: Who is in Charge at the Modern University.* Ithaca: Cornell University Press.

Rhoades, G. (1998). *Managed professionals: Unionized faculty and restructuring academic labor.* Albany: SUNY Press.

Ruch, R. S. (2001). *Higher Ed, Inc.: The Rise of the For-Profit University.* Baltimore: Johns Hopkins.

Rudolph, F. (1985). *Integrity in the curriculum.* Washington, DC: American Association of Colleges.

Sadlak, J. (2001). Globalization in higher education: Let us do it the smart way. *International Educator, 10*(4), 3–6.

Scott, P. A., & Conrad, C. F. (1992). A critique of intensive courses and an agenda for research. In J. C. Smart (Ed.), *Higher education: Handbook of theory and research, 8* (pp. 411–459). New York: Agathon.

Slaughter, S., & Leslie, L. (1997). *Academic capitalism.* Baltimore: Johns Hopkins University Press.

Vestal, T. (1994). *International education: Its history and promise for Today.* Westport, CT: Praeger.

Weisbrod, B. A. (1998). The nonprofit mission and its financing: Growing links between nonprofits and the rest of the economy. In B. A. Weisbrod (Ed.), *To profit or not to profit: The commercial transformation of the nonprofit sector* (pp. 1–22). Cambridge, United Kingdom: Cambridge University Press.

Winston, G. (1999, January/February). For-profit education: Godzilla or Chicken Little? *Change*, 12–19.

Winston, G. (1999, Winter). Subsidies, hierarchy and peers: The awkward economics of higher education. *Journal of Economic Perspectives, 13*, 13–36.

Winston, G. C. (1997). Why can't a college be more like a firm? In J. W. Meyerson (Ed.), *New thinking on higher education* (pp. 2–6). Bolton, MA: Anker Pub. Co.

Winston, G. C., Carbone, J. C., & Lewis, E. G. (1998). *What's been happening to higher education? A reference manual 1986–87 to 1994–95.* Working Paper. The Williams Project on the Economics of Higher Education, Williamstown, MA.

Yershova, Y., DeJaeghere, J., & Mestenhauser, J. (2000). Thinking not as usual: Adding the intercultural perspective. *Journal of Studies in International Education, 4*(1), 59–78.

Chapter 6

The Market for Higher Education at a Distance

Traditional Institutions and the Costs of Instructional Technology

Saul Fisher

INTRODUCTION

What are the root causes of the move by traditional institutions into the for-profit sphere? In this chapter I assess one such cause—or at least catalyst—of that move: an interest in exploiting new instructional technologies. Specifically, I suggest that some traditional institutions have made very optimistic estimations—indeed, they have been overly optimistic—about such technologies facilitating entry into a commercial higher education (HE) market. An unduly strong faith in the capacities of instructional technologies to allow for new, profitable revenue steams has led a number of colleges and universities to explore novel structures for delivering educational services to newer and broader audiences.

Thus, over the last five years, the HE landscape has seen the appearance of new, for-profit educational subsidiaries of traditional HE institutions (HEIs)—as well as growth among their close cousins, for-profit educational partner enterprises, and their older, disavowing siblings, nonprofit divisions or consortia created first and foremost as revenue-generating units. Familiar examples include NYUOnline (a for-profit subsidiary of NYU, now defunct); UNext (a for-profit partner of the University of Chicago and other institutions); and the Alliance for Life Long Learning (AllLearn; a nonprofit continuing ed consortium of Oxford, Yale, and Stanford universities; Princeton University was an initial partner but dropped out after one year). What makes these enterprises so new and strange is that traditional HEIs (tHEIs) are typically construed as "purely" nonprofit institutions ('pure' being defined variously).

To help understand these new roles that some nonprofits are undertaking, I sketch some pertinent elements of the higher education market, and examine the reasons why traditional institutions enter the for-profit sector of that market.[1] My focus is the projection of efficiencies produced by instructional technology, as a source of much promise vis-à-vis entry to broad student markets, and the ultimate disappointments resulting from overindulging such projections. What has been so widely promoted as an inexpensive means for tHEIs to expand their reach in fact bears tremendous costs—some hidden, others less so. It is reasonable to suppose, then, that such costs actually pose a barrier rather than an incentive to entering that once-heralded for-profit market.

I begin by describing a typology of the competitive landscape in which institutions look to costs to help make strategic decisions about their level of involvement in higher education online. Next, I assess a range of the motives variously attributed to tHEIs for entering those market sectors. I identify a single most likely motivation: the economic and technological judgment that instructional technologies yield efficiencies facilitating market entry for tHEIs. I then examine the most prominent individual claims to efficiency for instructional technologies, and suggest, more broadly, how the judgment that such technologies would facilitate market entry overlooked their true costs. Given the difficulties that a number of tHEIs have faced in that market sector, a more accurate assessment would be those costs that have represented barriers to entry. I close by offering observations regarding three issues: (a) sustainability in the for-profit online market (for tHEIs); (b) lessons for tHEIs in tending their fiscal planning and organizational missions in this terrain; and (c) the nature of technology as a facilitator.

One thing I do not offer here is a *postmortem* assessment, if only in the sense that there continue to be activities of the tHEIs in the for-profit and the near-for-profit arena. My goals here are to assess motivations among recent players in the market, identify the thinking behind at least one relatively plausible motivation—that instructional technologies made market entry feasible and desirable, and suggest how what transpired indicated that this last expectation was not plausible, after all.

PLAYERS IN THE ONLINE HIGHER EDUCATION MARKETPLACE: A TYPOLOGY OF MOSTLY TRADITIONAL INSTITUTIONS

In recent years, instructional technologies have enabled HEIs to offer online education in programs that extend beyond campus walls—and even across borders—to reach new groups of students as well as alumni. Perhaps the most dramatic breaching of borders is the crossing of the nonprofit divide, in the instance of for-profit distance-based higher education offered across the Internet. It is easy to overstate the role of tHEIs in pursuing profits from such enterprises, and a number of efforts in this direction have already ended after a short period of experimentation. What follows is a brief overview of select ways in which various (mostly traditional) players in the higher education sphere—old and new—have operated in markets opened up by online instruction.

OLD INSTITUTIONS PURSUING TRADITIONAL GOALS, BUT DIFFERENTLY

At a minimum, the online medium presents a new mode of delivering instruction of an otherwise traditional character. To be offered over the Internet, such traditional teaching materials and presentations may only need to be slightly altered. Such programs among esteemed institutions include Stanford's online master's degree in electrical engineering (http://scpd.stanford.edu/SCPD/programs/mastersHCP/msee.htm), Pennsylvania State University's PennAdvance program (http://www.sas.upenn.edu/CGS/PennAdvance), and the Duke University Fuqua School of Business's Cross Continent MBA—of which over 80 percent of the meeting time is online (http://www.fuqua.duke.edu/admin/cc/cc_home.html). The Stanford program replicates the preexisting traditionally taught program, the Penn program features online courses that correspond to identical general studies offerings, and the Duke program is closely modeled on the preexisting Executive MBA program, with an increased emphasis on international business. In each case, courses have been ported over to the Internet with few or no innovations in curriculum or pedagogy.

OLD INSTITUTIONS PURSUING NEW GOALS

Other sorts of programs pursued by traditional schools depart more dramatically from the usual organization or curriculum of higher education as conventionally conceived—though in some cases, these same schools also are pursuing more traditional goals through online education. A common feature of these programs is their orientation toward continuing education, either for members of the existing communities associated with those schools, or for new audiences. For example, Princeton, Stanford, Yale, and Oxford universities joined together in the Fall of 2000 to form the University Alliance for Life-Long Learning (http://www.alllearn.org), which is designed to offer courses for enhancement or for credit to alumni[2] and to other interested nonmatriculating students; as was already indicated, Princeton dropped out after one year. The novelty and strength of the alliance plan consisted in the creation of a continuing education program that draws on the teaching and curricular assets of four renowned institutions.[3] A more conventional approach, limited to a single school, is being pursued by Columbia University, which offers online courses and seminars, as well as course materials from on-campus classes, through its Columbia Interactive website (http://ci.columbia.edu/ci). These courses and seminars range over professional and technical fields as well as more mainstream disciplines in the arts and sciences. The audience includes nonmatriculants and current students, who may use the site as a portal to online components of their courses.[4]

NEW INSTITUTIONS PURSUING TRADITIONAL GOALS

One dramatic consequence of the development of online instruction has been the emergence of new schools and other ventures—with strong ties to tHEIs—that are run as for-profit enterprises. Some of the prominent new ventures include Cardean University (a division of UNext) (http://www.cardean.edu); Universitas 21 Global (http://www.u21global. com); and GEN, or General Education Network (http://www.gen.com). Each of these enterprises offers courses delivered across the Web that meet traditional curricular and pedagogical standards and are intended for matriculants, either within the context of the online school, or else toward credit that might be granted by a student's host institution.[5]

Cardean University courses have been designed by faculty from the University of Chicago, Carnegie Mellon University, Stanford University, the London School of Economics, and the Columbia Business School, under contract with UNext. Its business courses and degrees are offered to individuals and businesses, with the aim of capturing the market for high-end professional enhancement courses offered by companies to their employees.[6] Universitas 21 Global is the course-offering for-profit arm of the international consortium, Universitas 21 (http://www.universitas.com), which consists of eighteen HEIs including the University of Virginia and McGill University. This commercial consortium markets an online MBA and courses in information systems.[7] By contrast, GEN has tried to tackle what is often considered a difficult area for development or deployment in online education—liberal arts courses. Their goal has been to attract a wide audience that includes continuing education and current undergraduate students. These students would take GEN courses as convenient supplements to their on-campus course loads, or as a means of studying with particular professors who have impressive reputations in their academic disciplines.[8]

These institutions ostensibly compete with traditional higher education institutions, typically not directly with the core programs, but with extension, continuing education, and professional (usually business-related) programs of the traditional institutions.[9] GEN is unusual, however, in attempting to offer high quality courses in traditional subjects for undergraduate credit. Ventures of the sort represented by Cardean or Universitas 21 Global, typically focus instead on curricular offerings intended to attract student populations for whom the "classic" university or college education in a standard setting is an unlikely option. Like their counterparts among the for-profit institutions (FPIs) with no traditional roots, their target populations include single parents, nighttime and weekend students, and members of geographic communities underserved by existing nonprofit schools.[10] Whatever their various curricula, a common feature of all of these institutions is an attempt to provide educational offerings associated with some aspect of the tHEIs' missions—if only a peripheral one—through the new technologies and with the goal of meeting a bottom line.[11]

Several traditional institutions have given birth to for-profit subsidiaries charged with delivering courses typical to continuing education programs—these are hybrids, in a sense, of old and new institutions. Such hybrids include e-Cornell (http://www.ecornell.com), which offers executive and professional education in fields that correspond to established strengths of Cornell in hotel management and labor relations.[12] These spin-offs leverage the brand name of the parent schools, yet feature a flexibility and ability to raise capital that are characteristic of for-profit ventures.[13]

NEW INSTITUTIONS PURSUING NEW GOALS

The riskiest new ventures in online distance education are (or, in some cases, *have been*) those trying to use the new digital media to invent or extend novel concepts of postsecondary education, particularly with respect to pedagogy or curriculum. By doing so, their intentions have been to capture the attention of new student audiences, or to compete with existing institutions through new "product lines." Two such ventures include Fathom (http://www.fathom.com) —a for-profit—and Western Governors University (WGU) (http://www. wgu.edu)—a nonprofit. The primary partner in Fathom—now closed down— was Columbia. Working with ten institutional partners, Columbia created a wide range of minicourses for delivery to nonmatriculating students and alumni. Their goal was to sell continuing education directly as well as act as an online clearinghouse for other distance education courses provided by other institutions (for which Fathom received a percentage of tuition revenues).[14] Fathom's curriculum was aimed at a postsecondary audience. However, that curriculum was offered not in standard course units, but in bits and pieces, perhaps most analogous to alumni courses offered at some traditional institutions in "Deans Day" or "Alumni College" formats.

At some remove from traditional undergraduate institutions, we find the yet more radical Western Governors University, which dispenses altogether with credit-based curricular structures, for which they substitute competency-based degrees. Students who succeed at competency tests—on the basis of course materials delivered over the web, or even without having reviewed such materials—are eligible to pass through a series of gateways until they are judged fit to be awarded a degree or certificate. This sort of curricular structure is not a new invention. Rather, WGU models web-based instruction on the ways in which training is done in the information technology field, where competency-based certificates are common in the commercial model (as, e.g., in the certificates offered by Microsoft or Novell). While such new ventures as WGU (and, once upon a time, Fathom) represent competition for traditional institutions, their competitive strategies have not been as clear as those of new institutions offering educational services of a more familiar stripe. In dividing up traditional course offerings or changing the well-worn rules for acquiring degrees, the new experimental online institutions treat potential students as consumers with a wide variety of needs and preferences regarding the way in which to obtain postsecondary education. If such institutions discover a popular "formula"—and Fathom failed in precisely this regard—they stand to capture significant numbers of customers.

What joins all these varied enterprises—save for Western Governors University—is that they have been founded by, or are related to, traditional institutions (and even WGU uses curricular materials from such tHEIs as the Universities of Colorado and Hawaii).[15] Their varied educational and commercial goals suggest that these ventures must have had greatly different geneses. To a significant extent that is surely so. I am interested, however, in what might be a common feature of their origins, which may be identified in their underlying motivations for entering the for-profit (or near-for-profit) market for online education.

WHAT ARE THE HEIs DOING IN THE FOR-PROFIT SECTOR, ANYWAY? (ON THE IMPLAUSIBILITY OF MOST MOTIVATIONS)

There are many good reasons for tHEIs to retain nonprofit status for all of their instructional units. Why wade in the dangerous waters of the commercial education market? All of the usual reasons for caution appear to be relevant: financial risk; legal liability; threat to reputation; expense of time, energy, focus, and financial assets; unwanted government regulation; and erosion of political and social capital. These reasons are still more pressing when one considers that moving into for-profit ventures involves starting from historically well-established but often precarious fiscal and organizational status as non-profits. Much is at risk in any such for-profit enterprises.

Against this background, I find a bit wanting, the primary reasons that motivate tHEIs to move in these directions. Some of the more flawed candidates might help explain the broadly disappointing performance of such ventures (I do not explore that possibility in this chapter). I suggest that there is, in any case, an overall weakness in the general strategy pursued by many tHEIs in this domain, which highlights the inadequacies of the goals and motivations that are most frequently touted.

A list of the contending motivations and goals should include historical, social, fiscal, educational, technological, and economic claims.

> *Historical.* The possible historically oriented claims suggest that (i) such online ventures have their roots in the historical mission of the institution—given an *ethos of outreach and public education*—and the new ventures are an extension of the same; or (ii) institutions have a history of such moves—because they are *entrepreneurial.*

Historical examples of an ethos of public outreach include the continuing education or extension programs at many schools, and the correspondence course tradition (Bok, 2003, pp. 81–83). Examples of the second appeal to tradition, with historical commitments to entrepreneurial ventures, include the Carnegie Mellon Innovation Transfer Center and MIT Media Labs. Each of these historical motivations is well-rooted, then, in actual traditions, yet those traditions also demonstrate that such motivations rely on historical interpretation and its contingencies. Thus, if I think the ethos of outreach means "within the nonprofit sector," but you think otherwise, then we do not have common grounds for opting into for-profit ventures.

> *Social.* The possible socially oriented claims suggest that, in relation to other HE institutions or "clients," the pursuit of online ventures is expected, praiseworthy, required, mutually beneficial, or otherwise positively valued behavior.

To take the first such social motive, one might think that some of the selective private institutions felt a social obligation to widely distribute their instructional assets once that became technically feasible, as long as it was not a money-losing proposition. The same might hold, with an even greater sense of social obligation, for state HEIs. Furthermore, one might see AllLearn and Fathom as created for the mutual benefit of the partner institutions (though Fathom in particular seems to have been more straightforwardly an instance of diversifying assets and spreading risk). In the end, though, the putative social motivations are not likely very compelling unless they are literally mandates from the state. This is because there are other ways for tHEIs to plow their assets into socially valued enterprises.[16] Indeed, tHEI investment in for-profit ventures is heavily outweighed by their other projects undertaken in relation to other tHEIs, or to society on the whole.[17]

> *Moral.* The possible morally oriented claims suggest that the new online ventures are the right course to pursue, or that they bear the greatest social utility. Such claims include the belief (i) that free market competition is a moral imperative for great institutions, or (ii) that the HE learning community benefits best by such moves.

One might imagine a world in which such moral motivation could be sufficient reason for the University of Chicago to become a leading partner with UNext and Cardean—and in this fantasy, the Chicago School of Economics would be the great moral sages responsible for such investments. We know by the history of UNext that this is not in fact how things happened,[18] but they could and might well have at other institutions. The problem with this way of motivating investment in for-profit ventures is that however morally correct it may be, no one really invests on the basis of such reasoning. This makes it a poor choice of investment, a fact that is no doubt abundantly clear to university administrators. So even if they did think that one *should* invest the institution's assets in this way, fiscal responsibility would prevent them from doing so.

> *Fiscal.* One possible fiscally oriented claim suggests that responsible behavior entails investing where opportunities show a decisive advantage and an ability to capitalize on the market; otherwise assets are underutilized and a revenue stream is illogically passed by.

The thinking here is that for-profit online education simply represents a way for an HEI to invest its endowment funds while also boosting the quality and value of its instructional assets. For major research universities with large pools of teaching talent, it may seem tempting to create marketable courses using that readily available talent—and to try their best to beat the commercial competitors without such access to the right sorts of instructional expertise. Beyond temptation, it may appear to some that not pursuing such a path constitutes a failure to exploit a chance to build the endowment, and thus a failure to best satisfy the financial needs of the institution, including costs of traditional on-campus instruction (Bok, 2003, pp. 96–98). This view has a certain attractiveness: in times of irrational exuberance, once might well think it sufficient motivation for nonprofits to invest their own financial and intellectual capital in for-profit enterprises—for fear of losing out if one does not participate in the gold rush. Yet this view does not hold up to close inspection. Nonprofits in general and HEIs in particular, have special obligations to guard their assets closely and to follow rational and nonexuberant investment strategies—for the long-term fiscal health of the institutions. It is difficult to see why fiscal responsibility alone might be cited as a warrant for heavy investment in commercialization of an HEI's intellectual capital, when the vehicles for doing so—online educational ventures—require tying up and risking as much financial capital as they do.

> *Educational.* The possible education-oriented claims suggest that (i) intensively marketing education as a product is the best way to educate the greatest number of people—as it demonstrates the education's value and evinces students' greater learning energies, so that better learning takes place (a cynic might call this the University of Phoenix theory of learning); and (ii) if instruction at tHEIs is exposed to the world online and sold commercially, then consumers will render critical judgment as to the value of their purchased service. As a result, university instruction will no longer remain a hidden phenomenon, and its quality will rise markedly.[19]

I am not sure that any tHEIs would actually subscribe to this first view, much less admit to it (at least in this form). But it cannot be ruled out as a possibility, either, as that view has some currency with commercial players. In addition, if we attribute that view to certain institutions, it helps explain why they may have opted for one sort of online venture over another—if we also assume that *some* educational motive is at work.

The second view, about improving instruction by exposing it to market forces, is plausible if one thinks that instruction suffers from its opacity to students relative to quality, or if instructors feel no special pressure to meet standards of quality in their pedagogy. This complaint is voiced with some frequency, and there are even tales of such lack of pressure that have attained great infamy (resembling in form and accuracy politically motivated stories of welfare cheats). These tales seem to drive a great deal of resentment, sometimes taken up by university administrators. However, the opacity problem is prima facie suspect given that students are not shy about voting with their feet, and that most American HEIs place *some* sort of premium on quality instruction. So although some institutions might think putting instruction on the market will help improve it, it is hard to see how this could be a pervasive or persistent motivation for online commercial ventures.

Technological. The possible technology-oriented claims suggest that (i) we are doing this because we can (technology as enabler); and (ii) the culture of the new technologies is such that one only, or at best, learns from, market testing the instructional technologies.

There is no shortage of theories of technological change in the new information age, but surely these theories (i, ii) are the most prominent, especially relative to marketplace behavior. As regards (ii), one problem is its suggestion that the primary interest in employing instructional technologies is to refine them as technologies per se, rather than to achieve a given instructional task more efficiently. The technologies are thereby treated like ends in themselves. This unfortunate assumption at root takes a commercial market—instead of a "pure" teaching and learning environment—to focus one's attention on how the instructional technology "really" performs (here there is an analogy to the notion we saw in (e) of market testing the instructors and their practices). Such a view may be viable among unreconstructed instructional technologists. Yet tHEIs have no institutional interests driven by technological improvements for their own sake (except, perhaps, where a patent-driven revenue stream is anticipated) and so could not be thus motivated to explore online ventures.

The first view (i) may seem flawed for suggesting that well-managed tHEIs looking at their core activities of teaching and learning would exploit technological innovations simply because such innovations are available. Nonetheless, together with its economic corollary (see [g]), this view actually turns out to be the central motivation underlying institutional moves in this domain. Later on in this chapter, I focus on why this appears to be so.

Economic. The possible economically oriented claims suggest that (i) current market pressures demand that we do this (we will lose ground otherwise—for instance, students will go elsewhere); (ii) the future of HE is in this sector, so we need to be there soon, or first, to compete; (iii) we should capitalize on intellectual property (IP) of instruction, as is done with IP in the case of patents; (iv) we have a hybrid economic/ecological motivation: we are doing this because we can—the newly open market spaces, the possibility of expanding existing markets, low costs, and high returns allow tHEIs to take advantage of a niche.

The economic reasons are perhaps the most attractive on the face of the matter, simply because they are the only reasons that speak directly to the *for-profit* nature of the issue at hand. Derek Bok recently suggested that if one merely wants to improve instruction—even just in the specific environment of online education—then the mere presence of new FPIs offering similar online services to students should suffice as external competition that could drive pedagogical quality upward. If on the other hand, he notes, one wants to derive a revenue stream from online instruction, then the best way may be for tHEIs to pursue the for-profit route (Bok, 2003, p. 102).

Much has been written about the potential for competition with FPIs newly arrived in the higher education market (Garrett, 2003; Armstrong, 2002; Collis, 1999; Marchese, 1998). Is it truly plausible, though, that the FPIs represent market pressures that could either force tHEIs to improve the quality of their instruction, or pull tHEIs into the online education market, for fear that others will do it better and take away their students? Given that the degree to which FPIs *supplement* the position of tHEIs in the higher education market is minimal at best, the true level of competition between the different sorts of institutions should be minimal as well. In short, that the two sorts of institutions share a market according to an extremely broad definition is not by itself sufficient to motivate tHEIs to enter the for-profit market. Sharing a market might lead to tHEI market entry if the right sorts of specific conditions prevailed—for example, if there was direct, or at least meaningfully indirect competition, as per a scenario where the traditional market erodes in favor of a market favorable to the FPIs.

This raises the question of the future possibility that the sphere where tHEIs have always operated would dwindle away and give rise to a new and different one. In this new world, students opt for courses they happen to find on the Internet, perhaps à la carte but certainly with no attachment to traditional HE with its expensive overhead of room and board, student life, and the like. Such a view, once commonly touted by Internet enthusiasts and futurists, seems a little less popular after the dot-com bust, but should be seriously entertained. The principal question to ask in this regard is whether tHEIs gain anything from preparing for future competition with FPIs by staking out a for-profit approach at present.[20] If one thinks that the future of the HE market is in online education, even for what we today construe as the audience for traditional HE, then there is decent reason to start putting significant resources into online education. However, it does not follow from this that institutions can only, or even best, take on such a challenge by creating for-profit ventures to compete on a level playing field. The competition could well take place between organizations of different kinds—with nonprofits very plausibly winning over for-profits.[21]

A third economic candidate concerns intellectual property: the motivation for universities to enter the online education market in a for-profit mode, it is claimed, is to take advantage of the institution's IP as related to instruction. An important precedent for such a path is the great effort that HEIs have made to capitalize on research IP in the patents sector, since passage of the Bayh-Dole Act. This view of instructional IP, posited in numerous circles, is based on a poor analogy. The first complaint from any faculty member in this regard will be that, whereas the institution *might* own my research, it does not, and cannot, own my teaching, at least as considered as a performance. What the institution could end up owning is some form of the curricular materials—and such a claim has clearly been staked by MIT in its OpenCourseWare (OCW) project. In addition, the analogy between patent windfalls and instructional IP (copyright) windfalls falters, given the relative ease with which patent products can be brought to market—especially where the apparatus for commercialization (as in pharmaceuticals) already exists outside the HEIs. By comparison, hunting after profits derived from instructional IP requires a much greater investment in the university's own resources. While it is not implausible that tHEIs could turn such IP into a significant revenue stream, it is implausible to think that many such institutions would bank on this and turn their online educational efforts in the direction of for-profit ventures accordingly.

The last "economic/ecological" view echoes the Sixty-Minute MBA notion that the best business opportunities arise where one is well-suited to take advantage of a slice of the market in which one enjoys superior knowledge, experience, wherewithal, and resources. What enables tHEIs to do this, ostensibly, is that they are the oldest providers of higher education and so are poised to quickly corner any market for higher education, whether it is non-profit, quasi-for-profit, or full-blown for-profit. This sort of institutional confidence is important and ultimately to be cheered, but must be accompanied by the reality of proper market conditions or else it represents misplaced judgment, particularly in the cold and cruel for-profit market. Such a motivation could well drive tHEIs to the for-profit sector, if such institutions see the market conditions as appropriate.

What counts as "appropriate" here should be defined as some variation on the inexpensiveness of the costs and high nature of the returns. In the particular case of online education, I suggest, this inexpensiveness has less to do with the "education" part than the "online" part. For tHEIs, some think the *worst-case* scenario is that the educational component would be a fixed cost, differing not at all in traditional and online teaching environments. A best-case scenario would entail that porting courses to an online environment makes them highly replicable and capable of reaching broad audiences (as expansions of existing markets or inroads into new markets) for the same salary initially paid out to the instructor. This should result in impressive economies of scale and great labor savings. So far so good, but the tHEIs saw the real opportunity to lower costs not in lowering the costs of instruction per se, but in lowering the overall costs of *delivery* or (as the British say) *provision*. The difference, we will see, turns out to be significant.

In sum,[22] I have suggested that tHEIs have moved toward for-profit ventures in online education for two primary reasons, one technological and one economic. They both are some form of the notion that "we are doing this because we can," that the motivation to this market behavior consists in the mere ability to behave that way. However, assuming this as the primary motivation, it is not trivial after all; the market by orthodoxy is supposed to work in just this way.

Relative to such classical market behavior, the tHEIs exhibit a great deal of self-confidence in their building on instructional technologies, even though those technologies may look like a source of market friction given their standing as an asset for competing, online-based FPIs. Yet tHEIs view this putative source of friction as a potential source of strength, in light of the traditional academy's broad and deep knowledge base relative to pedagogy, information technologies, and specialized expertise in fields like educational technology and human-computer interaction. Indeed, many tHEIs subscribe to the view that instructional technologies facilitate their competitiveness because of built-in economies that can open up new markets and slash traditional costs of delivering education, thereby allowing tHEIs to develop for-profit ventures that are, so to speak, lean and mean teaching machines with a broad reach. So goes the argument that one should enter the market because one can. Unfortunately, to strike a meta-ethical tone, "can" does *not* imply "ought," and in any case not all parties among the tHEIs *could* pursue such objectives along these lines with any success. I look at why that is in the last two sections.

How Instructional Technology Was Supposed to Help Promote Traditional Higher Education—And Thereby Attract tHEIs to the For-Profit Sphere

I propose that the expectation that instructional technology should facilitate the operation of for-profit ventures by tHEIs is dependent, in two senses, on the notion that such technologies might facilitate traditional tasks of higher education. First, the former is dependent on the latter in the straightforward historical and technological sense that, as in many prior cases, the ability of a technology to yield efficiencies in a new business framework may depend on its track record in yielding like efficiencies in older, though similar frameworks.[23] Second, and more importantly, a number of tHEIs have behaved as though instructional technologies bear such an ability to deliver local, on-campus efficiencies *and* therefore provide a reliable guide to efficiencies in the broader, for-profit, distance education environment. If this judgment of tHEI behavior is accurate, then, it is important to know what instructional technology is *supposed* to be able to accomplish by way of the first, local efficiencies (on which the second, broader efficiencies depend). An optimistic perspective has it that there are some five such domains of potential efficiency.

Development. One highly efficient feature of web-based instructional tools and materials is that they are easily portable and can serve as building blocks for further development. Once the small pieces of a technology are built, you can aggregate, organize, and internally distribute them in many different ways—that is one of the most exciting aspects of toiling in code. The endless ways in which code components may be used means that the overall cost of development for any long-term use of such tools or materials as employ the code, is a diminishing number.

Delivery. Another great efficiency of instructional technologies is that they can be used to deliver instruction regardless of where students are located or when they might feel like coming to class; this is the promise of "anytime, anywhere" instruction. Thus, even if one deploys such technologies in an on-campus mode only, it is possible to increase course numbers at no or little cost of additional resources. This possibility has been of great interest to state institutions, which are faced with increasing enrollments as mandated by legislatures.

Labor Savings. One of the most intriguing aspects of using instructional technologies for labor economists has been the potential of such technologies to eliminate or reduce the costs of instructional labor. The theory is that instructional technologies enable the reduction of teaching time—sometimes to zero, depending on the perceived need for classtime—or "down-sourcing" to adjunct instructors, and automating or "down-sourcing" of grading and other administrative tasks. Such savings can be realized either through the elimination of teaching positions or in the growth of student cohorts without expanding the faculty (i.e., by increasing students in a particular course, or by increasing the number of courses, with fixed labor costs for instruction).

Renewable Use. Instructional technologies that are content-heavy offer a strong potential for efficient use over long periods of time. Once created, they may always be there for use in future classes by future instructors, with no expiration date in principle—a potential source of savings in curriculum development (especially for multiple use web-based materials) and professional (instructional) development for faculty.

Low Operating Costs. Once up and operating, one attractive prospect of instructional technologies is that they are very cheap to maintain per unit of technology (e.g., webpage, text database, and image bank). Thus, each resource should require only the marginal costs of (a) servers and networks used for all manner of purposes (including other instructional technologies) and (b) IT staff who maintain and support the technologies. As compared with the costs of maintaining classrooms or traditional library resources, the opportunities for savings are impressive.

One way to sum up the projected gains from these local efficiencies offered by instructional technologies is to tell a story about how online instruction becomes vastly less expensive over time—and thereby costs much less than any traditional instructional counterpart—once the preliminary production and fixed delivery costs are out-of-the-way. The story goes like this: The fundamental utility of online instruction consists in the capacity to deliver instruction over many sections or semesters and to ever-increasing numbers of students, with no costs added after hitting a defined point. In the case of cost per course section delivered, that point corresponds to the height of preliminary fixed costs x, plus whatever marginal costs y, there are in offering the course to each section; after this stabilizes at a given figure y_i for marginal costs, the course should never cost any more than $x + y_i$ to deliver. Indeed, at any point after the course is offered once, one of two circumstances will prevail: either the fixed costs will become some small fraction of x (because they represent largely preliminary expenditures) or else they go away altogether (because there are no more preliminary expenditures). In any case y_i represents the only significant costs and x is supposed to be negligible.

In the case of cost per student, the projected trend is far more dramatic: as a course is first rolled out for a few semesters or across a few sections, the preliminary costs of production and delivery move up quickly with more students taught, to a given apex—after which they tumble to a very low and stable marginal cost. The charm of this "ideal scenario" can be seen when you map the two trends on the same graph (Figure 6.1). For a short while, the growth in cost per student may greatly outpace the growth in cost per course section delivered. This much reflects the observation that the per-student cost of initially developing and deploying online technologies tends to be quite high. However, after only a few sections are delivered, the cost of delivery per student plunges well below the cost per course section delivered, and stays there for as long as the course is offered. In sum, not only are the costs of delivering the course stabilizing and the costs per student dropping, to an extremely low marginal value but, a yawning (and stable) gap opens up between what it costs the institution to offer a section of the course and what it costs them to add another student. This represents, among other things, the practical disappearance of additional, future instructional labor costs, and a

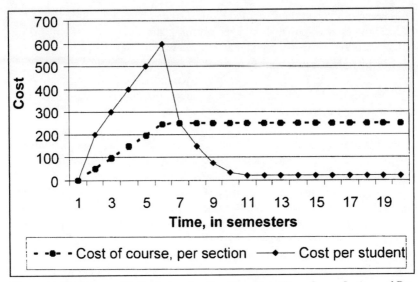

FIGURE 6.1. Total Costs of Online Instruction Over Time, for a Given Course Section, and Per Student

full-scale reduction in total costs of instructional labor. It *might* have a good payoff to add online sections (the costs of adding sections in the traditional, face-to-face environment also should stabilize, after all), but it will *certainly* have a good payoff to add students—whether sections are added or not.[24] Clearly, the more this scenario represents real possibilities—and the more it can be realized—the better the chances for exploiting online instruction to bring great efficiencies in instruction.[25]

Assuming that something like this ideal scenario is in the cards, let us turn to a second question regarding how such efficiencies as instructional technologies might promote tHEI provision in the for-profit sphere. The basic answer is that such lowered costs offered tHEIs the prospect of savings that would make palatable many of the other, extra costs of moving into the for-profit sector. These other costs include repurposing curricular materials, changing media, switching catchment and markets, sustaining clientele, altering the mission, and creating new organizations. In short, instructional technologies promised to make it attractive from a cost perspective, to enter a new sphere of activity in a new organizational guise. On a local, course-by-course level, teaching online offered the attractive possibility of cost-effectiveness. On a broader scale, the right level of initial investment in delivering *many* such courses—very possibly a considerable sum—would make it possible to realize a substantial Return on Investment (ROI).

Beyond this basic answer, there are two other likely motivations for tHEIs moving to develop for-profit projects, given the efficiencies promised by instructional technology. First, university administrators are aware of the fact that Instructional Technology (IT) costs typically run quite high. If there is a way to pursue technology-based projects that produce *any* savings or, in the best-case scenario, a revenue stream, then that will be recognized as the most attractive path. Second, by broadening the numbers of students for any given course—either in local, on-campus settings, or through expanding markets off-campus—the prospects are tantalizing for parlaying local efficiencies into extremely robust efficiencies and resulting in economies of scale.[26]

Problems. A dose of realism about costs and other features of using instructional technologies suggests some difficulties for the ideal scenario. First off, the prospective local efficiencies are, for the most part, either hard to realize or else offset by shifting costs that in some instances are greater than any savings won. To begin with, it is true that long-term development costs may diminish with the efficiencies of frictionless portability and aggregation of component code, yet the frequently high short- and medium-term costs of development may be the costs that matter most. This is because the shelf life of those components may not extend to the long term. In our era of the ultra-rapid product cycle, it may be highly inefficient to bank on development costs dropping in the event that one technology builds on its predecessor—the old technologies are often abandoned altogether in favor of entirely new structural approaches. A similar problem may plague efforts to maximize the benefits of a given instructional technology through renewed usage: just as these tools may be technically obsolete, so too may their content, or even format or presentation design, be outmoded. One need only look to fashions in textbooks to see that pedagogical trends do not stay still for too long. And the notion that repurposing existing materials is either easy or inexpensive is simply false: even with a canonical curriculum, instructors' interests yield great variation in reading selections, explanatory accounts, and modes of presentation.[27]

As for delivery, this brand of efficiency—which may increase student numbers for a given course, by removing constraints of time and place—is uncontestable. What is contestable, however, is whether the *quality* of the output can be raised proportionately to rises in the quantity of students so served, per input. This amounts to assigning a high value to the "effectiveness" in cost-effectiveness, and as I suggest in the next section, the cost-effective performance of instructional technologies is uneven on precisely that score.

Perhaps the greatest disappointment awaits those who place their faith in labor savings and in low operating costs. These two kinds of efficiency are unlikely in online education, because instructional technologies *may* cut the need for *instructors*, but they *almost always* increase the need for *technologists*. In fact, when one adds up the number of persons needed to design, develop, deliver, support, and sustain instructional technologies—not to mention the costs of licensing software, obtaining rights to intellectual property, and training faculty and staff—the comparable cost of the all-in-one faculty member found in traditional teaching environments begins to look far more attractive.[28]

Finally, let us consider the ideal scenario, which would have us assume that online instruction makes the provision of courses a proposition with little more than marginal costs to show for each iteration of the course, or for each student added, past some determinate number of instances for which the course is run, or past some threshold of students served. In particular, the ideal scenario has it that the cost per section delivered stabilizes after n iterations because whatever the preliminary costs represent fade away, never to be seen again. And the costs per student are supposed to plummet after a critical number of students pass through the course. However, neither element of the scenario is accurate just in case those costs taken to be solely preliminary, continue long after the initial stages of production and delivery.

What we should actually come to expect, it seems, is that the costs per course iteration stabilize, for short periods, before rising steeply once again as the cost of re-creating the course or repurposing its component parts becomes a necessary expenditure. Alternatively, if the course is allowed to "go stale," then the costs should rise even more dramatically in accordance with the rule of thumb that delivering an unwanted course is extraordinarily expensive.[29] Similarly, a more reasonable expectation vis-à-vis costs per students is that, after rising dramatically in the first few semesters, costs stabilize but at a moderate to high rate, as reflective of the huge expenses in support of maintenance and support of the technologies, and the occasional (and expensive) need to rework those technologies. It is completely conceivable, in fact, that the stabilizing rate for adding students will come out *above* that for adding course sections. In the end, though, it is counterintuitive that the two should be anything other than fairly closely tied together, even given the capacity of online education to deliver to many more people at a time. After all, all those people require some level of technology maintenance and support (and some require a great deal). One thing that does not disappear, then, are instructional labor costs—insofar as instructional tasks include upkeep of the quality of the curricular materials.

In sum, even assuming that some preliminary production and delivery costs disappear, those marginal costs remaining are wholly nontrivial. As a result, there can be no guarantees—or even rational expectations—that online instruction either becomes very inexpensive over time, or costs much less than traditional instruction.

The *same holds, mutatis mutandis, for* the proposed broader efficiencies of online, off-campus commercially marketed courses, which several for-profit ventures have touted. Many of the particular efficiencies that fail on the local level could be presumed likely to fail on the global level.[30] Thus, much work must (or at least *should*) go into revivifying online courses that are even one or two semesters old, sometimes in terms of content but almost always in terms of navigability, aesthetic appeal, informational design, teaching capacity, and ability to facilitate learning. This should be even more of a concern for courses that are globally marketed than for those that are plied on-campus only. Similarly, expected savings on labor and operating costs may prove to be elusive on the global, commercial scale. The broad picture is this: if the ideal scenario is simply a pipe dream, then tHEIs cannot plan on IT-based savings to offset their "switching costs" in entering the for-profit market. Indeed, if they have to plan on *increased* costs from heavy reliance on instructional technologies, then the allure of fashioning a commercial educational enterprise around their use is likely to wear off quickly.

WHAT WENT WRONG, OR, THE RISE AND FALL OF A BAD IDEA

Initially, investment in for-profit ventures by tHEIs may have seemed to be an especially good idea. Certainly there was a small bandwagon effect in the late 1990s to back such enterprises. I have suggested a primary reason—the projection of cost savings, and hope for a modest revenue stream—why such backing may have been attractive to institutional policy makers. The same reasoning likely held for the institutional investors as well.[31] For the most part, though, of late, there has been a retrenchment among tHEI investment in this area, and the common take is that such motivations as led them into the market, were in the end unsupportable, at least at this stage. Where exactly was such reasoning faulty? We have seen some of the particular flaws of the supporting assumptions—but the way those flaws crippled a number of for-profit ventures is a story, altogether unto itself.

The main thrust of this story is that the FPIs and tHEIs entering the for-profit market have faced different sets of challenges. For the tHEIs, there have been two obstacles to overcome in entry: a high standard of cost-effectiveness for instructional technology, and a high return on investment (ROI) overall for the entire operation. FPIs, by contrast, have only faced ROI as an obstacle, given that the cost-effectiveness barrier is much lower for them.[32] This is not so much a question of the cost end of the ratio as the effectiveness end. *Their* notion of pedagogical effectiveness is much easier to attain than the incumbent tHEI notion, since all the FPIs require, is that paying adult cohorts learn topics that generally require much less traditional and face-to-face instruction than those in the arts and sciences. Thus the distance in instructional quality and effectiveness from traditional teaching environments to their online counterparts is much shorter for the FPIs. As a result, cost-effectiveness of instructional technology for those institutions is a relatively minimal and short-lived worry.

The same cannot be said for the tHEIs, which are unable to offer any sort of inferior or even mediocre instruction—even in the context of a for-profit subsidiary—because of educational commitments, concerns for reputation, and political pressures, within and without the organization. A variety of concerned parties, including faculty senates, trustees, and funders, have demanded that tHEI ventures in online instruction be undertaken with the utmost pedagogical seriousness, and that institutional reputations not be wagered on inferior academic offerings. This is not great news for reducing costs: to the degree that on-campus university instruction through technological means can be as *effective* as its traditional counterpart, the costs of attaining that effectiveness can be at least as high as the costs of traditional means.[33] Indeed, the picture for distance education appears to be even starker, with cost-effectiveness a generally uphill struggle and victories typically achieved relative to effectiveness, not cost. The case of the Open University in the United Kingdom illustrates this point perfectly. The institution with the world's finest reputation for distance education (and an enormous student body) invests heavily in the quality and effectiveness of their courses, with uncontestable results. More students from the Open University go on to advanced degrees in the arts and sciences than from any other British HEI—and courses also cost more to deliver per student and per semester than at any other British HEI.[34]

And what of ROI? Here, too, the tHEIs are at a basic disadvantage in the for-profit online sector. To seek outside capital, tHEIs are required to create (or participate in) wholly new organizations, divorced from their main operations. Merely maintaining such separate organizational structures, though, eats into prospective ROIs—a set of circumstances that existing commercial entities do not bear. The FPIs can diversify their returns and spread investment needs in ways unavailable to tHEIs. But the main disadvantage for tHEIs relative to ROI, is that the FPIs can ethically take on the risk of entering a field that may require an ever-pressing need for investment and not worry about what the returns look like (naturally, this can produce variable results, as we saw in the dot-com bust). The tHEIs by contrast, must worry about such matters or else much more than a particular set of investments (with someone else's funds) is at stake. So if one were to gamble on the efficiencies of instructional technology, then one would be better off starting life as an FPI than a tHEI for-profit spin-off, because the spin for the traditional institutions is never very far-off.

If my assessment is correct, though, the underlying reason why ROI—and for that matter, cost-effectiveness—faces troubling prospects in this case, is that instructional technologies represent a cost sink which, far from predictably diminishing over time, may well expand—at a predictably high rate. And as such costs climb, they prevent institutions used to doing business in their traditional form and fashion from changing to another, very different mode of operation. In this sense—at least for those institutions without the deepest pockets—it seems unavoidable that instructional technology should represent a barrier to entry for tHEIs looking to crack the for-profit online educational market.

Perhaps it is unsurprising, then, that those institutions pursuing online ventures in the for-profit domain have included a number of the best, or at least *better*, endowed HEIs: NYU, Columbia, Penn State, Duke, and Cornell, to name some prominent instances. Some of these institutions have declared victory and retreated, whereas others remain in the market. But for just such institutions, determining that they are unable to compete in this domain, instructional technology costs per se should not have posed a barrier to entry. By contrast, they should have posed a barrier for other, less-well endowed tHEIs seeking to participate in this market, like the University of Maryland (in its for-profit guise) or SUNY Buffalo. Sizable expenditures on somewhat risky ventures are supposed to be more manageable by the well-off institutions. Yet if my analysis is correct, then costs of instructional technology were also a central factor in the inability of those better-endowed players to successfully enter the for-profit online education market. This further suggests that comparable tHEIs may have avoided entry altogether on the same grounds, whether they explicitly articulated those reasons or not.

SOME OBSERVATIONS

I conclude with three brief observations on recent tHEI experiences in the for-profit market for online education.

First, where the costs for instructional technologies are covered through external support, there may well be higher expectations of cost-effectiveness. Projects funded by the government (e.g., Fund for the Improvement of Post-secondary Education or National Science Foundation) or private foundations (e.g., Mellon, Hewlett, Sloan, or Pew) may well show strong measures of cost-effectiveness (a project like MIT's OpenCourseWare, which in its first phases is largely funded by external means, is one clear case). However, appealing to such funders to support the initial stages of a broad online enterprise is not by itself a sustainable solution. To build sustainable solutions on top of such external funding generally requires mature business models—not yet a feature of most such ventures (though the Fuqua virtual program and eCornell are counter-examples, neither having received external funding). On the other hand, a deep institutional commitment to an online venture may supplant the requirement for revenue, as transpired in the OpenCourseWare case. This can only happen, however, where the institution has equally deep pockets and is willing to enter the competitive market for distance or online provision of higher education without committing to playing the commercial game.

Second, I propose two broad economic and mission-related lessons for the tHEI community.

No Magic Elixirs. One may well suppose that, in some instances, fiscal interests have played an important role in the decision of some tHEIs to create for-profit online ventures that compete with FPIs. Yet even if this were so, it need not contradict my suggestion that common sense generally prevails at tHEIs and does not let market trends drive institutional investment. In short, the tHEIs' interpretations of their fiscal interests would not necessarily have been irrational or exuberant. A prudent institutional investor might carefully weigh risks and benefits of entering the commercial online market, with the supposition that instructional technology expenditures would be cost-saving assets, not liabilities. I have argued here that such a supposition would be wrong. But the basis for assuming that it is correct, would not likely have been the vision of a vastly expanded endowment. Rather, one might suspect at root, that such putative cost savings would make the difference between successful and teetering commercial enterprises. We ought to be wary of such judgments that promote magic elixirs, as well.

Playing to Your Strengths. One may also surmise that no one bothered to adequately forecast the long-term costs of online education. The big hole in any such forecasts appears to have been the costs of sustaining and renewing the technologies themselves, a large piece of which is connected to pedagogical enhancement. This is a tragic missing piece, because the ostensible strength of the tHEIs in the online market for higher education is their pedagogical capacity. If that capacity does not make the transition to the virtual environment—and stay ahead of the for-profit competition—then a major strategic advantage is squandered.

Third, the domain of science and technology studies offers this important bit of wisdom: Technology may be, in a narrow sense, a *work* facilitator—indeed, that is a mark of its success. But it is not necessarily an *economic* facilitator in a broader sense, and may even act as an inhibitor. Lurking behind-the-scenes here is the answer to the "Productivity Paradox." It is not surprising, after all, that technologies thought capable of boosting productivity, add to overall costs of production. This is because they were not so much intended by their designers to boost total productivity conceived in traditional terms as to *enrich* existing output, or to *enable* new sorts of efficiency. Such enriching and enabling facets of improved productivity may easily increase costs. To take the case at hand, instructional technologies enable tHEIs to do business very differently, but the price of doing business in these new ways may be prohibitive, one main reason being the long- and even medium-term costs of those same technologies. It is conceivable that those costs may diminish, or that other factors may push or pull tHEIs further into the for-profit market in the future. In the meantime, traditional institutions should consider means of entering or staying in markets for distance or online provision in ways that sustain their missions and ethos, yet do not as a consequence increase their costs.

NOTES

Portions of this chapter were delivered at the Mellon Cost Effective Use of Technology in Teaching conference, Northwestern University (November 2002) and at TeachersCollege, Columbia University (April 2003). Many thanks to my former colleagues at the Mellon Foundation and to Marianne Bakia and Sarah Turner for helpful comments and suggestions.

1. My remarks concerning nonprofit universities and colleges are limited to tHEIs: R1s, R2s, and LACs (as organizational types), generally in the arts and sciences and engineering (as discipline-types). The R1s and R2s are the Research 1 and Research 2 research and doctoral universities identified in the 1994 and 1996 Carnegie Foundation classifications; the LACs are the Liberal Arts Colleges identified in the same classifications (Carnegie Foundation for the Advancement of Teaching, 1994). My remarks concerning for-profit institutions are limited to those that serve broad, geographically diverse student populations (through distance education, for the most part).

2. Fuchs (Andrew W. Mellon Foundation) has suggested that such online courses for alumni may serve as "maintenance contracts" on traditional undergraduate degrees.

3. In the fall of 2001, Princeton withdrew from the Alliance, effective in 2002. The Alliance—now called "AllLearn" for short, has since opened its enrollment to all interested parties, much as was the case with Fathom.

4. A different sort of novel effort by traditional schools is the establishment of international partnerships that are facilitated through online instruction. Thus, for example, MIT collaborates with two Singaporean schools in the Singapore-MIT Alliance (http://web.mit.edu/sma).

5. Another similar venture—with no relations to tHEIs—is the University of Phoenix Online (http://online.phoenix.edu). Like the brick-and-mortar University of Phoenix, the online division aims its programs at nontraditional students who are typically adult learners and full-time employees: courses tend to be in professional areas, with a strong focus on business courses and, more recently, on teacher training.

6. UNext also offers minicourses without credit and not toward the MBA granted by Cardean (Carr, 2001).

7. A like effort, called UK eUniversities Worldwide (UKeU), drew only on British institutions and attempted to market British education globally on a collective basis. UKeU failed to attract enough students, though, and closed operations in 2004.

8. While GEN is still a going concern, their current offerings on the web are few in number.

9. The place or "niche" of FPIs in the established market for higher education is defined primarily by their *complementing*—rather than supplementing—tHEIs. For FPIs to significantly supplement the tHEIs in terms of providing a commonly available alternate source of education, there would need to be some critical mass of FPIs offering such provision. Their numbers, however, have never been that great—even at the height of the dot-com era, there were not so many. (Much depends, of course, on how one counts FPIs—in this chapter, the focus is on those offering a bachelor's degree or higher.)

In any case, FPIs could not, in principle, supplement the *core* missions of the tHEIs, because any such FPIs that set out to do what the tHEIs do would share at least some aspects of the same missions, relative to the criteria for "traditional" I have stipulated. Except for the fact that they are organized as for-profit corporations, they would then *just be* tHEIs. Assuming that most FPIs rather *complement* (in some broad sense) the missions of the tHEIs, the pertinent question is whether they do so in any more meaningful way than, for example, trade schools.

As an example, if the General Education Network had survived in its initial form, its goal would have been to compete with existing LACs in the same typical disciplines—art history, English, and so forth. This is the flip side of the more commonly made point that—as is true of most of the FPIs—a singular focus on career advancement courses in professional disciplines like business, health care, and IT simply places the FPI missions outside the realm of, or market for, traditional higher education.

The most interesting ways in which FPIs complement tHEIs may not be relative to differences in organizational structure or disciplines taught, but in (a) audiences or cohorts served and (b) technologies employed. Thus, FPIs generally seek to reach nontraditional audiences such as working adults and returning students, the geographically remote, and housebound persons. The technologies employed—which accordingly serve remote users—generally include Internet, Integrated Services Digital Network (ISDN) videoconferencing, or satellite linkups to classrooms at a remove from the central campus (if one exists).

The noteworthy complementarities between FPIs and tHEIs therefore are not tied to the types of institutions they are or sorts of missions that flow from being institutions of those types—such differences are so great as to not merit discussion in this context. One intriguing difference consists in the FPI goal of thriving by *expanding* student cohorts and the tHEI goal of thriving (or sometimes just surviving) by *constraining* the size of their student cohorts. Another interesting difference consists in FPI explorations into, and use of, technology to promote distance versus tHEIs explorations into, and use of, technology either not at all or else to enhance on-campus education. It should be helpful to learn if, and how, all this reflects or helps shape the native markets for each institution type.

10. Other nontraditional populations—less sought after by online education ventures but representing great numbers of potential students—include handicapped and retired learners.

11. Those new entrants in the HE marketplace discussed here are connected in one way or another to tHEIs, and so are unlikely to undercut their overall presence in the HE market. By contrast, as some have suggested, new entrants wholly *distinct* from the tHEIs could threaten the market share of traditional institutions, by unbundling and discarding unprofitable elements of university-level instruction (Armstrong, 2002, 2000; Collis, 1999). Armstrong (2000) suggests that distance-learning institutions will be most competitive when they challenge the integrated functions of traditional institutions—teaching, research, and social community—and offer teaching alone at a high enough quality to make the other functions look superfluous and not worth the price of tuition (he cites the UK Open University in this regard). The response to such a challenge, he suggests, is to strengthen those traditional functions and their integration, and so offer education that continues to represent a clear advantage for the "education consumer," the potential student.

12. Another hybrid of this sort, NYUonline, was created by NYU in 1998 but closed down in 2001. The NYUonline courses focused on management and finance; these courses were subsequently offered by the NYU School of Continuing and Professional Studies (SCPS). In 2005, NYU announced plans to launch a similarly named "NYU Online," as a web-based degree program in management and social science—also under the aegis of the traditional and nonprofit SCPS.

13. With the collapse of the dot-com market, there have been doubts cast on the ability of the new for-profits to survive, much less pose a challenge to traditional institutions (Grimes, 2001). Yet some observers also suggest that education-oriented firms have some immunity to downturns in the technology sector (Blumenstyk, 2003; Ortmann, 2001). In any event, for-profit institutions are hardly new in higher education (the "offline" University of Phoenix was founded in 1976); what is novel is their greatly increased ability to reach large numbers of students with tremendous efficiency through technological means. Careful entry into the online market has rewarded the University of Phoenix, to cite that one particularly successful example, with strong enrollments and profitable returns (Symonds, 2003).

14. The University of Washington has also created a portal for entry to distance-learning courses, which is a nonprofit entity and features only institutions that are AAU members and are classified as "Research One" under the old Carnegie classification; see http://www.r1edu.org.

15. As the focus of this chapter is on traditional institutions, I have not addressed the other significant grouping of institutions in the market for online education, the relatively new, for-profit "service" institutions such as Capella University, Strayer University Online, or the University of Phoenix Online. Another group I have not discussed here is the nonselective tHEIs, which are less prominent in this market, at least on a nationwide basis (exceptions include SUNY Empire State College and University of Maryland University College). As Turner has suggested to me, the lower prominence of nonselective tHEIs is likely due to their relatively low market power, as a function of brand, reputation, quality, or location. An underlying factor here may be their inability to invest their resources in expanding that market power.

16. An anonymous reviewer notes that social motivations may be compelling without mandate, as is typically the case of HEI commitments to affirmative action. While this may be so globally, it is less clearly the case in the instance of developing online learning ventures, particularly of a for-profit nature. Such ventures are generally touted as delivering social benefits specific to the provision of instruction, rather than to any broader social benefits as are typically associated with affirmative action or with other extensive attempts at social transformation.

17. Another putative social motivation is the notion that there is great symbolism in online learning ventures, as they demonstrate to a wide public the leading roles of HEIs in the development and use of technology; thanks to an anonymous reviewer for this point. This motivation also has economic overtones, as brand equity through diffusion of intellectual property builds market recognition (see [g]). A problem with this proposed motivation is that there must be a fair guarantee of enormous symbolism and market recognition to offset the costs of starting up and maintaining such ventures, and most HEIs are unlikely to take chances, especially in a for-profit venture, without such guarantees. MIT was able to take a risk in this area—and to achieve great symbolic value and recognition—by launching its OpenCourseWare project with the help of private foundation funding. Without such outside support it is unclear that the ratio of expenditure to brand recognition would have motivated such investments.

18. Rather, it was a University of Chicago trustee, Andrew Rosenfeld, who teamed up with Michael Milken to found UNext—and then the two of them shopped around for high-status business school partners (Bok, 2003, pp. 79–81; Pizzo, 2001).

19. This view has been recommended by many advocates of TQM, particularly in the business world, but also by some academic proponents of instructional technology who see it as a route to quality through efficiency (Massy and Zemsky, 1995; Twigg, 1993). Bok (2003) offers a helpful overview of the merits and flaws of this view.

20. I am not suggesting that FPIs directly shape the broad motivations of tHEIs in the marketplace, even if some tHEIs have created for-profit and revenue-generating entries, as "inspired" by FPIs. There are, however, at least three other domains where FPIs may have had, or are likely to have, a clear-cut influence on tHEIs.

First, the institutional mission of tHEIs has been influenced, if only on the margins, in terms of some incipient recognition of the ability to serve wider audiences than have been served historically. Most selective tHEIs have rejected any deep, revolutionary expansion of their teaching missions; this is also true well beyond the selective institutions. Yet some tHEIs have begun to explore how modest expansions of those missions might be made to work. In most cases, this entails natural extensions of the traditional conceptions of such missions. One prominent exception to this stepwise sort of shift is MIT's project to place all their course materials on the web for free and public access; OpenCourseWare dramatically expands MIT's reach to the entire world.

Second, relative to teaching, instructors at tHEIs may feel no direct sense of competition with FPIs but many of them may be acutely aware of these new entities, and may be influenced by their uses of technology. One may suppose that this influence is derived not so much from a competitive spirit but as a way of simply learning from others' practices.

Third, relative to services for students, staff, faculty, and alumni, some FPIs have experimented with technology-based efficiencies, and the tHEIs may follow suit.

21. An interesting precedent for this exists in the area of scholarly communications. Here, such a nonprofit organization as Journal Storage competes successfully with for-profit publishers, which also aggregate journals and distribute them online to university libraries (though without constituting an archive per se).

22. It should be interesting to document these reasons in actual statements by HE administrators; that is beyond the scope of the present chapter.

23. Exceptions are no doubt rife, but there are enough cases where this is so to suggest that it is plausible to base expectations of the new efficiencies on the old ones.

24. Otherwise put, there are efficiencies to be gained over time from repeat uses of curricular materials across semesters, and even greater efficiencies to be gained at the same time—after fixed costs diminish—from economies of scale, where radically increased numbers of students are taught through use of the same materials and little or no increased instructional staff numbers.

25. Variations of this ideal scenario have been presented over the last decade by Jewett (2001), Massy (1995), and Twigg (1993), and and the scenario as painted here is undoubtedly an oversimplification of their views. One qualification Jewett (2001) offers, for example, clearly allows that the ideal scenario is not a foregone conclusion. "The effect of improvements in faculty productivity upon average costs is attenuated to the extent the value of the ssr [student staff ratio] does not change in a parallel manner" (p. 107); I argue in the next section that such attenuation is in fact the *likely* scenario.

Important precedents for the ideal scenario were outlined by Wagner (1982) and Wedemeyer (1981). Their notion—that at a particular number of students served, the unit cost per student drops dramatically—was related directly to distance learning, as against technology-enhanced instruction (and in any case both writers made this claim long before the emergence of the Internet).

26. Economies of scale should be particular significant where standardization of curricular materials and design are of great value, as with for-profit concerns like the University of Phoenix or DeVry University. For such institutions, there may be as much to gain—or more—from delivering curricular materials to many students at once, than from reusing the materials over time; thanks to an anonymous reviewer for this point. The same should not likely be true for tHEIs, however, because standardization is of less value for them. Such traditional schools are typically committed to one or more instructional styles that do not clearly benefit from homogeneity—so while there may be gain from any particular instructor reusing curricular materials over time, the benefit is not readily multiplied across instructors.

27. One possible way to get around the problem of repurposing electronic course materials is to break them into discrete parts, some of which may be more sustainable than others, and to make the parts widely available for instructors to adapt, combine or update, as they see fit. This is the strategy promoted by the Connexions project (http://www.connexions.org) founded at Rice University, and in use at several other universities.

28. The claim that online courses are likely to be more expensive than their traditionally delivered counterparts even enjoys support among instructional technologists; for example, see ITFORUM, April 2003 (http://www.listserv.uga.edu/cgi-bin/wa?A1=ind0304&L=itforum#17). For the instructional technologists who allow that teaching online is likely more expensive than traditional teaching, the reasons to deliver courses online are related to pedagogy, access, and mission, rather than to any projected costs savings.

29. The orthodox notion of economies of scale posits a U-shaped cost curve, where each upswing is followed by a downswing, returns to scale diminishing as production volume increases. Web-based services are supposed by their boosters to exhibit a departure from the orthodox vision, insofar as increases in production volume are accompanied by per-unit trivial costs. In this regard I am suggesting that, in the case of online higher education on a traditional, quality-based model, the per-unit costs never become trivial, blocking such a proposed departure from the orthodox picture.

30. Bakia points out that, while I argue for the failure of the "Ideal Scenario" relative to online course provision in a for-profit framework, similar arguments may be leveled against the visions behind many traditional institutions offering online courses in a nonprofit framework. Indeed, that is the take-home lesson of failures to sustain local efficiencies across multiple instantiations of a course or in the medium term, a result broadly (though not universally) indicated by the Mellon Foundation's CEUTT studies (cf. http://www.ceutt.org).

31. Ortmann (2001) provides a broader perspective on this matter.

32. This is not to deny that (as an anonymous reviewer notes) profitability or ROI rather than cost-effectiveness per se constitutes the actual market test. My point here is that profitability can be hampered by structurally low cost-effectiveness, as is the case for the tHEIs but not for the FPIs.

33. This is suggested by several of the Mellon Foundation's CEUTT studies; see in particular the George Mason University and UC Berkeley studies for careful documentation of costs.

34. For cost data, see Boyd-Barrett (2002).

References

Armstrong, L. (2002). A new game in town: Competitive higher education in American research universities. In W. H. Dutton and B. D. Loader (Eds.), *Digital academe: New media and institutions of higher education and learning* (pp. 87–115). London and New York: Routledge.

Armstrong, L. (2000). Distance learning: An academic leader's perspective on a disruptive product. *Change 32*(6), 20–27.

Blumenstyk, G. (2003, March 14). For-profit colleges attract a gold rush of investors. *Chronicle of Higher Education, 49*(27), A25. Retrieved from http://chronicle.com/weekly/v49/i27/27a02501.htm

Bok, D. (2003). *Universities in the marketplace: The commercialization of higher education.* Princeton: Princeton University Press.

Boyd-Barrett, O. (2002). Distance education provision by universities. In W. H. Dutton and B. D. Loader (Eds.), *Digital academe: The new media and institutions of higher education and learning* (pp. 185–205). London and New York: Routledge.

Carnegie Foundation for the Advancement of Teaching. (1995). *The Carnegie classification of institutions of higher education*, 1994 edition. Carnegie Publications.

Carr, S. (2001). Rich in cash and prestige, UNext struggles in its search for sales. *Chronicle of Higher Education, 37*(34), A33. Retrieved from http://chronicle.com/free/v47/i34/34a03301.htm

Collis, D. (1999). When industries change: Scenarios for higher education. In M. E. Devlin and J. W. Meyerson, (Eds.), *Forum Strategy Series, Forum Futures 2* (pp. 47–70). Washington, DC: Forum Publishing. Retrieved from http://www.educause.edu/ir/library/pdf/ffp9903s.pdf

Garrett, R. (2003). *Mapping the education industry. Part 2, Public companies—Relationships with higher education.* London: Observatory on Borderless Higher Education.

Grimes, A. (2001, March 12). The hope . . . and the reality. *Wall Street Journal*, R6. Retrieved from http://interactive.wsj.com/public/current/articles/SB984067378945390493.htm

Jewett, F. I. (2001). A framework for the comparative analysis of the costs of classroom instruction vis-à-vis distributed instruction. In M. J. Finkelstein, C. Frances, F. I. Jewett, and B. W. Scholz (Eds.), *Dollars, distance, and online education: The new economics of college teaching and learning* (pp. 85–122). Phoenix: American Council on Education and the Oryx Press.

Marchese, T. (1998, May). Not-so-distant competitors: How new providers are remaking the postsecondary marketplace. *AAHE Bulletin*. Retrieved from http://www.aahebulletin.com/public/archive/Not-So-Distant%20Competitors.asp

Massy, W. F., & Zemsky, R. (1995). *Using information technology to enhance academic productivity.* Washington, DC: Educom. Occasional Paper.

Ortmann, A. (2001). Capital romance: Why Wall Street fell in love with higher education. *Education Economics, 9*(3), 293–311.

Pizzo, S. P. (2001, September 10). Barbarians at the university gate. *Forbes ASAP.* Retrieved from http://www.forbes.com/asap/2001/0910/064s01.html

Symonds, W. C. (2003, June 23). University of Phoenix Online: Swift rise. *Business Week*. Retrieved from BW Online http://www.businessweek.com/magazine/content/03_25/b3838628.htm

Twigg, C. A. (1993). Can education be "productive"? *Educom Review, 28*(6). Retrieved from http://www.center.rpi.edu/ResArti/EdProd.html

Wagner, L. (1982). *Economics of educational media.* London: Macmillan.

Wedemeyer, C. A. (1981). *Learning at the back door.* Madison: University of Wisconsin Press.

Part 3

Political Economy

Chapter 7

Capital Romance

Why Wall Street Fell in Love With Higher Education

Andreas Ortmann

INTRODUCTION

The number of publicly traded degree-granting providers of postsecondary education in the United States grew at a steady pace throughout the nineties. Following the early example of DeVry, Inc. (DV) in 1991 and the Apollo Group, Inc. (University of Phoenix) (APOL/UOPX) in 1994, ten degree-granting providers of postsecondary education went public during the second half of that decade.[1] Most grew at a brisk pace, often through acquisitions. The last five years have seen more acquisitions (e.g., Blumenstyck, 2003) and con-solidation among the competitors constituting the field at the end of 1999, a remarkable new competitor, and the unstoppable emergence of a vibrant e-learning industry segment to which all major publicly traded degree-granting providers of postsecondary education laid claim to various degrees.[2] Together, the remaining publicly traded providers of postsecondary education currently command about 4–5% of the revenues flowing into higher education each year—most of it originating from Title IV programs—and from more than about 10% of the nation's campuses.

To sell to investors ownership in a new breed of companies that, in addi-tion, had to compete against incumbent providers that do not have to produce profits to please investors and are favored by numerous regulatory and tax breaks including tax-deductible donations (Facchina, Showell, and Stone, 1993), investment bankers and market analysts clearly had to have "compelling stories" to tell. This chapter presents an inventory of the reasons that analysts gave at the end of the nineties, that is, before consolidation started to reduce the number of competitors constituting the field during the year 2000. In a sense, the years before that consolidation—roughly the second half of the nineties—can be thought off as the take-off phase of the industry. Certainly, throughout those years the viability of a for-profit industry was not an uncontested idea.

Apart from compiling an inventory of arguments, I attempted to assess the relative importance of their reasons through a questionnaire that I sent to analysts who followed the education industry in 1999. I evaluated the merits of these arguments in light of modern economic and managerial theories of firms and markets. Drawing on portfolio recommendations of my correspondents, I also evaluated their predictive powers regarding the universe of companies discussed in this chapter.

The next section briefly reviews the role of market analysts and then describes how I collected and evaluated the arguments that analysts used to persuade investors, at the end of the takeoff phase of the industry. The third section summarizes the results of a questionnaire through which I attempted that evaluation. The following section discusses how analysts' view of the fledgling for-profit segment of postsecondary education compares to modern economic theories of firms and markets. In the conclusion I discuss briefly recent developments.

AN INVENTORY OF THE ARGUMENTS THAT
ANALYSTS USED TO PERSUADE INVESTORS

The Market for Market Analysts. In the fall of 1999, the education industry—although the second largest industry in the United States—was followed only by a small number of analysts. A *Wall Street Journal* article suggested that "half a dozen market analysts" (13 August 1999, p. A1) tracked education companies.[3] So small was the set of analysts that the *Wall Street Journal*'s 1999 installment of its annual "All-Star Analysts" section did not even list the education industry as one of its fifty-five industry categories. (It did list hospitals and HMOs—the largest industry in the United States and an industry that went through a process of privatization about a decade earlier that many consider a template of things to come in the education industry, e.g., Hansmann, 1994.)

What Do Market Analysts Do? Through the study of companies, managers, "business models," and the markets in which they are put to the test, market analysts try to identify likely "winners" and "losers."[4] The resultant "buy" and "sell" recommendations of various gradations are meant to help managers of mutual funds, pension funds, and retail customers to beat the market averages.

It is a well-established fact that an overwhelming number of mutual fund managers (and we can assume, pension fund managers) do not benefit on average from that advice (Carhart, 1997). Furthermore, the implosion of Internet companies during 2001 left many a retail customer with fractions of the value of stocks that analysts touted highly and publicly (but derided in drastic terms privately).[5]

The basic problem was that market analysts were often affiliated with securities houses that are involved in initial and follow-up public offerings ("underwriters").[6] Such an arrangement puts market analysts in a conflict-laden situation as they may feel obligated to promote those equities in which their investment bank has a vested interest rather than those that they consider better bets. The fact that, as in the case of Merrill Lynch, market analysts' compensation was linked to investment banking activities added to the incentive incompatibility of the situation.

Indeed, Lin and McNichols (1998) found—long before the bursting of the Internet bubble—that three-day returns to lead underwriter analysts' "hold" recommendations are significantly more negative than those by unaffiliated analysts, suggesting that lead underwriter analysts' recommendations are affected by the moral hazard problem they face. Lin and McNichols also found that lead and co-underwriter analysts' growth forecasts and recommendations were significantly more favorable than those made by unaffiliated analysts. These and similar findings by other authors reinforced the widespread view that market analysts are glorified salespeople who routinely paint too rosy a picture of the companies they promote (e.g., Chaney, Hogan, and Jeter, 1999; Amir and Ganzach, 1998; Loeffler, 1998; Brown, 1993). Interestingly, however, Lin and McNichols furthermore found that lead and co-underwriter analysts' earnings forecasts are not generally greater than, and postannouncement returns not significantly different from, those of unaffiliated analysts' recommendations.

There is by no means consensus on this issue: Keane and Runkle (1998) have contradicted the widespread view that stock market analysts' earnings forecasts and recommendations are too optimistic. Francis, Hanna, and Philbrick (1997) find, in addition, that stock market analysts do not seem to be easily swayed by management presentations, as these authors find no evidence that postpresentation forecasts are less disperse, more accurate, or less biased than their prepresentation forecasts.[7] One possible explanation for these results, if they survive replication with more recent data, is that reputation might constrain moral hazard in financial markets. Results suggestive of such an explanation exist (e.g., Clement, 1999; Nanda and Yun, 1997; Chemmanur and Fulghieri, 1994).

Constructing the Inventory of Arguments. The inventory presented here was compiled through a content analysis of fifteen interviews that the *Wall Street Transcript* (*WST*, www.twst.com) conducted between May 1997 and

April 1999 with a total of ten market analysts, eight on the "sell-side" and two on the "buy-side."[8] The arguments were then arranged in three sets: those related to the economics of the postsecondary education industry in general such as demographic and societal changes, those that suggest why one might want to invest in publicly traded postsecondary education companies, and those that suggest why investing in this fledgling segment of the education industry might not be a good idea.

Evaluating the Relative Importance of the Reasons. One way to evaluate the relative importance of arguments that are meant to entice pensions and mutual fund managers to invest in for-profit education providers is to count how often they were mentioned by the analysts participating in the *WST* interviews. However, a number of the interviews were conducted simultaneously, covered additional topics, and were semistructured;[9] frequency of arguments therefore is likely to be a noisy measure of their comparative importance.[10] Since I was interested in getting a sense of the relative merits of the arguments, I sent—in mid-September 1999—a questionnaire containing the three sets of arguments in the inventory to a set of ten analysts.[11] To make the evaluation criterion unambiguous, I told my correspondents that "with this present questionnaire we are trying to quantify the importance of the factors thus [= through the content analysis, A.O.] identified as being responsible for making postsecondary education a promising investment."[12] The analysts were asked to rate each reason on a 5-grade scale that runs from 1 to 5, 1 being "unimportant" and 5 being "among the 4 or 5 most important factors," with 2 = "less important," 3 = "important," and 4 = "more important." A small token of appreciation of twenty dollars was attached to each questionnaire. The cover letter and questionnaire are reproduced in the appendix in Ortmann (2001), and can also be accessed at home.cerge-ei.cz/ortmann/instructions.html.

Eight of the ten analyst correspondents returned the questionnaire, one of them anonymously.[13] Mean and median response was computed for all of the responses. On average, all reasons listed in the questionnaire were considered to be somewhat important as the lowest mean was 1.9 (less important). Given the relatively small number of correspondents (and therefore the possibility of outliers distorting averages) as well as the fact that the scale could be interpreted as noncardinal, I used the median to classify the answers of my correspondents. Specifically, arguments with medians of 4, I classified as the "most important"(***) ones, those with medians of 3 as "important" (**), and those with medians of 2 as "less important" (*).[14] Of the twenty-six arguments that I asked my correspondents to rate, nine garnered three stars, twelve two stars, and five one star.[15] While it is tempting to compute dispersion measures, due to the noncardinality of the scale it is not clear what such a measure would mean. Let me point out though that opinions ran the gamut on some issues (e.g., "barriers to entry") while on others they were tightly focused (e.g., "economies.")

THE RELATIVE IMPORTANCE OF THE ARGUMENTS THAT ANALYSTS USED TO PERSUADE INVESTORS

I will now integrate the arguments in a narrative that distinguishes the three sets of reasons that I identified through the content analysis. At the outset, it is interesting to note that almost all of the arguments concerned with the economics of postsecondary education and the reasons why one might want to invest in publicly traded postsecondary education companies were rated "most important" or "important." In contrast, most of the arguments reflecting reasons why one might not want to invest in those companies drew a "less important" rating.

The Economics of (Postsecondary) Education. The for-profit education industry had (and still has) plenty of competitors in the fight for investors. Most prominently, in the second half of the nineties there was the rush to settle cyberspace, which attracted massive and well-documented capital flows and capital gains (and a whole industry to comment on them, e.g., Multex.com). What then qualified (and still qualifies) the education industry, and in particular, the postsecondary education industry as a potentially attractive place for investments?[16]

The analysts agreed that a major driver of the emergence of for-profits was the shift to a knowledge-based and technology-driven economy that pays an ever higher income premium to those with Information Technology (IT)-related skills ("income premium"***). This income premium, and the underlying technological drivers, are seen as creating an increased demand for education on the part of adults ("career-oriented continued education"***) and as contributing to the increased demand for postsecondary education on the part of students who have just graduated from high school ("career-oriented education"***), with another driver of this development being the "baby boom echo" ("more education"**).

The analysts agreed that one of the features that make the education industry interesting is its very predictable revenues and earnings ("earnings visibility"***). That government funding is, and will be, a steady source of significant revenue was considered an important argument ("government funding"**). Even more important, in the eyes of the market analysts, is the widely held belief that the postsecondary education industry is essentially recession-proof, if not countercyclical, and therefore might reduce the volatility of one's portfolio ("a/countercyclicality"***). Analysts also believe that there is an increased need for IT-related skills internationally from which U.S. education companies could benefit ("international demand"**).

Why One Might Want to Invest in Publicly Traded Postsecondary Education Companies. The arguments so far suggest why the postsecondary education industry is likely to encounter favorable demand conditions for the foreseeable future. Such a friendly environment, however, while positive for public and private nonprofit higher education providers, does not necessarily translate into a promise that the stock price of publicly traded companies will fare well. After all, and to recall, not only do they have to deliver reasonable profits (= dividends and retained earnings) to please investors, but they also face competition from public and private competitors that do not have to produce profits to please investors, which are advantaged through numerous tax and regulatory breaks (see Facchina, Showell, and Stone, 1993), and that have access to resources such as foundation grants not available to proprietary schools.

Analysts work under the assumption that publicly traded companies are likely to have for the foreseeable future, in addition to their high earnings visibility, high revenues and earnings growth ("high growth"***). In the *WST* interviews, one analyst predicted 6–8% "same store sales" growth, and 12–16% overall growth rates as sustainable for well-managed companies. Other analysts seemed to agree with those estimates. Such growth would be, by all measures, a multiple of the growth of nonprofit competitors. In the *WST* interviews, another analyst suggested that a better performance measure of the underlying "business model" was returns on equity and that on those grounds the better players in the industry had done outstandingly well. In their questionnaire responses analysts confirmed that sentiment, qualifying "high returns" (***) as another of the most important reasons why one might want to invest in publicly traded postsecondary education companies.

The strong expectations of revenue growth and returns for for-profits prompted the question as to how they would be able to compete successfully in an industry populated with subsidized and otherwise advantaged competitors. Analysts suggested that for-profits understand, and understand better than their nonprofit competitors, that the education industry is a service industry first and foremost, and that those who want to survive have to focus on students' and their prospective employers' satisfaction instead of alternative priorities such as faculty research ("focus"**). According to the analysts, this is expressed in courses that are offered at convenient times and locations ("flexibility"**) and in the fact that for-profits pay religious attention to retention, graduation, placement, and referral rates ("attention"***), as reflected in for-profits' attempts to ferret out what prospective employers of their graduates are looking for.

While "focus," "flexibility," and "attention" may lead to increased revenues, they do not necessarily produce good earnings. Regarding the cost side, analysts consider it to be important (**) that publicly traded education companies operate under a "pricing umbrella" spanned by inefficiently run public and private nonprofits that allows them to increase prices at or above the rate of inflation. It is clear from the contexts of the *WST* interviews and roundtables (e.g., "focus"), that the use of the adjective "inefficient" refers to faculty paying too much attention to their research instead of teaching (see also Ortmann and Squire, 2000; and Herman et al., 1999).

The analysts in the *WST* interviews had identified as two key supply-side advantages of for-profits the significant economies of scale in marketing, regulatory compliance, and other functions that can be centralized and the fact that those publicly traded education companies who manage to navigate the regulatory environment successfully can rely on regulations as an effective barrier to entry for new enterprises. The questionnaire respondents agreed and classified these two arguments as important for the decision to invest in for-profit secondary education ("economies"**, "barriers to entry"***).[17] The argument that competition through new entrants is higher in the training segment of postsecondary education ("competition"**) was also considered important, and validated indirectly the claim that postsecondary education is, in key respects, different from other parts of the education industry.

While the claim that working adults represent the primary market for distance education programs ("primary market "**) was also considered important, the claim that distance education allowed publicly traded education companies to make end-runs around state education boards and accrediting agencies was considered less important ("end-run"*).

Why One Might Not Want to Invest in Publicly Traded Postsecondary Education Companies. It is in the nature of interviews and round-tables involving analysts that risk factors are featured less prominently. Still, several caveats were mentioned in the *WST* interviews and I included them as a third set of arguments in the questionnaire.

Surprisingly, market analysts considered as less important the argument that direct and indirect subsidies to private and public nonprofits puts for-profits at a competitive disadvantage ("subsidies"*). Likewise, differential enforcement of regulations was considered less important ("stricter enforcement"*) as a source of competitive disadvantage. Seemingly inconsistent with that assessment, the argument that state education boards and accrediting agencies are typically populated by nonprofit school officials and faculty who take a skeptical view of for-profit educational companies was considered important ("skeptical view"**).

Turning from external to internal problem potentials, analysts considered as important the fact that many degree-granting publicly traded postsecondary education providers have relatively short operating histories that complicate an assessment of the quality of the management ("short operating histories"**). That verdict is maybe not that surprising as it absolves the respondents to some extent from judgments that turn out to be mistaken. Seemingly inconsistent with analysts' assessments of the problems inherent with short operating histories, the fact that many for-profit managers have significant insider stakes was considered less important ("insider management and control"*), as was the oftenheard argument that the overwhelmingly practiced business model of leasing physical plant and hiring temporary and/or part-time faculty could represent a significant "contractual risk" (*).

Discussion. The picture that emerged from the questionnaire was, nuances aside, reasonably congruent with the kind of argument one typically found in the second half of the nineties (and still finds today) in company documents and analyst reports (for the best, and most "academic" among many, see Herman et al., 1999, an excellent primer that draws on U.S. Department of Education and National Center of Education statistics). One key difference is the degree of emphasis on risk factors that pervades Securities and Exchange Commission (SEC) filings but is not as highly rated by analysts.

It is still too early to assess the quality of the arguments that analysts used to persuade investors. Specifically, no satisfying studies exist about the value added of the educational offerings of publicly traded providers of postsecondary education. The stock market performance of these companies, until recently, has validated analysts' arguments (see also footnote 23). Specifically, the assumptions about enrollment, revenue, and earnings growth turned out to be underestimates for most of the companies that remain in competition, with some companies reporting extraordinary revenue and earnings growth (e.g., revenue growth: APOL for years ending August 2004 and 2003, more than 30% each, with enrollment and revenue growth for the online division being in excess of 50%; CECO for years ending December 2003 and 2002, about 50% each; COCO for years ending June 2004 and 2003, more than 50% each; EDMC for years ending June 2004 and 2003, about 30% each; and STRA for years ending December 2004 and 2003, about 25% each; earnings growth: CECO above 75%; COCO 25 and 70%, respectively; EDMC about 35%; ESI about 30%; and STRA 20 and 30%, respectively; all for the corresponding periods.[18])

HOW DO ANALYSTS' VIEWS COMPARE TO THOSE OF MODERN ECONOMIC THEORIES OF FIRMS AND MARKETS? AND HOW DO THEY MATCH THE FACTS?

Wall Street looks at profitability and earnings and that drives stock prices.
—An anonymous education industry analyst in the *WST* (May 18, 1998)

This money [aid programs that Ohio state legislators made available to students in for-profit colleges] is not necessarily going to educate more students or to improve education. It's a scholarship ultimately going into profits.
—Roderick G.W. Chu, chancellor of the Ohio Board of Regents

... we are pleased to be reporting record revenues and earnings for fiscal
1998. It is particularly satisfying that our graduates continue to achieve
high job placement rates and that their average starting salaries are increasing at substantially greater than the inflation rate. This is what our business
is all about.
—Robert B. Knutson, CEO, Education Management Corporation,
quoted in *Business Wire* (1988)

On Wall Street, we are told by one of the *WST* interviewees, it is earnings
and profitability that drive stock prices. It is the P-word that agitates people
like Chu (and many others, e.g., Burd, 2003). What Chu does not mention is
that state funds (and the substantial indirect subsidies through tax and regulatory breaks) go into something in nonprofits too, quite possibly into activities
that are not tied to the mission of nonprofit colleges and universities or into
outright wasteful activities (Ortmann and Squire, 2000; Ortmann, 1997;
Massy and Zemsky, 1994; James, 1978). The possibility of profits poses the
intriguing question of how earnings and profits can be generated by participants in an industry that is populated by directly and indirectly subsidized
competitors.[19] And it poses the equally intriguing question of how these new
entrants can produce for the foreseeable future both high growth in revenues
and high earnings.

One answer to that question is captured by the importance that analysts
assign, in unison with most companies' SEC filings, to the two key supply-side
advantages that for-profits are argued to have: the significant economies of
scale in marketing, regulatory compliance, and other functions that can be centralized ("economies"**) and the fact that those publicly traded education
companies who manage to navigate the regulatory environment successfully,
can rely on regulations as an effective barrier to entry ("barriers to entry"**).
Analysts' belief that competition through new entrants is higher in the training segment of postsecondary education reiterates the belief that those who
have successfully hurdled the regulatory barriers to entry in higher education
stand to reap significant advantages ("competition"**).[20] It is noteworthy,
though, that, although analysts agree on the importance of economies of scale,
they disagree on the importance of the barriers-to-entry argument, with
ratings running the gamut from "most important" to "less important."

Knutson gives another important answer to the question of why earnings
and profits are generated by publicly traded education companies in an industry that is populated by directly and indirectly subsidized nonprofit competitors. The essence of his demand-side argument is that postsecondary
education is an industry that is based first and foremost on quality and, since
the nature of education does not easily allow for an assessment of actual quality, on expected quality or reputation. This is why placement rates and

increasing starting salaries matter to Knutson.[21] Indeed, Knutson's conception of what his business is about flies in the face of widespread and popular conceptions that others have proposed as rationale for the raison d'être of higher education as we knew it (c.g., Winston, 1999, 1997) and that also underlies the dominant rationale for the existence of private and public non-profits (Ortmann and Kuhrt, 2000; Hansmann, 1996, p. 228; Oster, 1995, pp. 18–19; Young and Steinberg, 1995, pp. 20–21). In brief, the traditional view is that reputational equilibria can not work in markets where the quality of a good cannot be ascertained upon purchase because sellers of adjustable goods and services such as car repairs, organic fruit, education, and health, day, and elder care could, and would like to, rip off consumers by promising goods and services of high quality, collecting a corresponding price, and then delivering goods and services of inferior quality (Akerlof, 1970).

In a series of intriguing contributions, Hansmann (1996, chapter 12; 1980) suggested that the dire consequences of information asymmetries ultimately drove the emergence of entities that were constrained by a nondistribution constraint, that is, nonprofits. Sellers of adjustable goods and services, Hansmann argued, were prevented by the nondistribution constraint and its sidekick, the reasonable-compensation constraint, from ripping customers off. Being constrained from distributing profits, managers of nonprofits would have no incentive to maximize profits by ripping customers off where customers may refer to students (and their parents) as well as donors.

Akerlof's argument, and by implication Hansmann's, was countered by Heal (1976) who pointed out that the essence of the asymmetrical information problem could be framed as a one-shot prisoner's-dilemma-type game. Heal also pointed out that the likely outcome of an indefinitely repeated prisoner's dilemma game was very different from that of a one-shot game. Indeed, seller-buyer interactions tend to be of the indefinitely repeated kind, such as buying organic fruit at the local farmers' market or grocery store. Heal argued, furthermore, that even for car repairs, education, and health, day, and elder care (where sellers typically interact on a less frequent basis with any one customer), markets—possibly enforced by warranties and what not—would evolve effective means of reputational enforcement.[22] The ramifications of the argument are dramatic. As in the indefinitely repeated prisoner's dilemma game, it is now in the interest of the seller to provide the consumer with a product that matches her or his expectation. Heal's argument has become the cornerstone of modern theories of firms and markets all of which are built on reputational enforcement in exactly the kind of situations that allegedly require nonprofits to step in (Kreps, 1990a, Holmstroem and Tirole, 1989; 1990b; Klein and Leffler, 1981; see also Ortmann, 1999 for an analysis of the writings of an early contributor to that debate).

It is here where Knutson's sense of what his business is about comes into play. Increasing placement rates and increasing starting salaries beget more referrals which, in turn, reduce the costs of marketing and so on.[23] Educational institutions, in other words, are caught in repeated game scenarios and reputational equilibria that will be swiftly enforced. The argument here is similar to the argument that applies to financial markets. Analysts or fund managers who underperform will soon find the demand for their services dwindle. Just as systematically overestimating earnings is not evolutionarily stable for market analysts, not providing promised quality is evolutionarily not stable for for-profit companies (Ortmann, 1997). When analysts talk about "focus" and "flexibility" and "attention" as important arguments, this is what they talk about implicitly. As one of my correspondents (Soffen), succinctly put it, "When I'm trying to judge the quality of a company's product, one of the first data points I look to is the percentage of their new students derived from referral. . . . I would emphasize the importance of referrals as being a low-cost, high-conversion method of obtaining leads" (*WST*, May 18, 1998). An obvious consequence is that those for-profit providers that do not play the reputation game successfully won't stand a chance to collect "buy" recommendations.

Even if they do, though, they are not home free, as investors react quickly to both real and perceived problems. To wit, many of the companies in the universe we are concerned with here were way off their highs at the writing of the first draft of this chapter (October 1999), some dramatically so, and many are so these days for reasons I shall return to in the concluding discussion.[24] One of the interesting aspects of the decline in the stock prices of for-profit providers of higher education in 1999, has been that some firms have suffered more than others. Soffen sees the "tremendous flight to quality among the stocks" driven by reputations. "The stocks that have performed the poorest . . . have a cloud overhanging them. The stocks that have performed the best . . . are perceived by Wall Street to be clean as a whistle." Reputation, in other words, is the name of the game. It's a point that market analysts, and most of the companies represented in this study, seem to understand well. A for-profit education company that does not understand that reputation, and ultimately, expected quality matter, is likely to learn that lesson the hard way, as illustrated by the travails of companies such as EduTrek, Whitmann, or, Computing Learning Centers. Even companies like Sperling's APOL, Knutson's EDMC, or Larson's CECO (all of which have stellar reputations among analysts; see the off-record interviews published by the *WST,* April 26, 1999 and may 18, 1998) are highly susceptible to attacks on their reputation.[25]

In sum, based on my own research (Ortmann 2003, 2000; Ortmann and Kuhrt, 2000, Ortmann and Squire, 2000) and what I consider to be the essence of modern theories of firms and markets—"focus," "flexibility," and "attention"—I believe that analysts paint a reasonably accurate picture of threats and opportunities. There are two areas where I would quibble with analysts' view of things. First, I side with those analysts who believe that (regulatory) barriers-to-entry are an important issue.[26] Second, I believe that the contractual risk (in particularly as regards management and IT-faculty) is considerable and is not well understood by analysts.

CAPITAL ROMANCE: IS WALL STREET STILL IN LOVE WITH HIGHER EDUCATION?

Until fall 1998 most for-profit providers of postsecondary education had seen steady and rapid growth of revenues, earnings, and stock prices. Stock prices then started to drift downward dramatically, undermining for-profits' ability to use Wall Street as their readily available endowment.

The decline of stock prices during spring 1999 (see footnote 23) left many an analyst puzzled and experimenting with ex-post-rationalizations that were in some cases in marked contrast to the rather optimistic price targets the very same analysts predicted as late as April and May of that year. At a loss for a clear explanation, market analysts referred to "sentiments" that had turned negative. Among the more tangible reasons that market analysts paraded was that stock prices were not supported by enrollment and earnings numbers and that run-ins with regulators or very public suits filed by former and present students took their toll (Blumenstyck, 2000). Overall, the reasons for the decline seemed poorly understood and opinions about their justification were quite diverse.

To better understand analysts' commitment to degree-granting providers of postsecondary education, I asked my questionnaire respondents two allocation questions. I first tried to figure out how they rated the prospects of publicly traded degree-granting providers of postsecondary education relative to other areas such as K–12 and education products. I then tried to understand which publicly traded degree-granting providers of postsecondary education were still considered a good bet, and which not.

The detailed results of these two allocation questions may be found in Ortmann (2001). Interestingly, the analysts' responses contradicted the (then) actual flow of venture capital that steered away from postsecondary education while they had a strong preference for such investments. Of course, given their expertise, that was not that surprising.

Interestingly also, the analysts identified three groups of stocks into which they would invest sharply differing amounts of a hypothetical portfolio: APOL, DeVry, Inc. (DV), DV, and EDMC each garnered around 20%;

CECO, ESI, and STRA each garnered around 10%, with the other six candidates being distinctive also-rans (QEDC = 4%, EDUT = 3%, COCO = 2%, CLCX = 1%, WIX = 1%, and ARGY = 0%). As I document in Ortmann (2001), the differential allocation did not make much of a difference. Specifically, equally weighted portfolios drawing on these three groups of stocks would have performed more or less the same—a result that any believer in the efficient market hypothesis would have predicted. Specifically, analysts did not foresee the emergence of COCO as one of the remaining publicly traded providers of postsecondary education or of the acquisition of QEDC. That said, the six stocks that they implicitly predicted as survivors (APOL, DV, EDMC, CECO, ESI, and STRA) have done reasonably well indeed.

Conclusion

Market analysts' understanding of the reasons that drove (and continue to drive) the rapid emergence of a publicly traded for-profit higher education segment does not seem to give them much of an edge in predicting the success of individual companies. However, their arguments allow a compelling narrative about the reasons why Wall Street fell in love with postsecondary education in the first place and is likely to remain in love with it for the foreseeable future. Market analysts' interpretation of the universe of publicly traded degree-granting providers of such education are reasonably congruent with both facts and modern economic theories that emphasize incentive alignment problems and the importance of reputational enforcement of goods and services whose quality can be adjusted.

What, then, do we make of the flurry of lawsuits (from shareholders as well as from students) and government investigations (by seemingly everyone from the Securities and Exchange Commission, the Departments of Justice and Education, the California Attorney General, and accrediting bodies) that hit the majority of publicly traded providers of postsecondary education discussed in this chapter (specifically, APOL/UOPX, CECO, COCO, and ESI) through much of 2004? Never mind the pitiful *60 Minutes* segment in January of 2005 (see www.cbsnews.com/stories/2005/01/31/60minutes/main670479.shtml)?

I believe we see three forces at work. One force is, as in other areas of emerging industries, a well-organized set of lawyers at work who try to go after the obviously very deep, and increasingly deeper pockets of the ever fewer publicly traded providers of postsecondary education. The other force is an equally well-organized lobby of traditional providers of colleges and universities, often well connected with sympathizers at the Departments of Justice and Education and at the accrediting bodies (as well documented in Sperling, 2000). This lobby tries hard to influence the outcome of the current reauthorization of the Higher Education Act. Specifically, this lobby tries to prevent publicly traded providers of postsecondary education from gaining access to federal funds other than grant and loan money (e.g., Burd, 2005, 2003). Some well-sowed doubts about the trustworthiness of the publicly traded providers of postsecondary education might go a long way in that battle. It is hard to explain the sudden flurry of damaging claims and sensationalist actions (e.g., the ESI raid or the *60 Minutes* "investigation") any other way.

Third, publicly traded providers of higher education do walk a knife-edge in trying to maintain their reputations *and* to demonstrate to Wall Street that they can continue to produce stable and high returns (which is, of course, what made them Wall Street's darlings in the first place). Sometimes, as they make the transition to more elaborate management structures, and as they lose the direct input of founders who had a good grasp of reputational issues (e.g., Sperling, 2000 at APOL), they may temporarily forget that their business is, first of all, about trust and trustworthiness of their products. In this respect, occasional shareholder and student lawsuits[27] as well as government investigations of aspects such as recruiting practices at APOL/UOPX are useful. It is the potential of such investigations to trigger dramatic losses in market valuations that adds to the enforcement that reputation, quite efficiently, provides in any case.

As far as I am concerned, it is only to be hoped that the same tough standards (of truth in advertising and whatnot) currently applied to publicly traded providers of postsecondary education will also be applied to traditional providers of postsecondary education which, in their blatant inefficiency (see Ortmann and Squire, 2000; Ortmann, 1997), have failed the nation for a long time and that have made possible the tremendous success story that publicly traded providers of for-profit education in the United States have, without doubt, become. Not just on Wall Street.

NOTES

An earlier version of this chapter was published under the same title in *Education Economics* 9, pp. 293–311 (see Ortmann, 2001). The current version has been significantly updated and rewritten during March 2005; we thank Routledge (www.tandf.co.uk), for permission to do so. Financial support by the Alfred P. Sloan Foundation (through the Curry School of Education at the University of Virginia) is gratefully acknowledged, as is the hospitality of the Program on Non-profit Organizations at Yale University and of the Center for Adaptive Behavior and Cognition at the Max-Planck-Institut fuer Bildungsforschung in Berlin that the author was visiting while writing the original draft of this chapter. Thanks are in order to David Breneman, Ralph Hertwig, Brian

Pusser, Sarah Turner, Gordon Winston, and two *Education Economics* referees for their comments on earlier versions of the manuscript. The usual caveat applies. A special thank-you to the market analysts who responded to the questionnaire.

1. These ten degree-granting providers were The Argosy Education Group (ARGY); Career Education Corporation Education (CECO); Computer Learning Centers (CLCX); Corinthian Colleges (COCO); Education Management (EDMC); EduTrek International (EDUT); ITT Educational Services (ESI); Quest Education Corporation (QEDC, formerly EDMD); Strayer Education (STRA); and Whitman Education Group (WIX). Capital letters in parentheses denote the symbol under which these companies are, or were, traded; in the present text these symbols are also used as shorthand to denote these companies.

2. As regards consolidation, ARGY was acquired in September 2000 by EDMC; EDUT was acquired in October 2000 by CECO; QEDC was acquired in July 2000 by Kaplan Inc., a subsidiary of the Washington Post Company (WPO); and WIX was acquired in June 2003 by CECO, while CLCX—brought down by the incompetence of its management—filed in January 2001 a chapter 7 bankruptcy petition that halted all of its operations. No comparable companies went public during that time. This has left, as of March 2005, as the dominant publicly traded providers of postsecondary education providers, APOL (with its University of Phoenix online subdivision for which it issued a tracking stock that traded independently between September 2000 and August 2004 under the symbol UOPX on the NASDAQ), CECO, COCO, DV, EDMC, ESI, STRA, and Laureate (LAUR, until May 2004 SLVN for Sylvan Learning Systems, Inc.). The latter is a remarkable new competitor because it established its postsecondary education credentials though a string of fast-growing and apparently quite profitable universities located in Europe as well as in Central and South America (see, however, the important caveat in Smith, 2004); it then—per acquisition and after a failed attempt to make its own Caliber Learning Systems (CLBR) a success—moved into e-learning with the acquisitions of Walden University and National Technical universities. It is noteworthy that all publicly traded providers of for-profit education now have e-learning divisions, although it took some a couple of years to realize that they could not do without it, as some initially had claimed (Ortmann, 2003, 2000). As of mid-March 2005, the eight companies just enumerated, all had market capitalizations in excess of $1 billion, ranging from APOL ($13.7 billion) to DV ($1.4 billion).

3. Indeed, according to *Multex.com* (www.multexinvestor.com), an average of six analysts followed the publicly traded degree-granting companies at the writing of the first draft of this chapter, ranging from one for smaller ones such as EduTrek International, Inc., to fourteen for the Apollo Group, Inc., by all measures the largest one at the time.

4. While market analysts have somewhat different functions from those of their colleagues who engineer equity offerings, or venture capitalists, it is likely that the pros and cons of a particular proposition are more or less the same across these three groups of market participants. The most important difference is that venture capitalists are the ones to come into the game early, and hence face a higher degree of uncertainty and

risk that is reflected in venture capitalists' higher hopes for returns (KnowledgeQuest, 1999a).

5. The Investment Protection Bureau of the New York State Department of Law provided numerous examples of such misrepresentation when it went after Merrill Lynch in April 2002. In May 2002 New York State Attorney General Spitzer and Merrill Lynch announced an agreement that reformed investment practices in key aspects (e.g., a prohibition of investment banking input into analysts' compensation); it also levied a $100 million penalty on Merrill Lynch; see www.oag.state.ny.us/press/2002/may/may21a_02.html).

6. See, for example, Block (Banc of America), Cappelli (Credit Suisse First Boston), Gay (Thomas Weisel Partners, formerly Montgomery Securities), Locke (Banc of America), Peterson (US Bancorp Piper Jaffray), Soffen (Legg Mason Wood Walker), and Stefan (ABN-AMRO). These affiliations are as of 1999.

7. In light of Abrahamson and Park's (1994) finding that managers tend to conceal negative organizational outcomes, the skepticism reflected in stock market analysts' reactions seems appropriate.

8. Cappelli, Gay, Hermann, and Craig (Everen); Odening (Salomon Smith Barney, formerly Hambrecht & Quist); Saltzman & Stefan (ABN-AMRO); and Soffen are from the sell-side, and Ankrum (Janus) and Cheseby (T. Rowe Price) are from the buy-side. Three of the market analysts (Cappelli, Gay, and Odening) were interviewed twice, one (Soffen) thrice; all affiliations are as of 1999.

9. Among the multiple-participant settings were two round tables with four participants each and two interviews with two participants each.

10. It turns out that a simple counting of arguments led to a similar assessment of their relative merits, especially as regards the first two sets of questions.

11. Among these correspondents were all those sell-side analysts that participated in the *WST* sessions. Since Saltzman and Stefan (ABN-AMRO) and Herman and Craig (Everen) were in the same firm, I only sent them one questionnaire. In addition, I sent a questionnaire to four analysts who I had become acquainted with during my research (Bloch, Locke, Paris, and Peterson).

12. I also specified that the investment should be promising for "the forseeable future" and instructed the analysts that "when rating the reasons listed below, please use a 5-year perspective." This specification was meant to reduce possible ambiguities among my correspondents about the relevant time horizon.

13. Thanks are in order to Gregory Cappelli, Jerry Herman, Michael Locke, Alex Paris, Robert Peterson, Matthew Stefan, Scott Soffen, and the anonymous correspondent.

14. There were six cases where the median required averaging. The classification of these arguments was done through rounding that relied on the mean. Clearly this is a somewhat arbitrary procedure. The classification, however, is rather robust to various specifications and does not in any significant manner affect the narrative that will be constructed presently from this inventory.

15. A ranking of the responses according to mean is highly congruent, as the first draft of this chapter (see home.cerge-ei.cz/ortmann/recentWPs.html) demonstrates. Classifying arguments with means between 3.8 to 4.3 as the "most important" ones, those with means ranging from 2.8 to 3.6 as "important" (**), and those with means ranging from 1.9 to 2.5 as "less important"(*), leads to 7 triple-, 14 two-, and 5 one-star classifications. In fact, only two of twenty-six arguments switch their classification, namely, "attention" and "barriers to entry," both of which are upgraded.

16. After the implosion of Internet companies during much of 2001, there was a general unwillingness of investors to invest at all in a market whose slide seemed unstoppable. After a year-long drought, education venture capital investments quadrupled (both in number of transactions and volumes) in the second quarter of 2002 relative to the first quarter according to market research firm Eduventures. The $50 million investment of two private equity firms in the third quarter of 2002 in newcomer U.S. Education Corporation—a company that since then has tried to acquire private career colleges offering information technology and allied health associate and certificate programs—was another indication that, after the drought and the accompanying consolidation phase documented in footnote 2, funds were more easily accessible again. As of mid-March 2005, the company (www.useducationcorp.com) has acquired four colleges; it may go public within a couple of years. See also Blumenstyck (2005) which summarizes recent, and not so recent, Eduventures investment data.

17. This poses the interesting question of why these advantages are suddenly central drivers of growth. Three explanations come to mind. The most likely explanation is, as evidenced by the fact that most initial and follow-up public offerings have happened since December 1994, that proprietary providers have gained the critical mass that allows them to capture those economies. Second, it is quite possible that the advances in information technology that we witnessed over the past decade (e.g., McKinsey, 1993, 1992) were a *conditio sine qua non*. Third, the public perception of for-profit education has clearly changed (KnowledgeQuest, 1999b; 1999a); for-profits have won respect even in Congress (Burd 2003, 2001, 1998).

18. The data are computed from income statements.

19. A referee noted that "federal subsidies to higher education have been shifting from demand-side to supply-side (tuition) subsidies in the united States, and that the latter subsidies have been opened up to for-profit institutions to a substantial extent, providing a considerable boost to the demand for their services. State-level subsidies remain heavily on the supply side, but are evidently declining on a per-student basis and seem likely to continue to decline, and may ultimately be converted in many cases to demand-side subsidies as well." True. This should, however, not distract from the fact that for-profits have to produce profits to please their investors and that they do not have available to them numerous regulatory and tax breaks including tax-deductable donations and foundation grants. While in other words, the playing field is less uneven, it is not level yet. I have little doubt that the ability of for-profits to emerge, and thrive, in what should be a hostile environment to them, was possible only because of the appalling inefficiency and inefficacy of traditional providers of postsecondary education.

20. The following are two representative views:

This industry by definition is one with very high barriers to entry. . . . it's perhaps one of the most heavily regulated industries in the economy. . . . If you want to talk about what keeps us awake at night, it's the concern about the shifting sand of this regulatory oversight and our ability to adapt to it and stay on top of it. . . . If there's one thing that I really watch, that's the piece. (Moore, president and CEO, Corinthian Colleges, Inc., in a *WST* interview, June 4, 1999)

Regulation is both a benefit and barrier. There are significant costs and administrative burdens for being in this regulated industry. But by the same token, it also raises the hurdle rate for potential or would be competitors to enter the market." (Herman, analyst, in a *WST* interview, April 26, 1999)

21. Knutson's argument is prominently mentioned by most companies and their CEOs, for instance, Strayer's Bailey: "Producing satisfied graduates who have successful careers increases our referral rates and strengthens our reputation" (*WST*, June 4, 1999). In fact, reading SEC filings and message boards it becomes quickly clear that it is management's lack of understanding of reputational issues that did in companies such as CLCX. See also footnote 23.

22. There is a widespread misconception that repeated games do not apply in a context in which people only invest in something like a college education. Theoretically, it does not matter whether a firm plays against the same person all the time or against a series of people (Kreps, 1999b, pp. 66–72) if, and that is an important conditional, the firm has a reputation to protect and the value of that reputation always exceeds the short-run gains it could obtain from sullying its reputation. I have argued elsewhere that this is indeed the situation in which many a higher education firm finds itself these days (Ortmann, 1997). One might object that it takes time to build a reputation. It is therefore interesting to note how quickly for-profits have managed to overcome the negative connotations that were attached to their enterprise certainly in the first half of the nineties (Burd, 2003, 2001, 1998).

23. In their SEC filings the companies enumerated in footnote 1 typically claim(ed) that between one third and two-third of their students come from referrals.

24. Had one bought one share of each of the stocks mentioned in footnote 1 plus APOL and DV at their 52-week high (in most cases early in 1999), one would have paid a grand total of $275. At the end of September 1999 this amount would have been worth less than $150, for a loss of approximately 45% of the original investment and not taking into account the opportunity cost of investing that money elsewhere. That said, it is noteworthy that shareholder returns since the IPOs equaled 4–11 times that of the S&P 500 Index and that the comparative returns of a market cap weighted postsecondary index beat the S&P 500 Index by a factor of more than 3 (Herman et al., 1999, pp. 52–53). Also, between the last trading day in September 1999 and the last trading day in September 2000, the stocks enumerated in footnote 1 plus APOL and DV approximately doubled in value. Between the last trading day in September 2000 and the last trading day in September 2001, a portfolio of 1 share each of APOL,

CECO, COCO, DV, EDMC, ESI, STRA, and WIX would have appreciated approximately 45%—a remarkable performance by any standard but in particular in light of the abysmal performance of U.S. stock markets during that time (which includes the implosion of Internet stocks). Finally, a portfolio of one share each of APOL, CECO (including WIX), COCO, DV, EDMC, ESI, and STRA, kept through mid-March 2005, would have again more than doubled in value since the last trading day in September 2001, outpacing by a wide margin all relevant market indexes that during that time moved essentially sideways. In fact, only one of the education stocks would have produced losses during that period (DV) with all others increasing in value roughly two to three times—a spectacular performance by any measure. These results are robust to different ways of computing performance such as measures that weigh price with market capitalization (e.g., see the Chronicle Index of For-Profit Higher Education, www.chronicle.com whose origin goes back to discussions that the present author had with a *Chronicle* writer at a workshop in the fall of 1999).

25. As regards APOL, in the fall of 1999 (at the time the questionnaire was sent out) its stock price was about 50% off its high. This development was attributed by several analysts to a two-year investigation that the Department of Education (DE) had undertaken. However, APOL's stock price did not recover significantly upon the news that the final program review determination letter essentially exonerated APOL: "(The DE) largely agreed with Phoenix that many of the university's problems in managing federal student aid funds were the result of its rapid expansion of the past several years" (*Chronicle of Higher Education*, August 13, 1999, A43) As regards EDMC, its stock got pounded after it announced, in September 1999, that 145 Houston-area students had brought a suit against the Art Institute of Houston, alleging that they were defrauded by their school. EDMC's stock price (which in mid-1998 was above $35) fell, in late 1999, and for several months was below $10. It has recovered significantly since then. Most recently, and in fact through much of 2004, a flurry of lawsuits (from shareholders as well as from students) and government investigations hit APOL/UOPX, CECO, COCO, and ESI, with ESI losing temporarily half of its value after FBI federal agents, equipped with search warrants and grand-jury subpoenas, invaded its headquarters and ten of its campuses, while CECO and COCO lost—less temporarily—about two-thirds and three-fourths of their value over the summer in reaction to various lawsuits and government investigations, as well as missed earnings estimates.

26. My view is supported by KnowledgeQuest's 1999 ranking of quality of management and regulatory environment as the highest risks. Note that this ranking is based on surveys of venture capitalists, that is, people who put their money where their mouth is.

27. Alternatively, actions such as those of Bostic, a large shareholder who ran the American Intercontinental University schools before selling them to CECO in 2001, might help publicly traded providers of postsecondary education to remember what their business was supposed to be all about. According to Reuters (March 24, 2005), Bostic—through a proxy filing with the Securities and Exchange Commission—recently called on shareholders to improve corporate governance and to remove or alter many of CECO's antitakeover provisions. Specifically, he proposed that shareholders

vote to eliminate a stockholder rights plan or poison pill, and change restrictions on shareholders' ability to call special meetings and to switch to an annual reelection of directors from the currently staggered board.

REFERENCES

Abrahamson, E., & Park, C. (1994). Concealment of negative organizational outcomes: An agency theory perspective. *Academy of Management Journal, 37,* 1302–1334.

Akerlof, G. A. (1970). The market for lemons. *Quarterly Journal of Economics, 84,* 488–500.

Amir, E., & Ganzach, Y. (1998). Overreaction and underreaction in analysts' forecasts. *Journal of Economic Behavior & Organization, 37,* 333–347.

Blumenstyck, G. (2005, March 25). Investments in privately held higher-education companies doubled from 2003 to 2004, report says. *Chronicle of Higher Education (Today's News).*

Blumenstyck, G. (2003, March 14). For-profit colleges attract a gold rush of investors. *Chronicle of Higher Education,* A25.

Blumenstyck, G. (2000, January 7). In 1999, the bull market rurned into a bear for publicly traded higher-education companies. *Chronicle of Higher Education,* A47.

Brown, L. (1993). Earnings forecast research: Its implications for capital markets research. *International Journal of Forecasting, 9,* 295–320.

Burd, S. (2005, March 11). Lawmakers are urged to 'go slowly' on loosening rules for for-profit colleges. *Chronicle of Higher Education,* A24.

Burd, S. (2003, September 5). For-profit colleges want a little respect. *Chronicle of Higher Education,* A23.

Burd, S. (2001, November 9). For-profit colleges praise a shift in attitude at the Education Department. *Chronicle of Higher Education,* A24.

Burd, S. (1998, September 4). For-profit trade schools win new respect in Congress. *Chronicle of Higher Education,* A47.

Business Wire (1998, August 6). Education Management Corporation Reports Fiscal 1998 Fourth Quarter and Year End Financial Results. Retrieved from http://www.findarticles.com/p/articles/mi_m0EUN/is_1998_August_6/ai_20994092.

Carhart, M. M. (1977). On persistence in mutual fund performance. *Journal of Finance, 52,* 57–82.

Chaney, P. K., Hogan, C., & Jeter, D. C. (1999). The effect of reporting restructuring charges on analysts' forecast revisions and errors. *Journal of Accounting and Economics, 27,* 261–284.

Chemmanur, T., & Fulghieri, P. (1994). Investment bank reputation, information production, and financial intermediation. *Journal of Finance, 49,* 57–79.

Chu, R. G. W., Chancellor, Ohio Board of Regents. Quote from Ohio Board of Regents Board Meeting, 1999.

Clement, M. B. (1999). Analyst forecast accuracy: Do ability, resources, and portfolio complexity matter? *Journal of Accounting and Economics, 27,* 285–303.

Facchina, B., Showell, E., & Stone, J. (1993). Privileges and exemptions enjoyed by nonprofit organizations. *University of San Francisco Law Review, 28,* 85–121.

Francis, J. J., Hanna, D., & Philbrick, D. R. (1997). Management communications with securities analysts. *Journal of Accounting and Economics, 24,* 363–394.

Hansmann, H. (1996). *The ownership of enterprise.* Cambridge: Belknap Press of Harvard University Press.

Hansmann, H. (1994). Organization of production in the human services. Working Paper 200. Yale University, Program on Non-profit Organizations.

Hansmann, H. (1980). The role of nonprofit enterprise. *Yale Law Journal, 89,* 835–901.

Heal, G. (1976). Do bad products drive out good? *Quarterly Journal of Economics, 90,* 499–503.

Herman, J. R., Craig, R. L., Pollak, L. D., & Basel, K. A. (1999). *Educational services industry* 2d ed. Chicago: EVEREN Securities.

Holmstroem, B. R., & Tirole, J. (1989). The theory of the firm. In R. Schmalensee and R. D. Willig (Eds.), *Handbook of industrial organization, 1.* New York: North-Holland.

James, E. (1978). Product mix and cost disaggregation: A reinterpretation of the economics of higher education. *Journal of Human Resources, 13,* 157–186.

Keane, M. P., & Runkle, D. E. (1998). Are financial analysts' forecasts of corporate profits rational? *Journal of Political Economy, 106,* 768–805.

Klein, B., & Leffler, K. (1981). The role of market forces in assuring contractual performance. *Journal of Political Economy, 89,* 615–641.

KnowledgeQuest. (1999b, September 17). *1999 KnowledgeQuest ventures survey of education venture capital.* Paper presented at the 4th Annual EI Finance & Investment Institute, Boston.

KnowledgeQuest. (1999a, July 30). *Venture capital investment in the education industry.* Paper presented at EDVentures '99, Madison, WI.

Kreps, D. M. (1990b). *Game theory and economic modeling.* Oxford: Oxford University Press.

Kreps, D. M. (1990). Corporate culture and economic theory. In J. E. Alt and K. A. Shepsle (Eds), *Perspectives on positive political economy.* Cambridge, United Kingdom: Cambridge University Press.

Kronholz, J. (1999, August 13). After a Shaky Start, Push Toward Academic Profits seems Poised for a Surge. *The Wall Street Journal,* p. A1.

Lin, H. W., & McNichols, M. F. (1998). Underwriting relationships, analysts' earnings forecasts and investment recommendations. *Journal of Accounting and Economics, 25,* 101–127.

Loeffler, G. (1998). Biases in analyst forecasts: cognitive, strategic or second-best? *International Journal of Forecasting, 14*, 261–274.

Massy, W. F., & Zemsky, R. (1994). Faculty discretionary time: Departments and the "academic ratchet." *Journal of Higher Education, 65*, 1–22.

McKinsey Global Institute. (1993). *Manufacturing productivity.* Washington, DC: McKinsey & Company.

McKinsey Global Institute. (1992). *Service sector productivity.* Washington, DC: McKinsey & Company.

Nanda, V., & Yun, Y. (1997). Reputation and financial intermediation: An empirical investigation of the impact of IPO mispricing on underwriter market value. *Journal of Financial Intermediation, 6*, 39–63.

Ortmann, A. (2003). The economics and industrial organization of E-learning: An introduction. Paper presented at the NCSPE conference, Teachers College, Columbia University. New York.

Ortmann, A. (2001). Capital romance: Why Wall Street fell in love with higher education. *Education Economics, 9*, 293–311.

Ortmann, A. (2000). The emergence of a for-profit higher education sector: Recent developments. Paper presented at the ARNOVA Conference (1998), Seattle.

Ortmann, A. (1999). The nature and causes of corporate negligence, sham lectures, and ecclesiastical indolence: Adam Smith on joint-stock companies, teachers, and preachers. *History of Political Economy, 31*, 297–315.

Ortmann, A. (1997). How to survive in post-industrial environments. Adam Smith's advice for today's colleges and universities. *Journal of Higher Education, 68*, 483–501.

Ortmann, A., & Kuhrt, K. (2000). *Why a college is like a firm.* Paper presented at the AEA Meeting (2001), New Orleans.

Ortmann, A., & Squire, R. (2000). A game-theoretic explanation of the administrative lattice in institutions of higher learning. *Journal of Economic Behavior and Organization, 43*, 377–392.

Oster, S. (1995). *Strategic management for nonprofit organizations.* New York: Oxford University Press.

Smith, R. (2004, February 23). Sylvan's financial maze. *The Motley Fool.* Retrieved from www.fool.com/Server/FoolPrint.asp?File=/news/mft/2004/mft04022309.htm

Sperling, J. (2000). *Rebel with a cause.* New York: Wiley.

Winston, G. (1999). Subsidies, hierarchy and peers: The awkward economics of higher education. *Journal of Economic Perspectives, 13*, 13–36.

Winston, G. (1997, September/October). Why can't a college be more like a firm? *Change, 29*, 32–38.

Young, D. R., & Steinberg, R. (1995). *Economics for nonprofit managers.* New York: Foundation Center.

Chapter 8

A Crowded Lobby

Nonprofit and For-Profit Universities and the Emerging Politics of Higher Education

Brian Pusser and David A. Wolcott

INTRODUCTION

Over the past decade there has been a significant increase in research on for-profit providers of degrees and training in higher education (Pusser and Turner, 2004; Kirp; 2003; Pusser, 2002; Newman and Couturier, 2001; Winston, 1999). Much of that work has turned attention to the possibility of for-profit expansion, with a particular focus on price and subsidies (Hoxby, 1998; Winston, Carbone, and Lewis, 1998); technology (Newman and Couturier, 2001); barriers to entry (Winston, 1999); and regulation (Eaton, 2001, Marginson, 1997). While the growth of for-profit providers in general, and of the widely publicized University of Phoenix (UOP) in particular is impressive, it comes from a small base. By any measure, the for-profit degree institutions remain a very small portion of total postsecondary activity (Breneman, 2005; Pusser and Doane, 2001). At the same time a separate literature has emerged which suggests that for-profits have considerably more influence and potential than the number of institutions or their enrollments would suggest (Berg, 2005; Kirp, 2003; Ruch, 2001; Munitz, 2000; Sperling, 2000; Tooley, 1999). While these authors cite a number of drivers of change, they fundamentally argue that for-profit corporations will use large amounts of capital, technology, and market forces to reshape the higher education arena. These arguments were perhaps best summed up by the title of Ted Marchese's (1998) widely cited article in the AAHE Bulletin, "Not-so Distant Competitors: How New Providers are Remaking the Postsecondary Marketplace."

Subsequent work in this arena has argued that new providers are not remaking the marketplace; rather, they are effectively capitalizing on shifts in student demographics, and labor market demands. That work suggests that for-profits are more accurately characterized as beneficiaries—rather than drivers—of change (Pusser and Turner, 2004; Pusser and Doane, 2001; Ruch, 2001). However, there is one arena in which we suggest that for-profit higher education providers and other corporations involved in postsecondary provision do have a very real chance of altering the postsecondary landscape. It is in the political arena, through the use of lobbying and direct campaign contributions to shape regulations and policies, that for-profits may ultimately prove to be of the greatest significance. The foremost for this is that a great many postsecondary institutions are public institutions, and, as such, are particularly salient in local, state, and federal political processes (Pusser, 2003). As public institutions, and to a lesser degree private institutions which receive public subsidies, have become increasingly central to state and national political contests, the level of institutional political activity has greatly increased, as has the degree of interest group participation. Our research shows a substantial increase in such political activity at the state and federal levels by both public and private nonprofit institutions, and by for-profit providers, and a high level of turbulence in the higher education policy arena. In this chapter, we examine the growth in postsecondary political activity, the comparative advantages enjoyed by different institutional forms, and how those advantages might reasonably be deployed in some of the key contests ahead. We begin with a brief analysis of the historical role of institutional political activity in higher education.

INSTITUTIONAL CONTROL AND THE AMERICAN POSTSECONDARY SYSTEM

The higher education system in America is fundamentally a nonprofit system, with 85% of two- and four-year degree-granting institutions registered as nonprofits (Goldin and Katz, 1999), and fewer than 4% of baccalaureate degrees awarded by for-profit institutions. It is also worth noting that baccalaureate degree production in for-profits is the domain of a few institutions, with DeVry, Strayer and the University of Phoenix awarding nearly 80 percent of all for-profit baccalaureates (Breneman, Pusser, and Turner, 2000).

To a similar degree, postsecondary students are disproportionately served by public institutions. While 56% of the degree-granting institutions are private, over 80% of enrollments are in public, nonprofit institutions (Goldin and Katz, 1999). There has been some disagreement in the literature over whether to describe the institutional array in the United States as a system (Clark, 1983). Despite the tendency of public policy research to treat the "system" as fifty state systems, given the importance of Pell grants, guaranteed student loans, and federal tax credits, the federal role in aid and regulation is essential to the success of state institutions. It is fair to conclude that if there is a system in the United States, it is historically based in direct public provision through state-chartered institutions (public supply), augmented by state and national subsidies to virtually all accredited institutional types (public subsidy).

Public supply refers to the provision of higher education in public non-profit institutions. Public subsidy refers to the allocation of public funds to public or private, for-profit or nonprofit institutions. Public subsidies may either be provided by state or federal entities to an institution as direct institutional grants (supply side subsidies), or to students in the form of grants, loans, tax credits, and the like (demand side subsidies), which may be used at any accredited institution. Over the past two hundred years, publicly incorporated institutions that have been publicly funded and regulated have become the dominant sites of postsecondary enrollment and the provision of postsecondary degrees. State and federal entities, through the establishment of nonprofit public universities, the provision of public funds to nonprofit public and independent institutions, and the establishment of accreditation and oversight functions, have long served as providers, subsidizers, and regulators of American higher education. As we will argue later in this chapter, a key political and policy battle is emerging in various states over efforts to shift the state role in higher education from public supply to public subsidy (Pusser, 2006).

HISTORICAL APPROACHES TO POLITICAL ACTIVITY IN HIGHER EDUCATION

From the earliest efforts to establish state charters, through the Morrill acts, the GI Bill and the Higher Education Act of 1965 (HEA), postsecondary institutions have argued that they operate in the state interest, or in the national interest, but not as a special interest (Cook, 1998; Hawkins, 1992). The conceptualization of higher education as a public good permeated political contests in the nineteenth century over the chartering of many large state postsecondary institutions and state systems (Pusser, 2002; Douglass, 2000). Along with concerns over public investment efficiencies, information asymmetries and moral hazards, the dedication to the public interest also helps explain the evolution of the nonprofit organization as the dominant institutional form. The promotion of higher education as a public good, and of the institutions as providers of a key social function, also contributed to the rise of state flagship universities to political economic prominence (Kerr, 2001).

THE GI BILL

One of the first significant twentieth-century congressional debates over non-profit and for-profit postsecondary education concerned the degree to which proprietary and other types of postsecondary institutions would be included under the GI Bill. After considering a number of competing proposals, the Veterans Affairs Committee approved an omnibus bill that included proprietary schools and that supported a wide variety of veterans and types of institutions. Congressional support for students in other-than-vocational programs was a departure from earlier policies, as disabled veterans of World War I had been provided with stipends only for attendance at vocational institutions (Loss, 2001; Olson, 1974).

THE HIGHER EDUCATION ACTS

The Higher Education Act of 1965 constituted a key component of Lyndon Johnson's Great Society programs, and unlike the Morrill Acts or the GI Bill, it was seen as a new structural component of federal policy that would be renewed through congressional reauthorization on a regular basis (Gladieux and Wolanin, 1976). Title IV of HEA created the Guaranteed Student Loan program (GSL), which established a federal role in promoting individual human capital investment and the portability of financial aid. Over time, it has grown to become "the largest and most important student aid program in America" (Breneman, 1993, p. 386). HEA also created Equal Opportunity Grants (EOG) designed to insure access and opportunity for low-income students. The reauthorization of HEA in 1972 was equally influential in shaping the contemporary politics of federal support for higher education. At that reauthorization, a contest was waged over whether the focus of federal financial support should be on institutions (a position supported by the major higher education associations) or on direct student aid (a position supported by a group of legislators led by Senator Claiborne Pell). Pell carried the day, and the Basic Educational Opportunity Grants (BEOG) created at that time were later renamed "Pell grants." Negotiations over HEA 1972 also resulted in the passage of Title IX, a nondiscrimination clause that continues to have significant impact on policies in those postsecondary institutions, both public and private, that are the recipients of federal funds (Dubrow, 2003).

The political struggles over HEA 1965, and its first reauthorization, revolved in part around partisan conflicts that shape the contemporary postsecondary political debate. Through its commitment to student aid over institutional aid, Congress endorsed the concept of higher education as a private good, as an investment in personal human capital. At the same time, the commitment to eliminating underinvestment through loan guarantees and the attention to equity and access signaled support for higher education as a public good. The debate reflected the ascendance of human capital theories in policy making (Becker, 1964) and was neatly summarized in a Carnegie report released in 1973 entitled, "Higher Education: Who Pays? Who Benefits? Who Should Pay?"

At the same time, HEA was a referendum on public supply and public subsidy. Reflecting the growing interest in models of choice and public institutions (Friedman, 1962), Title IV created portable financial aid that students could use at virtually any public or private nonprofit postsecondary institution. With the adoption of BEOG as student aid, rather than institutional aid, Congress ensured a greater degree of student mobility and institutional choice. The 1972 reauthorization also greatly expanded the range of institutions that were eligible under Title IV, including many forms of proprietary institutions. While federal support was firmly established as student, rather than institution centered, the states continued on the opposite tack, directing the vast majority of state support for higher education to individual institutions. The tensions between the vision of higher education as a public or a private good and of the relative utility of institutional and individual aid are not only at the center of federal and state policy debates today, but they also have significantly shaped the way in which postsecondary lobbying has evolved over the past two decades.

HIGHER EDUCATION AND POLITICAL ADVOCACY

A number of significant challenges emerge in attempting to describe the extent of postsecondary political advocacy. First, the higher education arena is extremely diverse in character and is not easily encompassed by prevalent models from other policy domains. More important, little research in higher education to date has been turned to building a political theory of higher education. Following on Moe's (1995) assessment of the dearth of positive political approaches to elementary and secondary education, Pusser (2003) suggests that the study of higher education has relied on organizational theory to describe institutional politics, and consequently has adopted an endogenous approach to understanding such contests in higher education. In turn, this has led to a dearth of higher education research that conceptualizes postsecondary institutions, particularly the public ones, as political institutions, sites of contest over the allocation of politically salient costs and benefits. What research there is on political advocacy in higher education has focused on the role of professional interest groups (Cook, 1998) and on institutional efforts to use federal policy to increase targeted revenues (Slaughter and Rhoades, 2004; Savage, 1999; Slaughter and Leslie, 1997).

THE BENEFIT TYPOLOGY

There are a number of models from social science research that address the broader rationale behind public advocacy, and some shed light on the higher education policy domain. Clark and Wilson (1961) distinguished between interest groups based on the types of benefits that accrue to the actor. Sabatier (1992) defined the elements of their typology as (1) material benefits (tangible, usually monetary, rewards); (2) solidary benefits (rewards from social interaction); and/or (3) purposive benefits (psychic/moral satisfaction from pursuing official goals related to public welfare). This suggests that nonprofit institutions fundamentally pursue purposive benefits. Nonprofits have historically viewed themselves as working to advance the broader public good and have been wary of losing their "privileged status in society" (Murray, 1976, p. 90) through partisan political activity. Gladieux summed up this perspective on nonprofit lobbying a quarter century ago in his comment that "distaste for the art and practice of politics is mixed with genuine concern that aggressive political actions would somehow be inappropriate to the academic enterprise and might even be counterproductive" (1977, p. 43). As one would predict, for-profit postsecondary institutions have adopted a different approach to political activity. For-profits have generally pursued direct benefits such as favorable tax laws, reduced regulatory oversight, and policies that increase profits, or in the case of publicly traded proprietary institutions, that maximize shareholder interests.

THE DELIBERATIVE THEORY

Mansbridge (1992) suggests three empirical models of interest group deliberation, with some utility in evaluating political activity in the postsecondary realm. They are competitive deliberation, collaborative deliberation, and corporatist deliberation. Under competitive deliberation, actors have fixed preferences. Interest groups "implicitly assume the existence of a truth (or a good public policy), the system being designed to elicit the best result through a competition constrained by rules of fair play" (p. 38). Under collaborative deliberation, actors attempt to influence the preferences of fellow interest group elites to shape the policy arena in their collective favor. Mansbridge states, "By giving some groups privileged access to decision-making, they exclude others more or less permanently and rigidify the system of interest representation" (p. 41).

Under this model, nonprofit institutions of higher education can be located in both the competitive deliberation and collaborative deliberation models. Alternatively, for-profit postsecondary institutions emerge in the corporatist category, which "links interest groups directly with state lawmaking and law-enforcing processes" (Mansbridge, 1992, p. 41). For example, unlike nonprofits, for-profit institutions have exploited the art of direct campaign contributions. Over the past decade, for-profit higher education providers have made significant direct financial contributions to political leaders and entities at the center of the higher education policy debate. For-profits have also aimed to integrate their organizations with legislative and regulatory entities. In February 2001, the Apollo Group (the parent company of the University of Phoenix) nominated the former chair of the House Committee on Education, to the university's corporate board. In October 2001, Sally Stroup, then chief Washington lobbyist for the Apollo Group, was appointed the Assistant Secretary of Education (Lobbyist Watch, 2001).

At first glance, the political interests of for-profit firms seem apparent—advocate policies that serve the firm's financial interests. However, Plotke (1992) argues:

> Contrary to prevailing views, political efforts by business cannot be explained solely in terms of strategic calculation aimed at realizing economic interests. Rather, such political efforts are conceived and pursued when economic phenomena are interpreted in the light of normative political and cultural commitments. (p. 175)

Coupled with, or perhaps a result of, the cooperation among businesses is the growth of market approaches to the reform of public policies. The rise in the early 1980s of neoliberalism, a philosophy based on "market deregulation, state decentralization, and reduced state intervention into economic affairs in general" (Campbell and Pedersen, 2001, p. 1), greatly enhanced the stature and relative position of market models in the broader political economy. In its first budget, the Reagan administration argued, "The most important cause of our economic problems has been the government itself" (White House, 1981). Speaking to its faith in the market, the administration went on to state, "Many special interests who had found it easier to look to the Federal Government for support than to the competitive market will be disappointed by this budget" (Ibid.).

RESEARCH ON CONTEMPORARY LOBBYING

In the most comprehensive contemporary study of nonprofit postsecondary lobbying to date, Cook (1998) interviewed a number of university presidents who suggested that the key to their approach was to emphasize the role of higher education as a public good. One comment epitomized their tone:

"Higher education is significantly different from other sectors and special interests. It is not self-serving, it is other-directed, it serves society; and it does little special interest pleading" (p. 140). Another president put it more succinctly, "We wear white hats" (p. 141). Whether legislators were ever as enamored of the concept of higher education as a public good as these presidents indicate, political actors are likely to be less so today. The combination of declining discretionary resources at the state level, the rise of market-based social policies, and the attendant challenge to government provision of social services, has increased legislative demands for a clear return on dollars invested in higher education. Nonprofit postsecondary political activity over the past decade has reflected a shift in approach, one designed to more effectively respond to the changing political economy of higher education.

HOW THEY LOBBY: NONPROFITS—THE BIG SIX

Despite the existence of a myriad of postsecondary advocacy organizations in the capital, over the past several decades, nonprofit postsecondary institutions have relied primarily on a set of associations known as the "Big Six." These organizations, the American Council on Education (which serves as the coordinating body for the six), the Association of American Universities, the American Association of Community Colleges, the American Association of State Colleges and Universities, the National Association of Independent Colleges and Universities, and the National Association of State Universities and Land Grant Colleges, represent the vast majority of nonprofit two- and four- year institutions. According to Cook (1998): "These six major associations differ from most other Washington higher education associations in that they are presidentially-based. In other words, the presidents of colleges and universities are designated as the principal institutional representatives" (p. 10). Cook suggests that at the federal level the Big Six postsecondary associations practice "public good" lobbying on behalf of higher education writ large. Although the associations do not stand out for the amount of money they spend in support of legislation (at least relative to the individual institutions), they do provide what has been termed "in-kind" contributions to political leaders. The associations, through their institutional members, represent blocs of voters and have created powerful alliances with state industries and economic enterprises (Ansolabehere and Snyder, 1996). The institutions themselves also allocate important benefits (e.g., jobs, often unionized) in the congressional districts, and the most selective institutions often educate powerful constituents of the various members of Congress. The associations also provide expert testimony, informal and formal contacts with congressional leaders, planning and drafting of legislation, and grassroots organization in support of particular bills.

INSTITUTIONAL EFFORTS

In a significant shift that has taken place over the past three decades, institutions have rapidly increased other avenues for promoting their causes at the state and federal levels. At the state level this has been manifest in increased institutional expenditures for legislative liaisons and membership in state associations of colleges and universities. At the federal level the transformation has been apparent in the growth of individual governmental relations offices in the capital, and the increased use of lobbyists. At both the state and federal levels the nonprofits also rely heavily on the efforts of institutional constituents, alumni, employees of colleges and universities, parents, and not the least, students, who act individually and in concert to bring pressure to bear on legislators. Over the past decade, a number of institutions have also benefited from the efforts of state level political action committees (PACs).

These efforts have resulted in major shifts in the types of representation and in the levels of funding brought to bear on behalf of nonprofits. The most significant of these has been the growth in institutional lobbying efforts aimed at garnering congressional earmarks. Savage (1999) has defined earmarking as "specifically designating funds for a particular recipient in appropriations, legislation and reports (p. 62). A central aspect of this process is the act of registering institutional lobbyists and/or hiring registered lobbyists to work on behalf of the institution. The number of registered higher education lobbyists increased nearly 2000% from 1981 to 2003 (Figure 8.1). As a consequence of this effort, the number of earmarks generated for designated colleges and universities also grew significantly over the same period, increasing by a factor of 94, from 21 earmarks in 1980 to 1,964 in 2003 (Figure 8.2).Similarly, the total dollars generated by earmarks in federal appropriations bills also grew rapidly between 1980 and 2003 (Figure 8.3), from some $16 million to over $2.0 billion per year.

These impressive gains have come at an economic and political price. As Figure 8.4 demonstrates, 15 registered institutions spent an aggregate of over $8.8 million on lobbying expenditures for the year 2003 (lobbying expenditures do not include individual, PAC, or soft money campaign contributions). The political costs of earmarking are more difficult to measure, as they have generated intense scrutiny within and outside of Congress, with a significant number of critics suggesting that they are both a device that avoids peer review of federally funded programs, and a questionable allocation of taxpayer dollars (Savage, 1999).

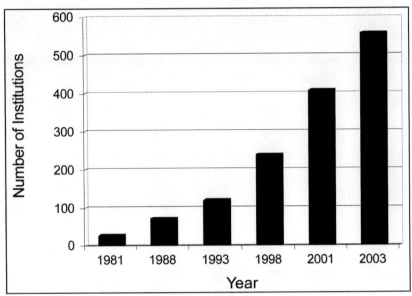

FIGURE 8.1. Number of Higher Education Institutions Using Lobbyists
Note: Includes institutions that represent their own interests and/or retain a firm to represent such interests.
Sources: Savage (1999) and Brainard (2004).

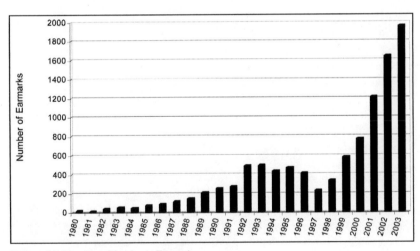

FIGURE 8.2. Number of Academic Earmarks
Sources: Savage (1999) and Brainard and Borrego (2003).

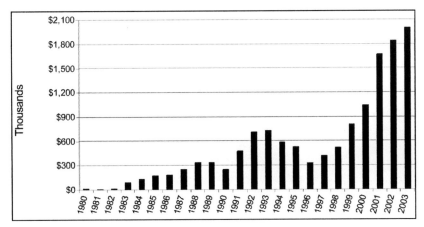

FIGURE 8.3. Amount of Academic Earmarks
Sources: Savage (1999) and Brainard and Borrego (2003).

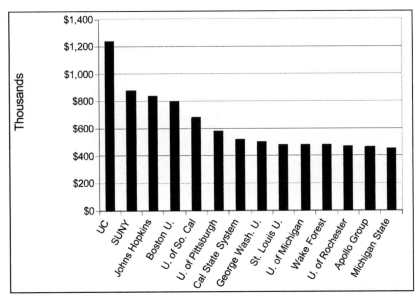

FIGURE 8.4. Lobby Expenditures: Top 15 Education Organizations (2003)
Source: Brainard (2004).

The Role of Individuals and PACs

A more indirect element of the nonprofit postsecondary lobbying effort consists of individual, PAC, and soft money donations to candidates and political parties. Because 501(c)(3) charitable organizations are not allowed to make direct contributions to candidates with state or federal funds, these data are more difficult to interpret for higher education than for other policy realms. Figure 8.5 portrays the growth over time in higher education-related campaign contributions for the period 1990 to 2004. From a low of just over $2 million, these funds totaled more than $32 million in the year 2004 electoral cycle. There is a clear upward trend of expenditures across presidential election cycles.

Campaign dollars are also the nonprofit dollars that are distributed in the most partisan fashion. Figure 8.6 shows the 15 largest higher education-related campaign contributors for the year 2004. This figure reflects primarily individual contributions for which the individual listed an educational organization as place of employment. Those affiliated with the University of California ranked first, with some $1,800,000 in contributions. As one measure of partisanship, 93% of those dollars went to Democrats. Second on the list, those affiliated with Harvard University, generated nearly $1,000,000, 96% of which went to Democrats.

Postsecondary For-Profits: How They Lobby

The universe of for-profit postsecondary lobbying organizations is similar in many ways to that of the nonprofits. Associations, institutions, individuals, and PACs all play significant roles in shaping the policy environment. A fundamental distinction is that individual for-profit institutions are not constrained from donating directly to individual candidates or to political parties and consequently they rely more heavily on PACs and on soft money contributions.

Associations

The largest and most visible association of for-profit postsecondary institutions is the Career College Association (CCA). CCA represents some 950 two- and four-year for-profit institutions. CCA ranked first among Education PAC campaign contributors in 2004, contributing 64% of its dollars to Republicans. Most of those dollars were from CCA's PAC, which was the largest higher education PAC for that cycle (Figure 8.7).

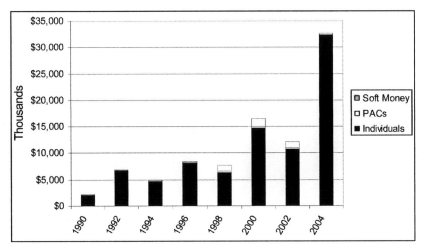

FIGURE 8.5. Higher Education-Related Campaign Contributions
Note: Includes individual, PAC, and soft money donations to candidates and political parties.
Source: Center for Responsive Politics (Federal Election Commission data).

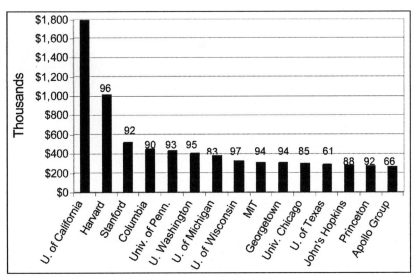

FIGURE 8.6. Top 15 Higher Education Campaign Contributors: 2003–2004 Election Cycle
Percentage of Total Contributed by Democrats (Above Bar)
Note: Includes individual, PAC, and soft money donations to federal candidates and political
parties by individuals who listed a university as their employer. Total from all contributors is
$25,631,680.
Source: Center for Responsive Politics (Federal Election Commission data).

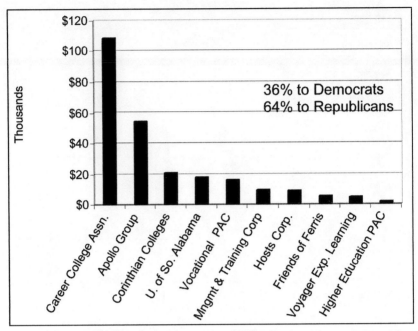

36% to Democrats
64% to Republicans

FIGURE 8.7. Contributions from Top Ten Education PACs: 2003–2004 Election Cycle
Note: Includes all PACs classified by the FEC under "education."
Source: Center for Responsive Politics (FEC data).

INSTITUTIONS

As noted earlier, a handful of for-profit degree-granting institutions produce the majority of degrees granted in the entire sector. The leader in this group by nearly any measure is the University of Phoenix and its parent corporation the Apollo Group. In 2004, Phoenix enrolled over 239,000 students and in 2005 had gross revenues of over $2 billion. Not surprisingly, the Apollo Group has been extremely active in state and national politics ranking fifteenth in higher education campaign contributions for the 2004 cycle (Figure 8.6). As shown in Figure 8.8, Apollo's campaign contributions have been steadily increasing since it went public in 1995. Apollo contributed over $265,000 in 2004, nearly seven times what it contributed in 1994. About one-fifth of those funds came from Apollo's higher education PAC (Figure 8.7).

As shown in Figure 8.9, Apollo was the leading postsecondary institutional contributor of soft money (donated to parties, rather than to individual candidates), having given $140,000, with 68% of that money directed toward

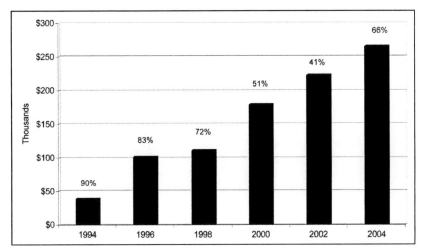

FIGURE 8.8. Apollo Group Campaign Contributions
Percentage of Total Contributed to Democrats (Above Bar)
Note: Includes individual, PAC, and soft money donations to candidates and political parties.
Source: Center for Responsive Politics (FEC data).

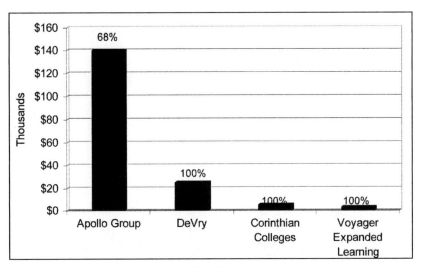

FIGURE 8.9. Education Soft Money: 2001–2002 Election Cycle
Percentage Contributed to Republicans (Above Bar)
Note: Includes only select soft money contributors classified by the FEC under "education."
Source: Center for Responsive Politics (FEC data).

Republican candidates. DeVry, another postsecondary for-profit, gave a smaller amount in federal soft money contributions, as did Corinthian Colleges. Each of those institutions gave their entire contributions to Republican candidates, not surprising given that party's majority in the House and Senate. Soft money was banned in April 2002 when the U.S. House of Representatives passed the Shays-Meehan Campaign Finance Reform Bill.

These data support Cook's (1998) critical distinction between nonprofits and for-profits, the willingness to become directly involved in the legislative process. The for-profits have made direct campaign contributions and targeted them at key legislators. Six members of the House are of particular interest in this case, Howard "Buck" McKeon, Robert Andrews, Johnny Isakson, George Miller, and David Wu, all members of the House Committee on Education and the Workforce. Three members of the Senate Committee for Health, Education, Labor, and Pensions were among the top ten education PAC recipients, Patty Murray, Chris Dodd, and Judd Gregg. Senator Arlen Specter is a member of the Senate Appropriations Subcommittee for Health, Education, Labor, and Pensions. Figure 8.10 indicates the estimated total PAC contributions from for-profit postsecondary organizations to each of these ten legislators. As Figure 8.10 illustrates, when looking at the education PAC contributions in the 2004 election cycle, a number of familiar names emerge, including Apollo, CCA, Corinthian, and Vocational PAC. It should be noted that these are not particularly large amounts of money in light of the total amount of annual interest group contributions. In the 2003 election cycle, the National Association of Realtors was the top PAC contributor with $3,771,083 in contributions (48% Democratic, 52% Republican).

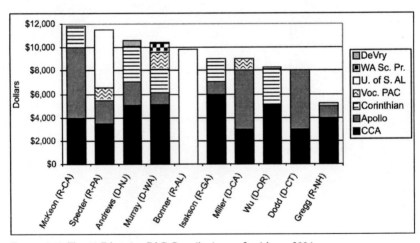

FIGURE 8.10. Top 10 Education PAC Contributions to Legislators 2004
Source: Center for Responsive Politics (FEC data).

NONPROFITS AND FOR-PROFIT LOBBIES:
CONVERGENCE AND DIVERGENCE

Predictions of how nonprofit and for-profit political activities will shape the higher education arena going forward rely on an assessment of their respective comparative advantages in the process, and the ways in which the broader political economy views their respective efforts. If nonprofits and for-profits share common cause on an issue, variations in their approach to access and expenditures in the political process may produce useful complementarities. Where they diverge, significant costs to both parties and ineffective policy transformations may well result. Our analysis of postsecondary policy contests over the past three decades points to four key areas of contest that will loom large in the future: (1) regulation and barriers to entry; (2) finance; (3) the role of entrepreneurial revenue generated by individual institutions; and (4) the tension between public provision and public subsidy. While in each of these categories there are a number of points of contest and convergence, a few key examples will demonstrate the respective positions of nonprofits and for-profits.

REGULATION AND BARRIERS TO ENTRY

Regulation has been seen in much of the literature on nonprofit and for-profit competition in higher education as a source of protection for nonprofit organizations (Ruch, 2001). However, our analysis suggests that contemporary policy contests reflect a certain commonality of interest between the leading for-profits and nonprofits. Prime examples of this are federal regulations controlling incentive compensation and student eligibility for aid. The incentive compensation contest addressed the method by which institutions pay admissions counselors and recruiters for delivering new student enrollments. In the late 1980s, challenges were raised concerning the manner in which some institutions were recruiting new students, and as a result, regulations were gradually strengthened. The issue garnered significant attention in 2000 due to allegations of fraudulent recruiting by a large for-profit provider, Computer Learning Centers (CLC). CLC subsequently declared bankruptcy amid calls for increased scrutiny of incentive compensation (Borrego, 2001). As a result, tighter regulations were imposed governing how institutions could compensate those who recruit students. During the drafting of new regulation in 2002, both nonprofit and for-profit institutions argued for a reconsideration of existing regulations, rather than the preservation of existing constraints. The final rule released in November 2002 presented twelve safe harbors within which institutions could offer incentive-based compensation, and was met with approval across institutional types (Farrell, 2002).

The contest over a key regulation defining student eligibility, the 12–hour rule, resulted in a similar convergence of interests. The Department of Education has historically relied on the 12-hour rule as a protection against fraudulent practice by distance providers of postsecondary education. It defined full-time enrollment as 12 hours per week of classroom-based instruction, a regulation that has been seen as a significant impediment to generating Title IV funds for students enrolled in distance programs. During debate over the rule in 2002, for-profit advocates were joined in opposition to the rule by such nonprofit entities as the American Association of University Professors, who argued that the rule limited innovation in online pedagogy. The rule was allowed to expire in November of 2002.

On a number of issues, such as the 50-percent rule, significant differences have emerged between the institutional sectors. The 50-percent rule mandates that colleges that enroll more than 50 percent of their students in distance courses can only offer federal financial aid with the permission of the Department of Education. As a result of nonprofit resistance to changes in the 50-percent rule, in November 2000, the University of Phoenix and another for-profit, Capella University, founded the Online-learning, Research, and Training Association. John Sperling, Chair of the Apollo Group stated, "a new trade group was necessary because existing higher education groups do not represent the interests of distance education" (Lobbyist Watch, 2000). In 2005, these and other political efforts led Congress to implement significant changes in the 50-percent rule and other policy shifts advocated by for-profit postsecondary organizations in the reauthorization of HEA.

One of the most controversial issues dividing nonprofits and for-profits, and one that is seen as a significant barrier to for-profit expansion, concerns the transfer of course credit. Indeed, when the Career College Association withdrew from the American Council on Education (ACE), it noted its disappointment with the lack of support from the ACE and its member institutions for the adoption of new guidelines to facilitate the transfer of academic credits from for-profit to nonprofit colleges (Borrego, 2002).

FINANCE

Perhaps the clearest area of convergence in political activities has been in the pursuit of increased federal funding for postsecondary education. Both nonprofits and for-profits have been in strong agreement over the need for increased federal contributions to student aid, although significant disagreements remain over what form the aid should take. Despite a general concern over rising levels of student indebtedness, both nonprofit and for-profit institutions advocated for an increase in loan limits in the 2004 HEA reauthorization (Morgan, 2002). While nonprofits would have preferred the support in different forms, both nonprofits and for-profits have been significant beneficiaries of the tax credits for students and families generated by the Taxpayer Relief Act (TRA) 1997.

A significant and unresolved dispute concerned regulations governing student eligibility for federal financial aid. Nonprofits advocated strict eligibility restrictions in the for-profit sector, while the for-profits argued that they should be subject to the same guidelines as nonprofits. On this issue, higher education associations suggested that Congress was giving preferential treatment to for-profits. Congressional action on the issue may well have been shaped by the growing influence of the for-profit lobby. Just over a month before the 1998 reauthorization, *The Chronicle of Higher Education* noted, "Now, the increased popularity of the University of Phoenix and other for-profit institutions is about to pay off on Capitol Hill as well, in the form of newfound respect from lawmakers" (Burd, 1998, p. 2).

ENTREPRENEURIAL REVENUE-GENERATING PRACTICES

A third key arena of political contest at the state and federal level revolves around entrepreneurial revenue-generating strategies in nonprofit institutions. Despite a general perception in the policy community that for-profit institutions are better positioned to capitalize on changing demographics and labor force training requirements, there is little empirical evidence of that. Over the past decade, nonprofit institutions have been rapidly increasing their provision of distance courses, offering greater numbers of certificates and degrees through continuing education and adult-learning programs, and expanding the use of contract education programs and industrial partnerships.

Taken together, these efforts constitute a significant convergence of institutional behaviors, an entrepreneurial wave that has the potential to create an array of hybrid institutions, the "for-profit nonprofits" (Pusser, 2000). As with the growth of academic earmarks, much of this transformation has taken place with little notice, in part because to date, it has required few state or federal resources. The rise of entrepreneurial nonprofits may soon challenge existing regulations governing postsecondary institutional behavior, and may also engender political challenges from for-profit providers.

PUBLIC PROVISION AND PUBLIC SUBSIDY

Of the emerging policy contests that will shape the future of nonprofit and for-profit political activities, perhaps none will figure as prominently as the struggle over public provision and public subsidy. The annual subsidy provided by the states directly to individual nonprofit institutions has long been the most important source of funds available to postsecondary institutions. It has also been a subsidy with unique characteristics, fundamentally directed to public nonprofits and a relatively unrestricted source of support for undergraduate education. It would not be an exaggeration to describe state block grants to institutions as the backbone of the contemporary postsecondary system. As Figure 8.11 demonstrates, state support for the postsecondary institutions in the fifty states now exceeds $63 billion annually.

State block grants also serve a key role in limiting the price of tuition, as a reduction in the former generally leads to calls for increases in the latter. State block grants are also generally considered the largest "discretionary" items in a state budget and consequently the site of continuous political contest and negotiation. The public provision of social services in the United States is currently contested to a degree unprecedented since the New Deal. Under the banner of markets, choice, and efficiency, over the past two decades a succession of interest groups and legislators have challenged the legitimacy of public provision (Pusser, 2002). The Bush administration, along with key members of the House and Senate, and the legislative leadership in a number of states, have begun to explore the transformation of public provision in higher education through an effort to shift the prevalent resource allocation model from public supply to public subsidy.

In FY 2003, states face the most severe fiscal crisis since the Great Depression. A number of state legislatures, most notably Texas and Colorado,

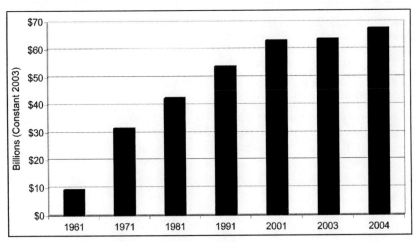

FIGURE 8.11. Aggregate State Support for Higher Education
Source: Grapevine—Center for Higher Education and Educational Finance, Illinois State University.

are considering legislation that would sharply reduce state block grants to public nonprofit postsecondary institutions in favor of direct student grants. These plans propose a dramatic restructuring of student financial aid policies, and demonstrate increased support for the creation of what might appropriately be termed higher education vouchers (Pusser, 2006). They also offer a significant opportunity to for-profit providers. In response, at the state level, institutional leaders have begun to make the case for public provision with renewed vigor, citing access and equity concerns, the role of public education in workforce development, and a host of other public benefits. However, given that both for-profits and private nonprofits have been traditionally disenfranchised from state grants to institutions, there would seem to be considerable potential for a new political coalition in favor of a shift away from public provision to public subsidy.

IMPLICATIONS

There is a tendency in much of the contemporary literature on postsecondary organization to take for granted an impending ascension of markets and competitive forces (Berg, 2005; Kirp, 2003; Newman and Couturier, 2001; Ruch, 2001; Goldstein, 1999; Duderstadt, 1998), and given that ascension, to also take for granted a subsequent transformation of the finance and provision of higher education. That transformation would also seem to favor the expansion and success of for-profit providers, and many venture capitalists have invested in that proposition in pursuit of an increased share of what has been estimated as a roughly $300 billion industry (Blumenstyk, 2003). Given the popularity of market-based social policies in the current Congress and in legislatures across the country, the conclusion that nonprofits are in serious trouble is understandable. It may not, on the other hand, be an accurate prediction of the future. As we have argued, there is a significant increase in political activity and lobbying by nonprofit associations and institutions, and by organizations concerned with the future of nonprofit higher education. There is also considerable evidence that nonprofits are succeeding in a variety of entrepreneurial revenue-generating pursuits, and that they are making a case for protecting those revenue streams.

There is another issue that emerges from this research, one that may be a useful indicator of the future of the political struggle over postsecondary policy between nonprofits and for-profits. That issue is the continued inability of for-profit enterprises to establish significant market share in the American K-12 system. Since the publication of Chubb and Moe's *Politics, Markets, and America's Schools* (1990), over a decade ago, many public policy advocates, political leaders, interest groups, and venture capitalists have advocated a shift of the K-12 system from one that is essentially nonprofit, marked by public provision, to a hybrid mix of nonprofit and for-profit institutions, with a reduction in public provision and an increase in public subsidy. It would be fair to say that they are not there yet, and that there is little that predicts they will get there soon.

Despite the myriad distinctions between the two sectors, there are a number of lessons from the political contest in the K-12 arena that offer insight into the future of political action in the postsecondary arena. First, building coalitions contributes to political success. Nonprofit postsecondary institutions have been characterized over the decades by a peculiar form of political isolation and atomization, both on campuses and in external relations. Despite critical claims that higher education has suffered politically for its inability to "speak with one voice," advocates of nonprofit public provision at the K-12 level have garnered significant political influence by speaking not with one voice, but through a coalition of interested voices. That coalition has included parents, community leaders, representatives in Congress and the state legislatures, and unions.

Unions are playing an increasingly active role on many university campuses, in support of a wide variety of employees including maintenance workers, clerical staff, faculty, and graduate students (Rhoades, 1998). Figures 8.12

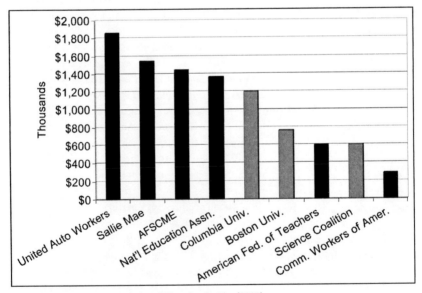

FIGURE 8.12. Lobby Expenditures: Education Lobby (2000)
Note: Overall lobbying expenditures, both in-house and external. Grey denotes organizations classified under "education" by the FEC. Black denotes organizations classified under "labor" or 'finance/credit' by the FEC.
Source: Center for Responsive Politics (FEC data).

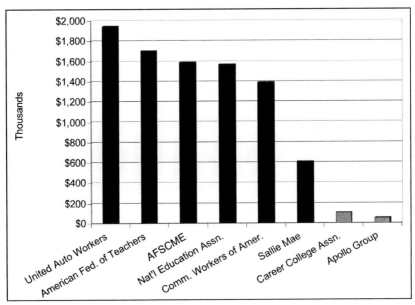

FIGURE 8.13. Key Education PACs: 2003–2004 Election Cycle
Note: Gray denotes organizations classified under "education" by the FEC. Black denotes organizations classified under "labor" or "finance/credit" by the FEC.
Source: Center for Responsive Politics (FEC data).

and 8.13 portray the lobbying expenditures of a number of organizations with postsecondary affiliations. The United Auto Workers (UAW), currently active in organizing graduate student unions, spent nearly $2 million on its lobbying activities. The American Federation of State, County, and Municipal Employees (AFSCME), which represents staff on a number of campuses, spent over $1.5 million. The Communication Workers of America (CWA), also active in organizing graduate student unions, spent another quarter of a million dollars. The degree of investment of these organizations is further evidenced by their PAC contributions (Figure 8.12). AFSCME spent $1.6 million on candidates in the 2004 election cycle. The UAW contributed $1.8 million and the CWA just under $1.4 million. At this point only a small portion of these contributions is linked to postsecondary lobbying efforts, but these relationships give an indication of the potential influence that may be brought to bear one day, particularly if the contest is over the future of many billions of state dollars for higher education.

When contemplating the potential for postsecondary political organizing, it is useful to keep in mind the scale of the nonprofit postsecondary sector. As one example, there are approximately 150,000 students in the University of California (UC) system, 350,000 in the California State University (CSU) system, and over 1,000,000 in the California Community College System. UC has about 75,000 full-time employees, CSU over 40,000, and the Community College System just over 60,000. Taken together they constitute nearly 2 million individuals directly linked to the public nonprofit institutions in one state. They may well be 2 million actors with quite different political orientations and social locations, but they may also represent the building blocks of a significant new political coalition.

In the period since World War II, the public postsecondary institutions in California and across the country have enjoyed an astonishing period of investment, growth, and success. Over the past decade, major reductions in state support have severely threatened those gains and the quality of life on campuses. Posed against three centuries of postsecondary provision in the United States, it is unclear whether the past decade represents an anomalous moment or a vision of the future. The nonprofit postsecondary system in the United States has, politically speaking, long been something of a sleeping giant. Given the emerging shifts in state and national policies, and the potential conflict between nonprofit and market models, it appears there are now significant incentives for the giant to awaken.

REFERENCES

Ansolabehere S., & Snyder, J. M. Jr. (1996). *Money, elections, and candidate quality.* Unpublished Manuscript. Department of Political Science, MIT.

Bayh-Dole Act of 1980. Title 35, U.S. Code, §200.

Becker, G. S. (1964). *Human capital: A theoretical and empirical analysis* New York: Columbia University Press.

Berg, G. A. (2005). *Lessons from the edge: For-profit and nontraditional higher education in America.* Westport: Praeger.

Blumenstyk, G. (2003, March 14). For-profit colleges attract a gold rush of investors. *Chronicle of Higher Education*, p. A25.

Blumenstyk, G. (2002, October 25). Court ruling revives patent lawsuit against Duke U. *Chronicle of Higher Education*, p. A33.

Borrego, A. M. (2002, October 7). Association of for-profit colleges pulls out of the American Council on Education. *Chronicle of Higher Education*. Retrieved October 8, 2002 from www.chronicle.com

Borrego, A. M. (2001, February 2). For-profit and nonprofit colleges alike criticize U.S. rules on compensating recruiters. *Chronicle of Higher Education*. Retrieved December 10, 2002 from www.chronicle.com

Brainard, J. & Borrego, A. M. (2003, September 26). Academic pork barrell tops $2-billion for the first time. *Chronicle of Higher Education*, 50(5): p. A18.

Brainard, J. (2004, October 22). Lobbying to bring home the bacon. *Chronicle of Higher Education*, 51(9): p. A26.

Breneman, D. W. (2005, Spring). Entrepreneurship in higher education. In B. Pusser (Ed.), *Arenas of entrepreneurship: Where nonprofit and for-profit institutions compete.* New Directions for Higher Education, *129*, 3–9.

Breneman, D. W. (1993). Guaranteed student loans: Great success or dismal failure. In D. W. Breneman, L. L. Leslie, & R. E. Andersen (Eds.), *ASHE reader on finance in higher education.* (pp. 377–387). Needham Heights, MA: Pearson Custom Press.

Breneman, D. W, Pusser, B., & Turner, S. E. (2000, April). *The contemporary provision of forprofit higher education: Mapping the competitive market.* Working Paper. Charlottesville: Virginia Project on the Economics of Higher Education.

Burd, S. (1998, September 4). For-profit trade schools win new respect in Congress. *Chronicle of Higher Education.* Retrieved December 10, 2002, from www. chronicle.com

Campbell, J. L., & Pederson, O. K. (2001). The Rise of Neoliberalism and Institutional Analysis. In J. L. Campbell & O. K. Pederson (Eds.), *The Rise of Neoliberalism and Institutional Analysis* (pp. 1–24). Princeton: Princeton University Press.

Carnegie Commission on Higher Education. (1973). *Higher Education: Who Pays? Who Benefits? Who Should Pay?* New York: McGraw-Hill.

Chubb, J.E. & Moe, T. M. (1990). *Politics, Markets, and America's Schools.* Washington, DC: The Brookings Institution. 318 pp.

Clark, B. R. (1983). *The higher education system: Academic organization in cross-national perspective.* Berkeley: University of California Press.

Clark, P. B., & Wilson, J. Q. (1961). Incentive systems: A theory of organizations. *Administrative Science Quarterly, 6*, pp. 129–166.

Cook, C. E. (1998). *Lobbying for higher education: How colleges and universities influence federal policy.* Nashville: Vanderbilt University Press.

Dougherty, K. J. (1994). *The contradictory college.* Albany: SUNY Press.

Douglass, J. A. (2000). *The California idea and American higher education.* Stanford, CA: Stanford University Press.

Dubrow, G. (2003). Higher education act. In J. Forest & K. Kinser (Eds.), *Higher education in the United States: An encyclopedia* (pp. 299–302). Santa Barbara: ABC-CLIO.

Duderstadt, J. J. (1998). Can colleges and universities survive in the information age? In R. N. Katz (Ed.), *Dancing with the devil* (pp. xxx–xxx). San Francisco: Jossey-Bass.

Eaton, J. (2001). Distance learning: Academic and Political Challenges for Higher Education. *CHEA Monograph Series* Number 1.

Farrell, E. F. (2002, November 4). Education Department eases rules on incentive payments to college recruiters. *Chronicle of Higher Education.* Retrieved November 4, 2002, from www.chronicle.com

Friedman, M. (1962). *Capitalism and freedom.* Chicago: University of Chicago Press.

Gladieux, L. E. (1977). Education lobbies come into their own. *Change, 9*(3), 42–43.

Gladieux, L. E., & Wolanin, T. R. (1976). *Congress and the colleges: The national politics of higher education.* Lanham, MD: Lexington Press.

Goldin, C., & Katz, L. (1999). The shaping of higher education: The formative years in the United States, 1890–1940. *Journal of Economic Perspectives, 13,* 37–62.

Goldstein, M. B. (1999). Capital ideas. *University Business, 20,* 46–53.

Hardy, C. (1990). Putting power into university governance. In J. C. Smart (Ed.), *Higher education: Handbook of theory and research* (pp. 393–426). New York: Agathon Press.

Hawkins, H. (1992). *Banding together: The rise of national associations in American higher education, 1887–1950.* Baltimore: Johns Hopkins.

Hoxby, C. (1998). *How the changing market structure of U.S. higher education explains tuition.* NBER Working Paper 6323.

Kerr, C. (2001). *The uses of the university,* 5th ed. Cambridge: Harvard University Press.

Kirp, D. L. (2003). *Shakespeare, Einstein and the bottom line.* Cambridge: Harvard University Press.

Lobbyist Watch. (2001, February 2). University of Phoenix parent company names former GOP congressman to corporate board. *The Chronicle of Higher Education,* p. A21.

Lobbyist Watch (2000, November 3). Distance education institutions create advocacy group in Washington. *Chronicle of Higher Education,* p. A26.

Loss, C. P. (2001). *The best-informed soldier in the world: Adjustment, education, and the 1944 GI Bill of Rights.* Master's Thesis (University of Virginia).

Mansbridge, J. J. (1992). A deliberative theory of interest representation. In M. P. Petracca (Ed.), *The politics of interest* (pp. 32–57). Boulder: Westview Press.

Marchese, T. (1998, May-June). Not-so distant-competitors: How new providers are remaking the postsecondary marketplace. *AAHE Bulletin.*

Marginson, S. (1997). *Markets in education.* Melbourne, Australia: Allen & Unwin.

Moe, T. M. (1995). The politics of structural choice: Toward a theory of public bureaucracy. In O. E. Williamson (Ed.). *Organization theory: From Chester Barnard to the present and beyond.* (pp. 116–153). Oxford, United Kingdom: Oxford University Press.

Morgan, R. (2002, November 8). Are federal grants taking a back seat to student loans? *The Chronicle of Higher Education.* Retrieved November 5, 2002, from www.chronicle.com

Munitz, B. (2000, Janury-February). Changing landscape: From cottage monopoly to competitive industry. *Educause Review, 35,* 12–18.

Murray, M. A. (1976). Defining the higher education lobby. *Journal of Higher Education, 47*(1), 79–92.

Newman, F., &. Couturier, L. K. (2001, September/October). The new competitive arena: Market forces invade the academy. *Change,* 10–17.

Newman, F. & Couturier, L. K. (2001, March). *The new competitive arena: Market forces invade the academy.* Providence, RI: The Futures Project—Policy for Higher Education in a Changing World. Retrieved October 18, 2002 from http://www.futuresproject.org/publications/new_competitive_arena.pdf

Olson, K. W. (1974)/ *The G.I. Bill, the veterans, and the Colleges.* Lexington: University of Kentucky Press.

Ortmann, A. (2001). Capital romance: Why Wall Street fell in love with higher education. *Education Economics, 9*(3), 293–311.

Ouch #57 (2000) Big Banks on Campus *Public Campaign* September 8, 2000. Retrieved from http://www.publiccampign.org/publications/ouch-cpi/041–060 ouch057.htm

Plotke, D. (1992). The political mobilization of business. In M. P. Petracca (Ed.), *The politics of interest.* (pp. 175–198). Boulder: Westview Press.

Pusser, B. (2006). From ideology to policy: Choice programs in higher education. *La Revista de El Centro de Estudios y Dociumenticon sobre la Educacion Superior.* San Juan CEDESP.

Pusser, B. (2003). Beyond Baldridge: Extending the political model of higher education governance. *Educational Policy, 17*(1), 121–139.

Pusser, B. (2002). Higher education, the emerging market and the public good. In P. A. Graham & N. Stacey (Eds.), *The knowledge economy and postsecondary education* (pp. 105–125). Washington, DC: National Academy Press.

Pusser, B. (2000). The role of the state in the provision of higher education in the United States. *Australian Universities Review, 43*(1), 24–35.

Pusser, B. & Doane, D. J. (2001, September-October). Public purpose and private enterprise: The contemporary organization of postsecondary education. *Change, 33,* 18–22.

Pusser, B, Gansneder, B. M., Gallaway, N., & Pope, N. S. (2005, Spring). Entrepreneurial activity in nonprofit institutions. In B. Pusser (Ed.), *Arenas of Entrepreneurship* (pp. 27–42, 129). New Directions for Higher Education.

Pusser, B., & Turner, S. E. (2004). Nonprofit and for-profit governance in higher education. In R. G. Ehrenberg (Ed.), *Governing academia: Who is in charge at the modern university?* Ithaca: Cornell University Press.

Rhoades, G. L. (1992). Beyond "the State": Interorganizational relations and state apparatus in postsecondary education. In J. C. Smart (Ed.), *Higher education: Handbook of theory and research,* New York: Agathon Press.

Rhoades, G. (1998). Managed professionals: Unionized faculty and restructuring academic labor. Albany: SUNY Press. 351 pp.

Ruch, R. S. (2001). *Higher education, inc.: The rise of the for-profit university.* Baltimore: Johns Hopkins.

Sabatier, P. A. (1992). Interest group membership and organization: Multiple theories. In M. P. Petracca (Ed.), *The politics of interest* (pp. 99–129). Boulder: Westview Press.

Savage, J. D. (1999). *Funding science in America: Congress, universities, and the politics of the academic pork barrel.* Cambridge, United Kingdom: Cambridge University Press.

Slaughter, S., & Leslie, L. L. (1997). *Academic capitalism: Politics, Policies, and the Entrepreneurial University.* Baltimore: Johns Hopkins. 276 pp.

Slaughter, S., & Rhoades, G. (2004). *Academic capitalism and the new economy: Markets, state and higher education.* Baltimore: Johns Hopkins.

Sperling, J. G. (2000). *Rebel with a cause: The entrepreneur who created the University of Phoenix and the for-profit revolution in higher education.* New York: J. Wiley.

Tooley, J. (1999). *The global education industry.* London: IFC Press.

Turner, J. K., & Pusser, B. (2004). Place Matters: the distribution of access to a state flagship university. *Policy Futures in Education, 2*(2), pp. 388–421.

White House, The. (1981, February 18). *A program for economic recovery.* Retrieved December 9, 2002 from http://www.reagan.utexas.edu/archives/speeches/1981/21881c.htm

Winston, G. (1999). For-profit education: Godzilla or Chicken Little? *Change,* January-February, 12–19.

Winston, G., Carbone, J. C., & Lewis, E. G. (1998). *What's been happening to higher education: A reference manual, 1986–87 to 1994–95.* Working Paper. Williamstown, MA: Williams Project on the Economics of Higher Education.

Contributors

Dudley J. Doane directs the Office of the Summer Session, January Term, and the Center for American English Language and Culture at the University of Virginia. His research interests include the internationalization of higher education and higher education policy.

Saul Fisher is Director of Fellowship programs at the American Council of Learned Societies (ACLS). Before joining ACLS, he served as Associate program officer at the Andrew W. Mellon Foundation. He received a PhD in Philosophy from the Graduate School and University Center of the City University of New York and studied at the CNRD in Paris.

David A. Wolcott earned his doctorate in Higher Education at the University of Virginia in Charlottesville. His research interests cover state and federal higher education policy and the moral development of college students. Prior to entering the field of higher education, he was employed in the public policy sector in Washington, DC.

Andreas Ortmann is a Docent (Associate Professor) and senior researcher at CERGE-EI (Center for Economic Research and Graduate Education, Economics Institute), a joint workplace of Charles University and the Academy of Sciences of the Czech Republic. His research interests focus on the origin and evolution of moral sentiments, conventions, and organizations. His research has been published by *Economic Letters*, the *Journal of Economic Theory*, the *International Journal of Game Theory*, the *Journal of Economic Behavior and Organization*, *History of Political Economy*, the *Journal of Higher Education*, *Education Economics*, and *Behavioral and Brain Science*.

Brian Pusser is an Assistant Professor in the Center for the Study of Higher Education at the University of Virginia. His research addresses the political economy of higher education organization and governance. He is the author of *Burning Down the House: Politics, Governance, and Affirmative Action at the University of California* (SUNY Press).

David W. Breneman, Dean, University Professor, and Newton and Rita Myers Professor of Economics of Education at the Curry School of Education at the University of Virginia, serving since 1995. He was visiting professor at the Harvard Graduate School of Education from 1990 to 1995, where he taught graduate courses on the economics and financing of higher education, on liberal arts colleges, and on the college presidency; president of Kalamazoo College from 1983 to 1989; and Brookings Senior Fellow in economic studies from 1975 to 1983. He received his BA in philosophy from the University of Colorado, his PhD in Economics from the University of California at Berkleley.

Sarah E. Turner is Associate Professor of Education and Economics at the University of Virginia. She has published numerous works on the effect of financial aid on collegiate attainment and the link between higher education and local labor markets. In 2002 she received the Milken Institute Award for Distinguished Economic Research for her work on the paper, "Trade in University Training."

Index

Page numbers followed by *f* indicate figures; page numbers followed by *t* indicate tables.

political/social model and the public
good, 23–49; principles of, 24; prior
experience, 75, 90n7; quality, 39–40;
quantity/quality of learning, 65n4;
supply and demand, xii, 3–22; University of Phoenix model, 71–92; Wall
Street and, 145–66
Education Management (EDMC),
159n1
EDUT. *See* EduTrek International
EduTrek International (EDUT), 159n1,
159n3
Eduventures, 161n16
endowments, 65n5; per student, 54,
65n5
engineering: distribution of Associate
degrees awarded by control of institution and field, 2000–2001, 60*t*; distribution of Bachelor's degrees awarded
by control of institution, 2000–2001,
61*t*
English language and literature: distribution of Associate degrees awarded by
control of institution and field,
2000–2001, 60*t*; distribution of Bachelor's degrees awarded by control of
institution, 2000–2001, 61*t*
enrollment: at individual public AUSS
member institutions, summer, 97*t*; in
public and for-profit institutions and
population growth, 63*t*; in public and
for-profit institutions and population
growth, 1995–2000, 63*t*
entrepreneurial revenue generation,
93–94; definition, 93; practices,
185
EOG. *See* Equal Opportunity Grants
Equal Opportunity Grants (EOG), 170
ESI. *See* ITT Educational Services
ethnicity, 18, 72
exams: in major field, 76
Executive MBA program, 115
expenses: lobby expenditures, education
lobby in 2000, 188*f*; of travel, 53
experiential learning, 81

F
faculty: academic calendar, 77; additional
income, 95; full-time, 76; nontenured,
17n5; part-time, 17n5, 72–73, 76; pay
scale, 76–77; practitioner, 82, 91n12;
student staff radio, 139n25; during
summer session, 104, 106n4; tenured,
66n14, 87; at the University of
Phoenix, 72–73, 79–80, 91n12 (*See
also* teachers)
Faculty Curriculum Coordinator (FCC),
82
family: combining work and, 53
Fathom, 91n16, 117, 118, 119–20,
135n3, xiv
FCC. *See* Faculty Curriculum Coordinator
Federal funding, 64; amount of academic
earmarks, 177*f*; expenditures for top
15 organizations, 177*f*; lobbyists and,
184–85; number of academic earmarks, 176*f*; number of higher institutions using lobbyists, 176*f*
finance: collective versus individual,
27–29
financial aid, 28; merit-based, 39; portability, 36
Flexner report (1910), 5, 51
Florida: enrollment in public and for-profit institutions and population
growth, 1995–2000, 63*t*
foreign languages: distribution of Associate degrees awarded by control of
institution and field, 2000–2001, 60*t*;
distribution of Bachelor's degrees
awarded by control of institution,
2000–2001, 61*t*
for-profit institutions. *See also* higher
education institutions: distinction
between nonprofit institutions and,
10–11; distribution of Bachelor's
degrees awarded by control of institution and field, 2000–2001, 61*t*; distribution of degrees and certificates
awarded by control of institution, 55*t*;

for-profit institutions (*continued*)
distribution of degrees awarded by
control of institution and field, 60*t*;
economic model, 51–68; enrollment in
public and for-profit institutions and
population growth, 63*t*; enrollment in
public and for-profit institutions and
population growth, 1995–2000, 63*t*;
global, 10; growth markets, 59–64;
lobbyists and, 167–94; market and,
52–53; offerings, 58–59, 66n9; older
students and, 62, 66n12; supply of,
10–12, 17nn5–6; Title IV postsecondary institutions by control, 7*t*
Friends of Ferris: contributions from
education political action committees,
180*f*
Fund for the Improvement of Post-secondary Education, 133
Fuqua School of Business cross Continent MBA, 115, 133

G
GED certificate, 75
GEN. *See* General Education Network
gender equity, 15
General Education Network (GEN),
116–17, 135n5, 136n8
geographic markets, 53, 65n2; concentration of public and nonprofit colleges,
59, 62; definition, 53
George Mason University, 140n33
Georgetown University: higher education campaign contributors,
2003–2004 election cycle, 179*f*
George Washington University: lobby
expenditures, 2000, 177*f*
Georgia: enrollment in public and for-
profit institutions and population
growth, 1995–2000, 63*t*
GI Bill, 34, 53, 169, 170
global competence, 99, 101
grants: institutional, 35
Great Society initiatives, 5, 34, 170
GSL. *See* Guaranteed Student Loan
program

Guaranteed Student Loan program
(GSL), 170

H
Harvard University: endowment, 65n5;
higher education campaign contributors, 2003–2004 election cycle, 179*f*;
public policy, 54
Hawaii: enrollment in public and for-
profit institutions and population
growth, 1995–2000, 63*t*
HE. *See* higher education institutions
HEA. *See* Higher Education Act
health professions and related sciences:
distribution of Associate degrees
awarded by control of institution and
field, 2000–2001, 60*t*; distribution of
Bachelor's degrees awarded by control
of institution, 2000–2001, 61*t*
Hewlett Foundation, 133
Higher Education Act (HEA), 31, 36,
55, 169, 170–71, xv; amendments,
66n7
higher education institutions, 3–22. *See
also* distance learning; for-profit institutions; analysis, 9–14; as an industry, xiii;
competition between, 33; contributions
from education political action committees, 180*f*; costs, 11, 25; curriculum,
15; definition, 4, 17, 38; demand for
services, 13–14; distance learning and,
114–18, 135nn2–7, 136nn8–10; distribution of degrees and certificates
awarded by control of institutions, 55*t*;
distribution of Federal student aid by
institution control, 56*t*; endowment,
133; finance of, 25; for-profit education
analysis, 10–12; for-profit providers, 6,
16n2; for-profit sector demographics,
6–9; free market competition, 30,
31–32; future research, 14–16; historical approaches to political activity in,
169; history, 4–6, 16n1, 119; implications for traditional learning at the
University of Phoenix, 87–88; institutional commitment, 133–34; institu-

profits and for-profit, 183; number of higher institutions using, 176*f*; postsecondary for-profits, 178; research, 173–74; top 15 higher education campaign contributors, 179*f*
London School of Economics, 116
Louisiana: enrollment in public and for-profit institutions and population growth, 1995–2000, 63*t*

M
Maine: enrollment in public and for-profit institutions and population growth, 1995–2000, 63*t*
Management and Training Corporation: contributions from education political action committees, 180*f*
marketing: boundaries, 65n2; distribution of Associate degrees awarded by control of institution and field, 2000–2001, 60*t*; distribution of Bachelor's degrees awarded by control of institution, 2000–2001, 61*t*; geographic, 53, 65n2; market analysts, 146–47, 159–60n4, 159n3
Maryland: enrollment in public and for-profit institutions and population growth, 1995–2000, 63*t*; higher education campaign contributors, 2003–2004 election cycle, 179*f*; lobby expenditures, 2000, 177*f*
Massachusetts: enrollment in public and for-profit institutions and population growth, 1995–2000, 63*t*; higher education campaign contributors, 2003–2004 election cycle, 179*f*; lobby expenditures, 2000, 177*f*
Master's degrees: distribution of degrees and certificates awarded by control of institution, 55*t*; Fuqua School of Business Cross Continent MBA, 115; at Stanford University, 115; trends awarded by institution type, 9*t*; trends in awards by institution type, 8*t*
mathematics: distribution of Associate degrees awarded by control of institu-

tion and field, 2000–2001, 60*t*; distribution of Bachelor's degrees awarded by control of institution, 2000–2001, 61*t*
Max-Planck-Institut fuer Bildungsforschung (Germany), 158
"McEducation," 77–78, 82
McGill University, 116
mechanics and repairers: distribution of Associate degrees awarded by control of institution and field, 2000–2001, 60*t*; distribution of Bachelor's degrees awarded by control of institution, 2000–2001, 61*t*
media: effect on academic issues, 28–29
Mellon Foundation, 133; CEUTT studies, 140nn30, 33
Merrill Lynch, 147, 160n5
Michigan: enrollment in public and for-profit institutions and population growth, 1995–2000, 63*t*; higher education campaign contributors, 2003–2004 election cycle, 179*f*; lobby expenditures, 2000, 177*f*
Michigan State University: lobby expenditures, 2000, 177*f*
Microsoft, 118
military technologies: distribution of Associate degrees awarded by control of institution and field, 2000–2001, 60*t*; distribution of Bachelor's degrees awarded by control of institution, 2000–2001, 61*t*
Milken, Michael, 29, 138n18
Minnesota: enrollment in public and for-profit institutions and population growth, 1995–2000, 63*t*
Mississippi: enrollment in public and for-profit institutions and population growth, 1995–2000, 63*t*
Missouri: enrollment in public and for-profit institutions and population growth, 1995–2000, 63*t*; lobby expenditures, 2000, 177*f*
MIT: higher education campaign contributors, 2003–2004 election cycle, 179*f*; Media Labs, 119; online, 138n17